Reprints of Economic Classics

STUDIES IN PUBLIC FINANCE

Also published in

<u>Reprints of Economic Classics</u>

By Edwin R. A. Seligman

ESSAYS IN ECONOMICS [1925]
ESSAYS IN TAXATION [1931]
THE INCOME TAX [1911]
THE SHIFTING AND INCIDENCE OF TAXATION [1927]

STUDIES

IN

PUBLIC FINANCE

BY

EDWIN R. A. SELIGMAN

[1925]

REPRINTS OF ECONOMIC CLASSICS

AUGUSTUS M. KELLEY · PUBLISHERS
NEW YORK 1969

First Edition 1925

(New York: The Macmillan Company, 1925)

Reprinted 1969 by

AUGUSTUS M. KELLEY · PUBLISHERS

New York New York 10010

Library of Congress Catalogue Card Number

68-58013

PRINTED IN THE UNITED STATES OF AMERICA

by SENTRY PRESS, NEW YORK, N. Y. 10019

PREFACE

Between three and four decades ago I projected a work on Fiscal Science. Aware of the fact that a comprehensive book on general principles ought to come at the close, rather than the beginning, of a scholar's career and that many preliminary investigations would be needed, I began to make studies on a variety of related topics in the broad field. In 1895 some of these studies were collected as *Essays in Taxation,* a new edition of which has been called for every two or three years. During the next two decades other analogous studies, such as those on Progressive Taxation, on The Shifting and Incidence of Taxation and on The Income Tax, were elaborated into independent books, although my attention was temporarily diverted to topics in general economics, on which several volumes were published.

During the last decade a not inconsiderable number of other studies in Public Finance were made. Some of these, dealing particularly with the finances of the Great War, have been incorporated into later editions of the *Essays in Taxation,* which has been enlarged to almost double its original size. Some have been reserved for the *Principles of Fiscal Science* in three volumes which is almost ready for the press. Some have appeared in the official documents as reports of government or international committees. Some, of a more fugitive character, have been allowed to stand as originally published. But there still remain a number of contributions which do not fall into any of the preceding categories. I have accordingly ventured to make a selection of such contributions and to have them appear in the present work, as a companion volume to the *Essays in Economics,* published at the same time.

The contributions in the present volume, all of them with one exception the product of the last ten years, consist of articles in periodicals, chapters from books jointly edited, public addresses, association reports and hearings before legislative committees. They are almost equally divided between questions of fiscal theory and problems of fiscal policy. They appear substantially as originally composed. In only a few instances have any additions or comments been added, and these are always put in brackets, as is true likewise of the prefatory lines of introduction to each chapter. If the reception accorded to this collection is at all comparable to its predecessor, *Essays in Taxation,* I shall feel that the venture has been amply justified.

EDWIN R. A. SELIGMAN.

Columbia University, New York
October, 1925

CONTENTS

CHAPTER VI

CHAPTER VII

CHAPTER VIII

CHAPTER IX

CHAPTER X

CHAPTER XI

STUDIES IN PUBLIC FINANCE

STUDIES IN PUBLIC FINANCE

CHAPTER ONE

COMPARATIVE TAX BURDENS IN THE TWENTIETH CENTURY

[This was originally published in the *Political Science Quarterly*, vol. xxxix (1924).]

The question of the relative weight of taxation has of recent years attracted much attention. It cannot be said, however, that any satisfactory answer has thus far been given. It is the purpose of the present study to attempt such an answer, confining our attention to the United Kingdom, France, Germany and the United States.

In order to lead up to our conclusions, it will be necessary to present the facts as to the revenues from taxation. From that point of view it seems desirable to divide the subject into three periods: from the beginning of the century to the World War, the War years, and the *post-bellum* period.[1]

[1] The statistics in this study are not strictly comparable because of the varying fiscal years. The fiscal year in France is the calendar year; in Great Britain and Germany it ends on March 31st; in the United States on June 30th. Furthermore, the official statistics in Germany are for the year beginning, in the United States for the year ending, on the given date. Accordingly, the year 1913 means in Germany the year beginning April 1st, 1913; but in the United States the year ending June 30th, 1913. In the official statistics of the United Kingdom both years are generally mentioned, so that in the above case it would read 1913-1914. Occasionally, however, only one date is given, so that what would be 1913 in Germany would be called 1914 in Great Britain. Accordingly, for purposes of the comparative tables below, p. 139, we mean the fiscal years of the United Kingdom and the United States ending respectively on March 31st and June 30th of 1901, 1914, 1919 and 1922; but the fiscal year beginning April 1st, 1900, 1913, 1918 and 1921 in Germany, and the calendar year 1900, 1913, 1918 and 1921 in France.

In the state and local statistics in the United States the situation is also confusing. The *Census* of 1903 and that of 1913, as well as the annual *Sta-*

While the objection may be raised that the facts are presented in unnecessary amplitude and the figures set forth in wearisome detail our justification must be found in the almost complete absence of any such preliminary studies—an absence which explains the many inaccurate statements and untenable conclusions on this topic which have been widely accepted during recent years.

I. *The Situation in 1900*

United Kingdom. The revenues for the year 1900-01 were as follows, in thousands of £: [1]

Customs duties	26,489	House duty	1,720
Excise duties	38,335	Income tax	26,920
Death duties	17,195		
Stamps	7,825	Tax revenues	119,302
Land tax	755	Total revenues	140,124

The local revenues (exclusive of loans) amounted to £135 millions. Of this total, however, there are to be classed as taxation only the rates (51 millions) and the so-called tolls, dues and duties (5¼ millions)[2] or a total of some 56 millions. The other local revenues were derived from governmental contributions, the earnings of municipal monopolies, loans and miscellaneous sources. It appears, therefore, that

tistics of States and Cities, use the fiscal year ending June 30th, or the first fiscal period closing prior thereto. The *Census* of 1923, however, uses the calendar year 1922 for state and local statistics, but utilizes the fiscal year for federal statistics. As a result of all these discrepancies, the international comparisons can be only approximately correct.

[1] *Statistical Abstract for the United Kingdom*, 58th number, 1911, p. 2.

[2] *Ibid.*, p. 52. The so-called "tolls, dues and duties" are in part fees, but in larger part taxes, and should properly be included in the local tax revenues, as is recognized by Grice, *National and Local Finance*, p. 29. The failure to do this in not a few published reports renders the comparative figures inexact. The details of the "dues and duties" are found in Goschen's *Report on Local Taxation*, 1868, H. H. Fowler's *Report on Local Taxation*, 1893, and the *Report of the Departmental Committee on Local Taxation*, 1914. Among these dues and duties are the market dues, harbor dues, turnpike tolls, pilotage and light dues, city coal duty, local wine duty, license duties on automobiles, grain duty, dues for bridges and ferries, waterworks, piers and quays, sewerage works and other tolls and stallages. The fees are listed separately.

the total tax revenue of the United Kingdom in 1901 was about £175 millions.

France. The four direct taxes were the *contribution foncière* or real estate tax; the *contribution personnelle et mobilière,* a combination of a rentals with a poll tax; the tax on doors and windows; and the *contribution des patentes* or business tax.[1] In the same category were the so-called assimilated revenues (*taxes assimilées aux contributions directes*) which comprise a miscellaneous series of taxes and fees.[2] The indirect revenues (*impôts et revenus indirects*) comprise customs duties; taxes on transactions, including the registration of documents (*enregistrement*) and stamp taxes (*timbre*); the stock-exchange tax; the tax on securities (*impôt sur le revenu des valeurs mobilières*); and the so-called indirect taxes (*contributions indirectes*). These include taxes on spirituous and malt liquors, salt, vinegar, candles and playing-cards. The taxes on sugar, however, are separately listed. As will be seen from the table below, the revenue from the direct taxes in 1900 was about 524 million francs, while the indirect revenues amounted to 2,136 millions.

It must be borne in mind that the inheritance tax which in other countries figures as a direct tax is classed in France among the indirect revenues or registry taxes. On the other hand, the revenues from tobacco, matches and powder which in other countries form part of the indirect taxes are classed in France among the monopolies. In the table herewith will be found the figures for 1900 in millions of francs.[3]

[1] The French statistics are taken from the following sources: *Bulletin de statistique et de législation comparée,* Ministère des Finances, monthly (quoted hereafter as *Bulletin*) ; *Journal officiel de la République Française,* daily; *La France financière et économique,* Ministère des Finances, tome i, 1919, covering the years 1872-1913 (quoted hereafter as *La France financière*).

[2] Taxes on carriages, horses, mules, billiards and clubs; fees on goods in mortmain; mining rents; payments for the verification of weights, measures and alcohol meters; and charges for pharmacists' visits, factory inspection, and fraud repression.

[3] *La France financière.* Tome i, 119, pp. 232-236.

Direct revenues	524	Monopolies	746
Direct taxes	484	Post Office	270
Assimilated revenues	40	Public domain	81
Indirect revenues	2,136	Miscellaneous* and exceptional†	140
Registry taxes	573	Recettes d'ordre‡	157
Stamps and stock-exchange	184	Algiers	62
Tax on securities	79		
Customs	449	Total	3,815
Indirect taxes	668		
Sugar taxes	184		

* These include patent fees, repayments by localities for advances, and contributions for the construction of local roads and school-houses.

† These include indemnities, profits from the exposition of 1900, sale of surplus military material, and the like.

‡ These include university fees, fines, sums held back from official salaries for pensions, repayments by the railways for loans and guarantees, and contributions from the colonies toward military expenses.

It will be seen that in 1900 (which corresponds approximately to 1901 in the United Kingdom) the tax revenues including the fiscal monopolies [1] amounted to about 3,100 million francs, out of a total revenue of 3,815 millions. As to the local tax revenues there exist unfortunately no satisfactory statistics which show the exact division between taxes and other local revenues. However, we know [2] that in 1900, when the departmental revenue amounted to 317 millions of francs, about 189 millions consisted of the *centimes additionnels* or percentages added to the four direct state taxes. The rest came from a share of the state taxes on turnovers and automobiles, tolls, the public domain, and grants from the central government. The total communal receipts in 1900 amounted to 794 millions, of which the municipal customs duties (*octrois*) were 324 millions, the remainder being composed in large part of *centimes additionnels* (210 millions), together with a share of the turnover tax and of some

[1] Strictly speaking only the net returns of the fiscal monopolies ought to be included in the tax revenue. But the same objection applies to all the tax figures where no allowance is made for cost of collection. As our purpose is to ascertain the tax burden, it is legitimate to take the gross returns of the monopolies like the gross tax returns. The postal revenues are not included, partly because they are generally counterbalanced by the expenses, partly because in no other country are they comprised among the taxes.

[2] *La France financière*, pp. 318-335.

of the *taxes assimilées*.[1] The so-called *taxes municipales* are not included because they are not taxes.[2] The total tax burden, national and local, therefore, amounted in 1900 approximately to 3,900 million francs.

Germany. The German situation is analogous to that of the United States, inasmuch as we have to deal with both federal and state governments. In both countries, the federal government depended chiefly upon customs duties and excises. There was, however, one important difference. Since the customs and excises were inadequate, it was provided at the creation of the German Empire that, until the federal government should levy independent taxes, the expenses should be met by contributions from the states (*Matricular-Beiträge*) similar to the American requisitions levied from 1781 to 1789.[3] After 1879, however, the federal receipts exceeded the expenditures and the excess over 130 million marks was now allotted to the states; the contributions being set off against the allotments (*Ueberweisungen*) or federal grants. By the end of the century the increasing expenditures, especially for armaments, changed the surpluses into deficits, and the states had now again to make contributions to the Empire.[4]

[1] *Ibid.*, pp. 41, 330.

[2] The French *taxes* means fees and charges, not taxes. The term is rarely applied to veritable taxes. But the *taxes municipales* are almost entirely fees and charges. They comprise: *taxes de voirie* (*taxe de balayage, droits de place, permis de stationnement*), *redevances pour concession d'occupation, droits de pesage et de mesurage, concessions dans les cimetières*. *Cf.* Allix, *Traité élémentaire de science des finances*, 4th ed., Paris, 1921, p. 823.

[3] For an account of the German development in detail, see Seligman, *Essays in Taxation*, 10th ed., 1925, p. 436 *et seq.*

[4] The statistics for Germany are taken chiefly from the following sources: *Vierteljahrshefte zur Statistik des Deutschen Reichs*, quarterly, (quoted hereafter as *Vierteljahrshefte; Denkschriftenband zur Begründung des Entwurfs eines Gesetzes betreffend Aenderungen im Finanzwesen, zusammengestellt im Reichschatzamt*, 5 vols., 1908, covering the years 1872-1908 (quoted hereafter as *Denkschriftenband*); *Charge of Taxation in Germany, compiled in the Ministry of Finance* (*closed April 30, 1920*), *Translation without Responsibility*, Berlin, 1920, covering the period 1913-1920 (quoted hereafter as *Charge of Taxation*); *Memorandum on the Financial Position of the Reich* (no. 254), *The Reichsminister of Finance, To the Reichstag, N. St. 928.20*, Berlin, 29 July, 1920, *Translation without Responsibility* (quoted hereafter as *Memorandum*, no. *254*).

In the table appended will be found a statement of the federal revenues for 1900 and 1901:[1]

In thousand marks	1900	1901
Customs	465,797	494,388
Consumption taxes	340,716	321,980
Stamp taxes	80,362	85,083
Total taxes	886,875	901,451
Post Office	394,542	413,648
Contributions	527,662	570,993
Miscellaneous	189,017	189,466
Total revenue	1,998,096	2,075,558

Since the post-office revenues were almost entirely counterbalanced by the expenditures, and the state contributions by the allotments, the federal tax revenue amounted to only about 887 millions in 1900 and 901 millions in 1901.

Of the state and local taxes, unfortunately, there are no exact statistics available. We have, however, a statement of the state revenues for 1901 and of the communal revenues for 1907. In 1901 the revenues were as follows: [2]

In million marks	Empire	States	Total
Industrial revenues	542	2,582	3,124
Taxes and customs	1,057	574	1,632
Fees	10	172	182
Miscellaneous	655	825	1,479
Total	2,264	4,153	6,417

In 1907 the communal revenue was 3,138 millions, of which the tax revenue was 1,042 millions or about one-third.[3] Inasmuch as the communal revenue was increasing rapidly during the decade, it is safe to assume that the tax revenue in 1900 was about 800 millions. This would make the total tax revenues in 1900, corresponding exactly

[1] *Denkschriftenband*, i, p. 47.

[2] *Ibid.*, p. 448. The federal figures do not agree with those in the preceding table because they represent gross, not net, revenues.

[3] *Ibid.*, pp. 633 and 662.

to 1901 for the United Kingdom, about 2,200 millions (886 imperial, 525 state and 800 communal).

United States. In 1901 which, as we remember, corresponds roughly to the fiscal year 1900 in Germany, the federal revenues were as follows, in millions of dollars:

Customs	239
Internal revenue	307
Public domain	3
Miscellaneous	39
Total	588

The tax revenue was accordingly about 546 millions. It is to be noted that the post office has a separate budget and that only the deficit or surplus of post-office earnings is included in the Treasury statement.

So far as the state and local revenues are concerned, the figures for the nearest date are the census figures for 1903:

In millions of dollars	Federal	State	County	Local	Total
Revenues	567	189	199	719	1,663
Of which taxes	505	189	160	546	1,400

In other words, the state and local tax revenues in 1903 were about 895 millions. Making allowance for the growth of revenues between 1901 and 1903, and estimating the state and local tax revenues at about 850 millions, it may therefore be said that the total tax burden at the beginning of the century in 1901 was approximately 1,400 million dollars.

II. *The Development to the World War*

The United Kingdom. Owing to the Boer War, the tax revenue in the year 1901-2 stood at about £132 millions. These figures changed but little for the remainder of the decade. Then came the contest over the budget of 1909 and the agitation for augmented revenue, due partly to the prodigious addition to the naval estimates, partly to the legislation for old age pensions and national insurance. The result was, that by 1913-14, the last full year before the war, taxation yielded about £163 millions, as appears from the following table: [1]

	In thousands of £		In thousands of £
Customs duties	35,450	House duty	2,000
Excise duties	39,590	Income tax	47,249
Death duties	27,359	Land value duty.....	715
Stamps	9,996	Total tax revenue.	163,029
Land tax	700	Total revenue	198,243

Inasmuch as the local rates amounted to £82¼ millions, and the tolls, dues and duties to 10½ millions,[2] the total tax burden in 1913-14 may be put approximately at £256 millions (or exactly £255,678,288).

The salient facts in the character of taxation during this period deserve mention. Great Britain had for some time observed the policy of trying to keep a fair balance between direct and indirect taxes. When Lloyd George found in 1909 that he needed about fourteen millions more to carry out his program, he decided that a little over one-half should come from indirect taxes. He accordingly provided for an increase in customs duties, liquor and tobacco excises and in the motor-car tax as well as for additional stamp duties and a new tax on petrol or gasoline.

The chief interest of the budget lay, however, in the direct taxes. In 1907, the principle of differentiation was introduced into the income tax. That is to say, a distinction was now made whereby "unearned" was taxed at a higher rate than "earned" income. In the same year a considerably steeper scale of graduation, running up to 15%, was applied to the estate duty.

In the finance act of 1909-10, not only do we find an extension of differentiation but the graduated principle was now applied to the income tax, through the device of the so-called supertax, and abatements were introduced for chil-

[1] *Statistical Abstract for 1922*, p. 2.
[2] *Ibid.*, p. 57.

dren. Another change was the steeper graduation in the lower brackets of the estate duty, which now reached 15% on estates over a million instead of, as before, three millions. Since the legacy and succession duties, which applied to separate shares of the estate, were graduated according to relationship, with a rate ascending to 10%, the result was that the inheritance tax, or combination of death duties, now presented a graduated scale running up to 25%.

The most significant feature of the budget—and the true cause of the opposition by the House of Lords, which led to the epoch-making constitutional changes of the following year—was the introduction of the new land taxes: the undeveloped land duty; the increment-value duty; the reversion duty; and the mineral-rights duty. These taxes, however, met with a most obstinate resistance, so that the annual expenses of valuation exceeded the insignificant returns. As a consequence, all attempts to enforce the law were discontinued in 1920.

France. The situation in France during this period suffered but little change. The growing democratic movement, indeed, caused an increasing interest in the endeavor to abolish the four taxes on yield, or "real" taxes, and to replace them by an income tax.[1] It was not, however, until 1914 that the income-tax law was enacted by parliament. But the outbreak of the war caused its postponement until 1916. The income tax was to replace the four direct taxes, the assessment of which by the state was, however, to be continued temporarily for departmental and communal purposes. The law of 1914 provided for a 2% general income tax, with abatements on incomes under 25,000 fr., and with liberal deductions for children.[2]

The other changes of importance in the tax system of France during this period affected the inheritance tax and

[1] An account of the movement will be found in Seligman, *The Income Tax*, 2d ed., 1914, pp. 306-325.

[2] *Cf.* Just Haristoy, "L'impôt sur le revenu. Lois de 1914, 1915," in *Revue de science et législation financières*, vol. xiv (1916), p. 5.

the land tax. In 1901 and 1902 the scale of the inheritance tax (*droit de succession*) was increased, the direct tax rising to 5%, and the collateral tax to 20½%. In 1910, the direct tax was increased to a maximum of 6½% and the collateral tax to 29%. Finally, the law of 1914 converted the tax on land from an apportioned to a percentage tax, at the rate of 4% on the rental value; and the rate of the tax on improved real estate (which had for some decades been a percentage tax) was increased from 3.2% to 4%.

In the table below [1] will be found a statement of the revenues in 1913, the last full year before the war, in millions of francs.

Direct revenues	633.6	
Indirect revenues	2,890.2	
Registry taxes		834.3
Stamp and stock exchange taxes		157.5
Tax on securities		130.1
Customs		777.9
Indirect taxes		697.4
Sugar taxes		191.2
Total		3,523.8
Monopolies	1,035.1	
Post Office		311.2
Public domain	61.2	
Miscellaneous	71.3	
Exceptional taxes	185.2	
Recettes d'ordre	211.4	
Algiers	4.2	
Grand total	5,091.8	

It appears from this table that while the revenue from direct taxes had since 1900 increased only moderately, from 532 to 634 millions, the revenue from the indirect sources had increased very materially, namely from 1,964 to 2,890 millions, and that the revenue from monopolies had increased from 746 to 1,035 millions. Of this the tobacco, watch and powder monopolies yielded 610 millions, making the total tax revenues 4,134 millions.

The total local receipts were 613 millions departmental and 1,071 millions communal. The tax revenues formed, however, only a little more than one-half of this total. The *centimes additionnels* amounted to 290 millions in the departments and to 319 millions in the communes, while the municipal *octrois* amounted to 334 millions, making the en-

[1] *La France financière*, pp. 232-5.

tire local tax revenues 943 millions.[1] The total tax burden —state, departmental and communal—would thus be approximately 5,077 millions. In other words, the tax burden grew in this period from about four, to slightly over five billion (milliard) francs.

Germany. In 1906 the increasing needs of the federal government led to a number of new taxes, so that the federal tax system henceforth comprised customs duties, taxes on tobacco, spirituous and malt liquors, sugar, salt, playing cards, stamp taxes on securities, sales, lotteries, and railway transportation. A new feature, moreover, was the federal collateral inheritance tax, ranging from 4 to 25%. This, however, was to be levied by the separate states, which were now to abandon their own recently adopted inheritance taxes, and to turn over two-thirds of the yield of the new tax to the empire.

This change, however, did not suffice and the growing needs of the federal government were sought to be met by the laws of 1909. These provided for increased taxes and for the settlement of the fiscal relations between the empire and the states.

All the old taxes were increased and new taxes were imposed on dividends and interest (*Talonsteuer*), transfers of real estate, electric lamps, and bank deposits; three-quarters of the inheritance tax was reserved for the Empire; and the imperial grants were limited to the net yield of the tax on spirits. The unearned-increment or land-value tax which had begun as a local impost in Frankfort in 1904, had spread rapidly throughout Germany. The law of 1911 provided for a federal tax to replace all the former state and municipal taxes. To this extent the Empire now started on a policy of direct taxes.

A picture of the tax revenue of Germany in 1913 is afforded in the following table, in millions of marks: [2]

[1] *La France financière*, i, pp. 41, 318-336.

[2] *Charge of Taxation, etc.*, 1920, p. 36. These official figures vary considerably from those (derived from estimates) of *Taxation and National*

	Empire	States	Communities	Total
Direct taxes	0.8	893.	1,250.	2,144.
Income tax	—	(691)	(651)	(1,342)
Customs and excise taxes	1,589.	111.	35.	1,736.
Luxury taxes	40.	3.	24.	67.
Taxes on transactions	283.	108.	64.	456.
Taxes on inheritances	46.	24.	0.2	70.
Other indirect taxes...	—	—	3.4	3.4
Total	1,960.	1,140.	1,378.	4.478.

In other words the total tax revenue of Germany amounted to about four and a half billions (milliards) of marks.

United States. The relative increase in taxation here was less marked than in the other countries, the real significance of the period being found in the change in the character, rather than in the amount, of taxation.

After the Spanish War the American federal revenue system reverted to its customary form of customs and internal excises. The important changes of the period consist of the adoption of the corporate excise tax in 1909 and of the federal income tax in 1913; while in the states the movement for an income tax was inaugurated in Wisconsin in 1911.

The federal revenues in 1914, corresponding to 1913 in Germany and France, are seen in the following table:

	In millions of dollars
Customs	292.2
Internal revenue	330.0
Lands	2.6
Miscellaneous	61.9
Total	734.7
Post Office	287.2

The federal tax revenues were thus 672 millions.

Income, Research Report number 55, October, 1922, of the National Industrial Conference Board, New York. *Cf.* in general Dr. H. Koppe, "Die Reichssteuerreform in 1913," *Finanz Archiv,* vol. xxxi (1914), p. 254; and Dr. Rumpel, "Städtische Finanzen vor dem Kriege," *ibid.,* vol. xxxii (1915), p. 817. For the period prior to 1911, *cf.* Seligman, *Essays in Taxation,* 10th ed., 1925, pp. 500-515.

The figures available for an ascertainment of the total tax burden are derived from the census of 1913:

In millions of dollars

	Federal	State	County	Local	Total
Revenues (1903).........	657	189	199	719	1,663
Revenues (1913).........	954	368	370	1,108	2,799
Of which taxes (1903)....	505	189	160	546	1,400
Of which taxes (1913)....	661	304	306	849	2,180

From this it appears that the state and local burden of taxation was increasing during the decade at a faster rate than the federal burden, the former growing from 895 to 1,459 millions, the latter from 505 to 661 millions; but that the total increase of taxation—federal, state, and local—from 1.4 to 2.2 billions was not so rapid as in some of the other countries. The explanation is to be found in the fact that the outlays for military purposes were not growing to the same extent as in Europe.

Making allowance for the increase from 1913 to 1914, and estimating the state and local tax revenues in 1914 at 1,578 millions (compared to 1,459 millions in 1913), this would bring the total tax revenue in 1914 to about 2,250 millions.

III. *The Period of the War*

Hostilities began in August, 1914, and ceased in November, 1918. The war years are therefore taken as five years, 1914-18; and inasmuch as the fiscal years of Great Britain and the United States end on March 31st and June 30th respectively, the fiscal year 1918-1919 is counted in the war years of these countries.[1]

The stupendous expenditures of the war were met only in small part by taxation. In France the occupation of some of the richest provinces by the enemy, as well as the political conditions, rendered it impossible to defray any of the war expenses from taxation. The newly imposed taxes

[1] See above, the first note in this chapter.

were in fact scarcely sufficient to compensate for the deficit in revenues caused by the occupation. In Germany the expectation of speedy victory and of the imposition of tributes upon the conquered nations prevented for some time any increase of taxation; it was only after several years that substantial additions were made to the federal tax burden. In the separate states and communities, however, there was a great increase of the tax burden from the beginning. In England and the United States considerably larger sums were derived from taxation, although here also the overwhelming majority of the war expenses was met by loans. The proportion of net war expenditures defrayed from war taxes for the entire period of the war was in fact only about 17% in Great Britain and 21½% in the United States.[1] But so stupendous were the actual sums required that the burden of taxation in both Great Britain and the United States was enormously increased.

United Kingdom. The situation during the war is indicated in the appended table, in millions of pounds: [2]

	1914	1915	1916	1917	1918	1919
Customs duties	35	39	60	71	71	103
Excise duties	40	42	61	56	39	59
Death duties	27	28	31	31	32	30
Stamps	10	6	7	8	8	12
Land tax	0.7	0.7	0.7	0.6	0.7	0.6
House duty	2	2	2	2	2	2
Income duty	47	69	128	205	240	291
Excess profits tax	—	—	0.1	140	220	285
Land values tax	0.7	0.4	0.4	0.5	0. 7	0.7
Tax revenues	163	189	290	514	613	784
Total revenues	198	227	337	573	707	889

From this it appears that the tax revenues jumped from £163 millions in 1914 to £784 millions in 1919. The local taxes increased only slightly, until 1918, but very con-

[1] See Seligman, *Essays in Taxation*, 10th ed. (1925), pp. 758-767.
[2] *Statistical Abstract for 1922*, p. 2.

siderably thereafter, as appears from the following table, in thousands of pounds: [1]

	1914	1915	1916	1917	1918	1919
Rates	£82,343	85,375	87,737	84,705	87,978	114,200*
Tolls, dues and duties...	10,306	11,480	12,260	12,420	12,610	12,800†

* £103.6 millions without Ireland, where in the preceding year the rates were £9.9 millions.
† Estimated.

The total tax revenues of Great Britain, therefore, grew during the war period from £256 to about £911 millions.

On the eve of the war the income tax was fixed at 1s. 3d., with a supertax running up to 1s. 4d.; while the death duties were graded to a maximum of 20% (on estates over one million pounds.[2]) In November of the same year the customs on tea, and both the customs and the excise on beer were increased, while the income tax was doubled.[3] In the summer of 1915 both customs and excises on immature spirits were increased.[4] At the end of the year the customs duties were augmented on cocoa, sugar, molasses, glucose, saccharin, dried fruits, tobacco and motor spirits and were further raised on tea; the excise duties were increased on motor spirits and medicines, and both customs and excises were increased on coffee and chicory; new customs were imposed on motor cars, musical instruments, clocks, and cinematograph films; and new excises were laid on sugar, molasses, glucose and saccharin. The income tax was increased to 3s. 6d., with a supertax rising to the same rate; and a war-excess profits tax of 50% was imposed.[5]

[1] *Ibid.*, p. 59.
[2] Finance Act 1914, July 31, 1914; 4 and 5 Geo. 5, c. 10. An accurate statement of the detailed changes will be found in R. R. Kuczynski, "German Taxation Policy in the World War," *Journal of Political Economy*, vol. xxxi (1923), p. 763, in the appendix dealing with English War Taxation. The author calls attention to numerous inaccuracies, affecting both Germany and Great Britain, of Bogart, Friedman, Plehn and McVey.
[3] Finance Act 1914 (Session 2), Nov. 27th, 1914; 5 Geo. 5, c. 7.
[4] Finance Act 1915, July 29, 1915; 5 and 6 Geo. 5, c. 62.
[5] Finance (no. 2) Act 1915, Dec. 23d, 1915; 5 and 6 Geo. 5, c. 89.

In the spring of 1916 excises were levied on matches, table waters, cider and perry, with a somewhat higher customs duty on matches and a new tax on entertainments. In the summer of the same year came another comprehensive increase of both customs and excise on coffee, chicory, cocoa, sugar, molasses, glucose and saccharin, with new customs duties on table waters, cider and perry, and new customs and excise duties on mechanical lighters, together with a motor-spirit license duty. The income tax was raised to 5s., and the excess profits duty to 60%.[1]

About a year later the entertainment tax was increased, the tobacco customs and excises were augmented and the excess-profits duty was fixed at 80%.[2] Finally in 1918 the last of the war budgets increased the customs duties on spirits; raised both the customs and the excise duties on immature spirits, tobacco, beer, sugar, molasses, saccharin and matches; and augmented some of the stamp duties. The only decrease of taxation was a slight diminution of the duties on certain entertainments. But the income tax was now raised to 6s. with a supertax rising to 4s. 6d., or a total maximum of 52½%.[3] The result was that by the end of the war from a quarter to a third of very moderate incomes and over a half of the larger incomes were taken by the state; and in the last year of the war over three-quarters of the tax revenue was derived from direct taxes on wealth. The burden had now become a crushing one.

France. It was not until 1916 that the matter was taken energetically in hand. In April provision was made for setting the general income tax into operation.[4] In June the alcohol tax was increased and in July a war-profits tax of 50% was imposed.[5] Finally at the end of the year the so-

[1] Finance Act 1916, July 19, 1916; 6 and 7 Geo. 5, c. 24.
[2] Finance Act 1917, Aug. 2, 1917, 7 and 8 Geo. 5, c. 31.
[3] Finance Act 1918, July 30, 1918, 8 and 9 Geo. 5, c. 15.
[4] "Instruction du ministère des finances du 5 avril, 1916," in *Revue de science et de législation financières*, vol. 14 (1916), pp. 257 and 274.
[5] "La loi sur les bénéfices de guerre." *Ibid.*, p. 454.

called war taxes were introduced. The postal, telegraph and telephone charges were raised; increases were made in the taxes on sugar, tobacco, hygienic drinks and mineral waters; the tax on securities was increased from 4 to 5, 5 to 6, and 8 to 10 per cent respectively; and new excise taxes were imposed on amusements, pharmaceutical specialties, coffee, cocoa, tea, chicory, pepper and vanilla. Certain "assimilated" taxes were doubled, (carriages, clubs, billiards, mines and hunting); the war-profits tax was increased to 60%; the general income tax was now graduated from 1 to 10%, the maximum rate being applicable to incomes of 150,000 francs; and an "exceptional war tax" was imposed on those of military age, not called to the colors. This consisted of a flat payment of 12 fr. plus 25% of the general income tax.[1]

In July, 1917, the general income tax was raised from a maximum of 10% to 12½% and a series of taxes on income classified by source (*impôts cédulaires*) was introduced, to replace three of the four old impersonal taxes (*impôts réels*) —only the tax on real estate (*contribution foncière*) being retained, but with its rate increased from 4% to 5%. These new "schedule" taxes on income included those on agricultural profits (*bénéfices de l'exploitation agricole*) as distinguished from land ownership, at the rate of 3¾%; on industrial profits, 4½; on wages, salaries, pensions, life annuities and non-commercial professions, 3¾%; and on the interest on capital. Finally, a special turnover tax (*chiffre d'affaires*) was imposed on retail sales exceeding one million francs, rising from 1 to 5 per mill on sales over 200 millions.[2]

[1] For all these laws see J. Radouant, "Les impôts de guerre," in *op. cit.*, vol. 15 (1917), pp. 122-139. *Cf.* Just Haristoy, "L'impôt sur le revenu," *ibid.*, p. 53.

[2] For these laws see *op. cit.*, vol. 15 (1917), pp. 448-468. The account given by E. L. Bogart, *War Costs and their Financing*, 1921, pp. 247 *et seq.*, is inaccurate in several particulars. The taxes mentioned by him were imposed not "by Act of July 1, 1916," but by the succeeding act of Dec. 30th, 1916; and this latter act did not "raise in a drastic manner the rates" of those imposed by the act of July. Furthermore, the tax on securities was not "raised by 1%." but in some cases by 2%. As to the changes of 1917,

In October, 1917, the match tax was increased and at the end of the year further changes were made. A tax on payments was introduced at the rate of 1/5 of 1%, with 10% on certain luxuries; the war-profits tax was raised to 80%; and the inheritance tax was greatly increased, the estate tax (*capital net global des successions*) rising to 24%, and the tax on shares (*droits de mutation*) to 36%.[1] In January, 1918, the tobacco tax was further increased, and five months later the last of the comprehensive war-tax laws was enacted. The general income tax was now graduated up to 20%; an increase took place in the taxes on drinks, chicory, vinegar and sugar (by from 15 to 60%); some of the registration and stamp taxes were augmented, as was the "assimilated" *taxe de mainmorte;* and the tax on railroad passenger fares was raised to 35% (50% for *places de luxe*). New taxes were levied on insurance policies, shows and freight transportation (10%); and the luxury tax which had been imposed in March of the same year had some of its rates increased to 20%.[2] The results of these changes appear in the table on the next page.[3]

From this it will be seen that for the first two years of the war the yield of both the direct and the indirect taxes was actually less than before the war. In the subsequent years the chief increases came from the customs duties, the income tax and the war-profits tax. But even then, the total increase of taxes was comparatively slight, growing from 2,921 to only 5,308 millions. As a result of the war, moreover, the local revenues from taxation remained about the same, while the proceeds from *octrois* actually decreased, owing largely

Bogart is in error in stating that the income tax was increased by 20%. The maximum rate was increased 12½%. Furthermore, the half of one per cent turnover tax applied to sales not over $400,000, but over $40,000,-000. Finally, no mention is made of the increase of the land tax from 4 to 5% or of the important changes effected by the law of 1917.

[1] *Cf.* the law for the *création des nouveaux impôts de guerre,* in *Revue de science et de legislation financières,* vol. 16 (1918), p. 145.

[2] For these laws see *op. cit.*, vol. 16 (1918), pp. 454-479.

[3] *Bulletin de Statistique,* vol. 89 (1921), p. 625, and vol. 91 (1922), p. 849. This table differs from the preliminary figures found in various other statements.

In millions of francs

	1914	1915	1916	1917	1918
Direct taxes	611	547	550	730	696
Income tax	—	—	(51)	(254)	(547)
War profits tax	—	—	—	209	578
Registry and stamp taxes	815	610	685	896	1,143
Tax on securities	153	157	181	242	253
Tax on payments	—	—	—	—	112
Customs duties	579	764	1,400	1,511	1,186
Indirect taxes	604	517	530	752	954
Sugar tax	159	213	183	266	184
Monopolies (matches, tobacco, etc.)	571	549	616	712	710
Post Office	371	304	334	404	448
Public domain	60	114	110	120	148
Miscellaneous	273	355	343	344	379
Total revenues	4,196	4,130	4,932	6,186	6,791
Tax revenues *	2,921	3,013	3,811	4,914	5,308

* Including the monopolies, less the Postoffice.

to the occupied districts. The figures of local taxation are as follows: [1]

In millions of francs

	Centimes additionnels		Octrois	Total tax revenues
	Departments	Communes		
1914	308	323	268	899
1915	293	313	233	839
1916	304	334	224	862
1917	309	347	232	886
1918	326	411	174	911

The total tax burden in France at the end of the war period may therefore be put at 6,219 thousand millions or approximately six and a quarter billion (milliard) francs as compared with less than four billions (milliards) in 1914, and with over five billions (milliards) in the last year preceding the war.

[1] These figures are taken from successive volumes of the *Bulletin de statistique* and the *Annuaire statistique*, which contain in each case only the figures for the preceding year.

Germany. Already before the outbreak of the war,[1] in 1913, the government had provided for a non-recurring defense contribution (*Wehrbeitrag*) imposed on both property and income, the rate on property varying from 0.15% to 1½% (on sums over five millions), the rate on income varying from 1% to 8% (on incomes over a half million).[2] In the same year provision was made for the *Besitzsteuer* or tax (to be levied in 1917) on the increment of the value of property between 1914 and 1917. The rate varied from ¾ of 1% to 1½% on the increased value, with an addition graded from ⅒ of 1% to 10% according to the amount of the property (not of the increment).[3]

In the year following the outbreak of hostilities the Reichsbank was subjected to a war tax which increased from year to year.[4] In 1916 the matter was taken up seriously. An increase took place in the tobacco tax, in the stamp tax on bills of lading (*Frachturkundenstempel*) and in the postal, telegraph and telephone charges; and a tax of one per mill was imposed on sales or transfers of commodities (*Waarenumsatzstempel*).[5]

[1] For the situation at the outbreak of the war, see G. Schanz, "Uebersicht über die zur Zeit (1914) in den Deutschen Bundesstaaten und Gemeinden geltenden direkten Steuersystemen," *Finanz Archiv*, vol. 31 (1914), p. 236. *Cf.* Dr. F. W. R. Zimmermann, "Die Finanzwirtschaft des Deutschen Reichs und der Bundesstaaten zu Kriegsausbruch," *ibid.*, p. 194; and Dr. Rompel, "Städtische Finanzen vor dem Kriege," *ibid.*, vol. 32 (1915), p. 817. The best accounts of the changes year by year will be found in the articles by R. van der Borght, in the *Finanz Archiv*, vol. 33 (1916), p. 721; vol. 34 (1917), p. 747; and vol. 36 (1919), p. 182. *Cf.* the study by R. Jantzen on the direct tax of 1916, *ibid.*, vol. 34 (1917), p. 133; and the "Denkschrift des Reichministers der Finanzen Schiffer uber die Finanzen des Deutschen Reichs in den Rechnungsjahren 1914-1918," reprinted in *Finanz Archiv*, vol. 36 (1919), p. 183. A more general treatment will be found in R. R. Kuczynski, "Deutsche Kriegssteuerpolitik," *Annalen fur Sociale Politik und Gesetzgebung*, vol. vi (1918), p. 278. An English version of this is the same author's article mentioned above, p. 15, note 2.

[2] "Gesetz über einen einmaligen ausserordentlichen Wehrbeitrag von 3 Juli, 1913." *Finanz Archiv*, vol. 31 (1914), p. 320.

[3] "Besitzsteuergesetz," *Finanz Archiv*, vol. 31 (1914), p. 336.

[4] The bank tax for 1915 was 114 millions, together with three-quarters of the excess profits over the pre-war average. By 1919 it had reached 355 millions plus 80% of the excess profits. *Cf.* the laws in *Finanz Archiv*, vol. 33 (1916), p. 765; vol. 34 (1917), p. 834; vol. 35 (1918), p. 801, and vol. 37 (1920), pp. 658, 659.

[5] The respective laws will be found in *Finanz Archiv*, vol. 33 (1916), pp. 776, 781, 784, and 786.

Provision was now made for a war tax, consisting primarily of a levy on capital gains or the increment of property from 1913 to 1916, at rates varying from 5% to 50% (on increments over 400,000 mks.). The law included a tax of 1% on all property which had not suffered a decrease of at least 10%. Corporations (or companies) were subjected to a tax of from 5% to 30% of the excess profits over the five pre-war years, according as they amounted to from 2 to 30% of the capital; with a possible 50% increase of the tax, bringing the maximum rate to 45%.[1]

In 1917 the war tax was increased 20%, with abatements according to the number of children;[2] a 20% tax was put on coal, a 7% tax on freight traffic and a tax of from 10 to 16% on passenger fares.[3] Furthermore, in July, 1918, the duties on tea and coffee were raised; new taxes were imposed on wines, sparkling wines, mineral and artificial waters; an increase was effected in the beer tax as well as in the stamp taxes, especially the tax on bills on exchange; the postal, telegraph and telephone charges were again raised; the turnover tax was increased to ½ of 1%, together with a rate of 10% on certain luxuries; and the brandy monopoly was introduced.[4] Finally an extraordinary war tax was imposed on both property and income. The property tax varied from 1% to 5%, and the excess-income tax was graded from 5% to 50% (on an excess income of over 100,000 mks.). In the case of companies the excess-profits tax was graduated from 10% to 60%.[5]

As a consequence of the facts recited above the first two years of the war witnessed a diminution of the tax burden, the federal tax revenue falling from a little under 2½ bil-

[1] "Reichskriegssteuergesetz von 21 Juni, 1916," providing for the so-called *Ausserordentliche Kriegsabgabe*. *Cf. Finanz Archiv*, vol. 33 (1916), p. 767.

[2] *Finanz Archiv*, vol. 34 (1917), p. 820.

[3] "Reichsgesetz über die Besteuerung des Personen- und Güterverkehrs" and "Reichskohlensteuergesetz," *Finanz Archiv*, vol. 34 (1917), pp. 805, 813.

[4] *Finanz Archiv*, vol. 36 (1919), pp. 345, 404, 411, 428, 475, 487, 493, 501, and 518.

[5] "Reichsgesetz über eine ausserordentliche Kriegsabgabe für das Rechnungsjahr 1918, von 26 Juli 1918," *Finanz Archiv*, vol. 36 (1919), p. 530.

lions (milliards) of marks in 1914 to a little over 1½ in 1916; and the state tax revenues decreasing in 1915, and slightly increasing in 1916, making a total diminution of about 700 millions in the two years. From then on, however, came a notable change. The figures are found in the following table:[1]

In millions of marks

	Federal						State					
	Direct taxes	Customs	Indirect taxes	Taxes on exchange	Death taxes	Total	Direct taxes	Income taxes	Taxes on exchange	Death taxes	Total	Total
1914..	637	666	851	209	54	2,417	908	(711)	107	21	1,113	3,530
1915..	308	399	575	176	61	1,519	885	(676)	84	22	1,028	2,547
1916..	65	389	801	258	65	1,577	1,164	(933)	66	34	1,310	2,887
1917..	4,991	278	1,449	406	70	7,274	1,408	(1,167)	31	29	1,534	8,808
1918..	2,531	191	2,616	718	97	6,153	1,814	(1,545)	22	33	1,986	8,139

From this it appears that the federal taxes yielded almost three times as much in 1917 as in 1914, increasing from 2,417 to 7,274 millions and that the state tax revenues increased from 1,113 millions in 1914 to 1,986 millions in 1918, the major part of the increase coming from the income tax. The details of the income-tax revenue are shown herewith, in millions of marks.[2]

	1914	1915	1916	1917	1918
Prussia	396	373	553	696	909
Bavaria	51	49	67	90	126
Saxony	73	68	68	89	133
Würtemberg	25	25	42	55	72
Baden	16	16	16	11	14
All of the 26 states	711	676	920	1,153	1,527

As to the local taxes, exact figures are, unfortunately, not yet available. A fair estimate, however, based on the figures of 1913 and on the assumption that local taxes increased in a little larger proportion than the state taxes, would put the local tax burden in 1914 at about 1¾ billion (milliard) marks and in 1919 at about 3 billions (milliards).

[1] This will be found in *The Charge of Taxation*, 1920, and in *Memorandum, no. 254*.
[2] *Charge of Taxation*, p. 37.

This would bring the entire tax burden from about 5¾ billion (milliard) marks in 1914 to about 11¼ billion (milliard) marks in 1918, the period which corresponds to 1919 in the United Kingdom.

United States. Although the United States did not enter the war until 1917, the financial disorders in Europe so seriously affected current revenues that an addition was imperatively needed. The emergency revenue law of 1914 accordingly increased the taxes on beer and tobacco, and imposed a variety of stamp taxes. In 1916 the scale of progression in the income tax was made sharper and provision was made for an estate tax, running up to 10%, a munitions manufacturers' tax, an excise tax on corporations, and a series of special taxes. In 1917 an excess-profits tax of 8% was imposed and the scale of the inheritance tax was increased to a maximum of 15%.

After our entrance into the war in 1917 new taxes were imposed on excess profits, transportation, sales, stamps and admissions, together with a great increase in the taxes on income, tobacco and liquors. Finally, in 1918, the existing taxes were in many cases more than doubled, and a multiplicity of excise and miscellaneous taxes were imposed. The income tax, which in 1913 stood at the rate of 1% normal and 6% surtax was increased in 1916 to 2% normal and 13% surtax; in 1917, to a 4% normal and 65% surtax; and in 1918, to a 12% normal and 65% surtax, or a total of 77%. These were the highest rates yet reached by any country in the world. The results appear in the following table:

In millions

	1915	1916	1917	1918	1919
Customs	$210	$213	$226	$183	$183
Internal revenue	425	513	819	3,696	3,840
Miscellaneous	63	57	79	301	631
Total ordinary receipts	698	783	1,124	4,180	4,654
Postal receipts	287	312	330	344	365

From this it will be seen that by the end of the war, although the customs revenues had actually declined, the internal revenue had multiplied more than ninefold. Inasmuch as the only tax revenues included under the head of "miscellaneous" in the table on the last page were, in 1919, the tax on national bank circulation (3.8 millions) and the augmented postal charges (61.9 millions) it follows that the federal tax revenues increased from $637 millions in 1915 to $4,089 millions in 1919.

For the state and local revenues complete figures are, unfortunately, lacking. All that we possess are the statistics of state revenues and of cities over thirty thousand population. The state tax revenues for 1919 are given as $528 millions, and the cities' revenues as $875 millions, or a total of $1,403 millions.

The results of the 1923 census, however, enable us to make a reasonably accurate estimate of the entire state and local revenues in 1919. This estimate, as explained in the note, amounts to $2,617 millions.[1] Adding to this the federal revenues as above would bring the total tax revenues—federal, state and local—in 1919 to about $6¾ billions, or exactly $6,704 millions.

IV. *The Post-bellum Period*

Many of the war expenses did not cease with the armistice. It took some time for the armies to be demobilized and

[1] The pertinent Census figures are as follows:

In millions	*States*	*Counties*	*Local*	*Total*
1913	$304	$306	$ 849	$1,519
1919	528	...	....	....
1922	867	742	2,720	4,229

From this it appears that state revenues increased 73% from 1913 to 1919, and 64% from 1919 to 1922; or 285% from 1913 to 1922; and that total revenues increased 272% in the same period. Applying, therefore, to the total revenues slightly smaller intermediate percentages would give us a total revenue of $2,617 in 1919. That is, an increase of 71%. (in lieu of 73%) applied to $1,519 in 1913 would give $2,617 in 1919; and an increase of 62% (in lieu of 64%) applied to $2,617 in 1919 would give $4,239 in 1919, which is reasonably close to the actual census figure of $4,229.

The estimate differs only slightly from that of the *National Industrial Conference Board Research Report no. 55, Taxation and National Income,*

for conditions to return to a fairly normal state. Moreover, the stupendous war debts called for gigantic sums to provide for interest and amortization. As a consequence, the expenses actually increased in some of the countries; and especially with the falling-off in new loans, there was everywhere at first a necessity for augmented taxes. It was not until after a few years that it became possible to introduce a period of gradual reduction.

The increasing revenues immediately after the armistice were due to new and higher taxes. The result of the movement was a scale of graduation never before attained. By 1920 the progressive rate in the income tax had reached a maximum of 77% in the United States and of 60% in Great Britain, France and Germany. In the inheritance tax or death duties the rate in Great Britain had risen to a maximum of 50% (40% for the estate duty plus 10% for the legacy and succession duty); in Germany to 70%; in France to 80% and in the United States to 25%, to which should be added the state inheritance taxes, some running up to 15% direct and 30% collateral. The excess-profits tax which in Great Britain had been reduced in 1919 to 40% was increased to 60% and in Germany to 80%, at which figure it had stood in France. The capital levy was introduced into Germany in 1919 with rates of 10-65%, and in Italy in 1920 with the rates of 4½-50%. The high-water mark, however, was reached by the German property-increment tax of 1919 ranging from 10 to 100%. A similar tax imposed in Italy in 1920 (*imposta straordinaria sul patrimonio*) ran up to 80%.

The peak was reached in the United States in 1920, in England in 1921, in France in 1922. By that time the excess-profits taxes had been everywhere abolished and gradual remissions were being made in other taxes.

United Kingdom. In 1919 some taxes were increased,

Oct. 1922, p. 28, which is reached on a very different basis. The Board figures for 1919 are $6,742,020, as compared with $6,704,000 as above.

others lowered, but with a net increase of the burden. The income tax was raised to 6s.; the excess-profits duty was reduced to 40%. Increases were made in the customs on spirits, and in the customs and excises on immature spirits and beer; while the excises were reduced on tobacco, sugar, molasses, glucose, saccharin and chicory, and repealed on motor spirits and motor spirit licenses. Slight changes were made in the entertainments duty, and imperial preference in import duties was introduced.[1] In 1920 came some more notable increases. The supertax was raised to 6s. making a total maximum of 12s. (60%); the estate-duty was doubled, rising to a maximum of 40% on estates over two millions; the excess-profits tax was increased to 60%, and a 5% corporation-profits tax was introduced. The customs on spirits, wine and cigars were greatly augmented, as were the customs and excises on beer, while many of the stamp taxes were doubled. On the other hand, the duties on motor spirits and on land values were repealed.[2] In 1921 the additional 1920 duty on cigars was abolished, as was also the duty on mechanical lighters. The duties on sparkling wines were altered and on entertainments reduced, and provision was made for the termination of the excess-profits duty.[3] In 1922 the income tax was reduced to 5s.; the duties were lowered on tea, coffee, cocoa and chicory; the excises on sugar and on molasses made from domestic beets were repealed; the club duty was lowered; and relief was afforded from certain entertainment duties.[4] In 1923 the excise on cider was repealed and on table waters cut in half; the rebates on beer were greatly increased; further relief was afforded in the entertainment tax; and the income tax was reduced to 4s. 6d.[5] As a result of these changes the revenues were as follows, in millions of pounds.[6]

[1] Finance Act 1919, July 31, 1919, 9 and 10 Geo. 5, c. 32.
[2] Finance Act 1920, Aug. 4, 1920, 10 and 11 Geo. 5, c. 18.
[3] Finance Act 1921, Aug. 4, 1921, 11 and 12 Geo. 5, c. 32.
[4] Finance Act 1922, July 20, 1922, 12 and 13 Geo. 5, c. 17.
[5] Finance Act 1923, July 18, 1923, 13 and 14 Geo. 5, c. 14.
[6] *Statistical Abstract for 1923*, p. 2; *Finance Account* for 1923-24.

In millions of £

	1920	1921	1922	1923	1924*
Customs duties	149.4	134.0	130.0	123.0	119.9
Excise duties	133.6	199.8	194.3	157.3	147.9
Motor vehicles	—	7.1	11.1	12.2	14.7
Death duties	40.9	47.7	52.2	56.9	57.8
Stamps	22.6	26.6	19.6	22.2	21.6
Land tax	0.7	0.7	0.6	} 2.9	0.6
House duty	1.9	1.9	1.9		1.9
Income duty	359.1	394.3	398.8	379.0	329.9
Excess profits tax	290.0	219.2	30.5	2.0	—
Corporation profits duty	—	0.7	17.5	18.9	23.3
Land value duties	0.7	0.1	0.1	—	0.2
Total tax revenues	998.9	1,031.7	856.7	774.7	718.1
Non-tax revenues	340.7	394.2	268.2	139.3	119.1
Total revenues	1,339.6	1,425.9	1,124.9	914.2	837.2

* The figures are for Great Britain and North Ireland.

It was during this period that the great increase in local rates took place. In Great Britain alone (excluding Ireland) these amounted in 1922 to £192,008,000. Assuming that the total local taxes (including "dues") amounted to about £200 millions in 1921-22, to about £225 millions in 1922-23 and to about £250 millions in 1923-24; this would make the total tax burden in Great Britain in 1921 almost £1,250,000,000, in 1922 a little over a thousand (£1,060) millions, in 1923 about 950 millions, and in 1924 about 970 millions.

France. After the war was over it was decided that the excess-profits tax should cease after 1919.[1] But as additional revenue was needed to compensate for this, there was considerable discussion as to possible increases in the income tax.[2] The discussion eventuated in a law of June, 1920, which increased the graduation of the general income tax to a maximum of 50% with 10% additional for childless

[1] "Loi du 12 Août 1919 portant fixation du budget ordinaire pour l'exercice 1919," in *Revue de science et de legislation financières*, vol. 17 (1919), p. 477. *Cf.* "Les projets financiers du gouvernement en 1919", *ibid.*, p. 585.

[2] An account of the plans of Klotz, François-Marsal, Dumont and de Lasteyrie will be found in Just Haristoy, "L'impôt sur le revenu", *op. cit.*, vol. 19 (1921), pp. 96, 260, 491.

married persons, and 25% for bachelors and childless divorced persons. The rates of the scheduled income taxes were also increased—salaries and agricultural profits to 6%, industrial profits to 8%, real estate to 10% and mine profits to 20%. As a consequence the maximum possible rate on income was 82½%—50% global, 12½% additional for childless divorcés and 20% for the scheduled tax.

The same law fixed the date of expiration of the war excess-profits tax as June 30, 1920. The rates were increased in certain registry and stamp taxes, as well as in the taxes on drinks, alcohol, amusements, sugar, coffee, chocolate, tea, pepper vanilla, gasoline and automobiles. The payments tax on non-commercial transactions was increased to 10%, and the sales tax (*chiffre d'affaires*) to 1% and 3% with 10% on luxuries, plus an addition of one-tenth for local purposes, in which the departments were to share to the extent of one-third, and the communes two-thirds. The tax on securities was increased to 10%, 12% and 20%, respectively, and the inheritance tax was raised to a maximum of 39% on the estate, and 59% on the share. As this might mean a total tax of 98%, it was provided that the tax should in no event exceed 80%.[1]

In the two succeeding budgets for 1922 and 1923, only minor changes were made, barring a further increase in postal charges in 1923.[2] It was not until the great fall of the franc early in 1924, that a substantial further increase in taxation was considered.

As a result of these changes the revenues were as follows, in millions of francs: [3]

[1] "Loi du 25 Juin, 1920, portant création des nouvelles ressources," *op. cit.*, vol. 18 (1920), pp. 333-381.

[2] The laws of April 30, 1920; Dec. 31, 1921; and June 30, 1923, fixing the budgets for 1921, 1922, and 1923 will be found in *op. cit.*, vol. 19 (1921), p. 303; vol. 20 (1922), p. 163; and vol. 21 (1923), p. 439.

[3] The figures for 1919-1921 will be found in *Bulletin*, May, 1922. Those for 1922 and 1923 are taken from Clementel, *Inventaire de la situation financière*, 1924, p. 105.

	1919	1920	1921	1922	1923
Direct taxes	1,069	1,620	1,872	3,377	4,143
Stamp and registry taxes.	2,195	3,260	3,289	3.603	4,141
Taxes on securities	290	568	926	1,018	1,166
Sales tax†	269	1,256	1,911	2,301	3,031
Customs duties	1,477	1,596	1,197	1,615	1,609
Indirect taxes	1,779	2,612	2,919	3,762	3,912
Sugar taxes	377	444	365		
Monopolies	1,052	1,582	1,711	1,803	1,971
Post Office	589	921	1,071	1,285	1,319
Public domain	155	151	113	166	230
Miscellaneous	455	938	1,173	2,295	699
Total ordinary revenue.	9,707	14,948	16,547	21,225	22,221
War-profits tax	672	3,224	3,169	3,050	1,334
Sale of war material...	1,207	1,649	1,501	500	200
Total general budget..	11,586	19,821	21,217	24,775	23,755

† Including *impôt sur le chiffre d'affaires* and *impôt de luxe*, and for 1919 and 1920 the tax on payments.

‡ Post-office revenues and expenditures put into a special budget.

§ Including *recettes d'ordre* and miscellaneous.

From this it will be seen that the tax revenues[1] increased from a little over nine (9,180) milliards in 1919, to about seventeen and a half (17,359) milliards in 1921; grew to about nineteen and a half (19,529) milliards in 1922, and finally amounted to over twenty-one (21,307) milliards in 1923.

The figures of local tax revenues as far as available, are given herewith:[2]

In millions of francs

	Centimes additionnels		Octrois	Total
	Department	Communes		
1919	350	468	229	1,048
1920	508	719	379	1,606
1921	760	879	360	1,999

[1] The tax revenues are arrived at, as in the preceding section, by adding to the direct and indirect taxes the excess-profits tax and the revenues from monopolies, excluding the post-office.

[2] *Bulletin*, vol. 91, p. 114; vol. 92, p. 116. *Revue*, vol. 20 (1922), p. 593.

From this it would appear that the total tax revenues were in 1921 (corresponding to 1922 to the United Kingdom) about nineteen and a half (19,358) milliards. If we estimate the local tax revenues for 1922 at about 2¼ and for 1923 at about 2½ milliards, the total tax revenues for 1922 would be a little under twenty-two (21,775) billions (milliards) and for 1923 almost twenty-four (23,807) billions (milliards) of francs.

Germany. In 1919 the tax on tobacco was increased, as were also the postal, telegraph and telephone charges; new taxes were imposed on playing cards, illuminants (*Zündwarensteuer*) and transfers of real estate (*Grunderwerbsteuer*); and the turnover tax was raised to 1½%, with a rate of 15% on certain luxuries.[1] The inheritance tax now comprised an estate tax (*Nachlassteuer*) running up to 5%, and a tax on shares (*Erbanfallsteuer*) graded from 4% to 70% [2] The extraordinary war tax for the year consisted of a tax on excess income, graded from 5% to 70% and, in the case of companies, of an excess-profits tax running from 30% to 80%. A special tax was imposed on the increment of property (*Kriegsabgabe von Vermögenszuwachsen*) graduated from 10% to 100% (on all increments over 375,000 marks). Finally at the end of the year provision was made for an additional capital levy or so-called Emergency Sacrifice tax (*Reichsnotopfer*) on property, running from 10% to 65% (on property over seven million marks),[3] to be levied only once, but to be paid in thirty to fifty instalments. In the following year, however, the law was amended, requiring one-third of the levy to be paid in 1921, and abandoning the remaining two-thirds.

In 1920 the postal, telegraph and telephone charges were

[1] These laws will be found in *Finanz Archiv*, vol. 37 (1920), pp. 223, 243, 265, 276, 284, 287, and 289.

[2] *Ibid.*, p. 315.

[3] *Ibid.*, pp. 298, 306 and 559. For a discussion of this law, see v. Badulesco, "Le prélèvement sur le capital en Allemagne," in *Revue*, vol. 19 (1921), pp. 153, 333, 536, and J. Jastrow, "The German Capital Levy Tax," in *Quarterly Journal of Economics*, vol. 34 (1920), p. 462.

again raised, and the tax on sparkling wines was increased. The income tax was graduated from 10 to 60%; the corporation tax was fixed at 10% plus an addition of from 2 to 10% according as the profits exceeded 4 to 18% of the capital; and a 10% tax was imposed on interest (*Kapitalertragsteuer*).[1]

In 1921 another addition was made to the postal, telegraph and telephone charges, and the stock exchange tax (*Börsenumsatzsteuer*) was raised.[2]

In 1922 provision was made for a compulsory loan, with an obligation to subscribe from 1 to 10% of one's property. As this loan, like all the other German loans, has been completely wiped out by the worthlessness of the currency, it amounted to a pure tax. Slight changes were made in the income tax; the corporation tax was fixed at a flat rate varying from 10 to 20% according to each class of companies; and provision was made for an annual capital levy or property tax, graduated from 1% to 10%, with a possible doubling of the tax in the case of large estates; as well as for an annual capital-increment tax, graded from 1% to 10%. Finally a tax of 25% was imposed on house rents, to aid in the construction of new buildings.[3]

In 1923 additions were made to the taxes on beer, wine, mineral waters, artificial waters, transportation, tobacco and matches. The stamp taxes were raised, and the coal tax was doubled (to 40%). The turnover tax was increased to 2%, with 15% on luxuries. A tax on admissions was imposed and provision was made for taking account of the depreciation of the currency in the payment of taxes.[4]

[1] For these laws, see *Finanz Archiv*, vol. 37 (1920), pp. 573, 632, 639, 668, and 672.

[2] *Finanz Archiv*, vol. 38 (1921), pp. 616-656.

[3] *Finanz Archiv*, vol. 39 (1922), pp. 39, 211, 217, 233, 264, 277. A discussion of the compulsory loan will be found in E. Wellhoff, "L'emprunt forcé Allemand," in *Revue de science et de legislation financières*, vol. 21 (1923), p. 20.

[4] *Cf. Finanz Archiv*, vol. 40 (1923), pp. 473 (coal tax), 414 (turnover tax), 401 (amusements), and 280 (currency depreciation). For the other laws, *cf.* pp. 185-200, 265, 452-465 and 485. A study of the changes effected in 1922 will be found in J. Jastrow, "The New Tax System of Germany,"

The most important change, however, consisted in the centralization of the system. After 1920 all taxes except state taxes on land and business and communal taxes on land increments and minor sources were to be levied by federal officials. In order, however, to furnish an adequate revenue for state and local purposes, it was provided that a share of the federal revenues should be distributed to the localities. In the income and the corporation tax, the national government was to retain only one-third; in the inheritance tax the states received 20%; in the land-transfer tax 50%; in the sales tax 20% and the localities 5%. The German revenues since the war are given on the next page.

Adding to the federal figures the state and local tax revenues for which no exact figures are as yet available, and which may be estimated at some fifty billions (milliards), the total estimated tax burden in Germany for 1921 (corresponding to 1922 for the United Kingdom) would represent some 200 billions (milliards) of marks. It must be remembered, however, that this period witnessed the collapse of the German currency which assumed cataclysmic proportions in 1923. As a consequence not only were the actual receipts in paper marks far greater than the estimates here given, but owing to the violent daily fluctuations it is virtually impossible, without endless calculations, to reduce the actual revenues to gold marks.[1]

United States. The normal income-tax rate was reduced in 1920 from 6-12% to 4-8% and in 1922 the supertax was reduced from a maximum of 65% to 50%, so that the maximum total rate was now 58%. The excess-profits tax was lowered from 30-65% to 20-40%. On the other hand, the

in *Quarterly Journal of Economics*, vol. 37 (1923), p. 302. For a general survey of taxation from 1919 to 1923, see H. G. Moulton and C. E. McGuire, *Germany's Capacity to Pay*, 1923, pp. 160 and 187. A series of volumes, providing an exhaustive commentary on each of the new tax laws, is to be found in Schiffer, *Die Deutschen Finanz- und Steuergesetze in Einzelkommentaren.*

[1] Kuczynski, *Deutschland und Frankreich*, 1924, p. 89, gives the actual receipts in 1923 as 170 trillions (thousands of milliards) which, reduced to dollars, represents 204 millions, as compared with 430 millions in 1922.

In billions (milliards) of marks[1]

	1919	1920	1921	1922	1923*
Taxes on wealth and exchange:					
Income tax	—	10.2	29.7	243.	450.
Corporation tax	—	0.1	1.6	5.	7.
Capital tax (*Kapitalertragsteuer*)	—	0.9	1.5	2.	—
Emergency levy (*Reichsnotopfer*)	0.002	9.9	0.8	4.	—
Property tax (*Vermögensteuer*)	—	—	—	—	60.
Tax on possessions (*Besitzsteuer*)	0.08	0.01	0.1	0.116	—
Inheritance tax	0.09	0.3	0.6	1.5	2.
Turnover tax (*Umsatzsteuer*)	0.8	5.1	11.5	64.	500.
Real estate purchase tax (*Grunderwerbsteuer*)	0.06	0.7	0.7	1.2	1.4
Tax on dividends and interest (*Kapitalverkehrsteuer*)	—	—	—	6.	65.8
Motor vehicles tax	—	—	—	0.2	4.
Insurance tax	—	—	—	0.4	1.5
Race track and lottery tax	—	—	—	0.5	2.2
Stamp taxes	0.9	1.7	6.8	0.9	4.5
Transportation tax	0.5	1.4	2.2	11.1	520.
Non-recurring war taxes	1.2	5.6	5.4	—	—
Total	3.7	35.7	59.1	339.4	1,617.9
Taxes on commodities:					
Customs	1.1	2.2	5.9	31.4	500.
Coal tax	1.6	4.9	7.0	47.	2,750.
Other excises	1.7	4.1	8.3	29.	189.
Total	4.4	11.2	21.2	107.4	3,439.
Total direct and indirect taxes	9.2	53.0	149.6	446.8	5,640.9

* Budget estimates.

federal estate tax was increased from a maximum of 20% to 25%. Beginning with 1921 there came a reduction in some of the miscellaneous taxes, especially the taxes on communication and the "nuisance taxes." In the table on the next page will be found the tax revenues in millions of dollars.

To the customs and internal revenue we must add, in or-

[1] The figures for 1920-1923 are from the *Statistiches Jahrbuch*, 44th Issue, 1923, p. 317. Those for 1919 (not found in the published reports) are taken from a statement of the German Government furnished to the Bankers Trust Co. of New York, and kindly loaned by Mr. Harvey Fisk. Those for 1922 are from Kuczynski, *op. cit.*, p. 85, who also gives for 1923 the actual receipts in trillions.

	1920	1921	1922	1923	1924
Customs	$ 324	$ 308	358	$ 562	$ 545
Income and profits tax..	3,957	3,228	2,087	1,679	1,842
Other internal revenue..	1,121	1,351	1,121	946	953
Miscellaneous	1,302	694	538	660	544
Total ordinary	6,704	5,585	4,104	3,847	3,884
Post Office	437	463	485	533	573

der to present a complete picture of federal taxation, the following items included under the head of miscellaneous: federal bank tax ($59.8 millions in 1922, $10.8 in 1923, $3.8 in 1924; tax on bank circulation ($4.5 millions in 1922, $4.3 in 1923, $4.1 in 1924); and the immigrant head tax ($2.5 millions in 1922, $4.2 in 1923, $5.6 in 1924). The result is a total federal tax revenue of $3,630 millions in 1922, of $3,204 millions in 1923 and of $3,355 millions in 1924.

The new Census figures give the state and local revenues for 1922 as $4,227 millions.[1] On the assumption that they increased to about $4,350 millions in 1923 and to $4,475 millions in 1924, this would give a total tax—federal, state and local—of $7,851 millions in 1922, about $7,550 millions in 1923 and about $7,830 millions in 1924.

V. *Conclusion and Comparison*

In comparing the extent of the tax burden past and present, it is obviously necessary first of all to present the actual amounts of tax revenue. Assembling the figures which have been arrived at in the preceding pages and remembering, as explained above, that the dates given are only roughly comparable because the fiscal periods in some cases begin and in other cases end in the years mentioned in the respective columns, we should have the table on the following page.[2]

In the next place it is obviously desirable to ascertain the

[1] In the reduction of the foreign currencies to dollars the pound is taken as $4.87, the franc as 19.3 cents, and the mark as 23.8 cents.

[2] It must not be forgotten that the Census figures are for the calendar year 1922, and the federal figures for the fiscal year.

Tax revenues (in millions)

	1900-1901		1913-1914		1918-1919		1921-1922	
United States..	$ 1,400	$1,400	$ 2,250	$2,250	$ 6,704	$6,704	$ 7,850	$7,850
United Kingdom	£ 175	$852	£ 256	$1,237	£ 911	$4,437	£ 1,060	$5,162
France	fr. 3,900	$753	fr. 5,080	$ 980	fr. 6,219	$1,199	fr. 18,547	$3,580
Germany	mk. 2,200	$524	mk. 4,500	$1,071	mk. 11,250	$2,677	mk. 200,000	$47,600

taxation *per capita.* These figures, again only roughly comparable, will be found in the following table:

	1900-1901		1913-1914		1918-1919		1921-1922	
	Population millions	Tax per capita	Population millions	Tax per capita	Population millions	Tax per capita	Population millions	Tax per capita
United States.......	77	$18.18	98	$22.95	105	$63.84	109	$72.29
United Kingdom.....	42	20.28	46	26.89	46	96.45	48	107.54
France	39	19.30	39	25.12	39	30.74	39	80.97
Germany	57	9.19	67	15.98	60	44.61	62	767.74

According to the above figures the *per capita* tax had by the end of the war increased over five times in the United Kingdom, as well as in Germany, about four times in the United States, and only about one-half in France. On the other hand, by 1922 the figures were reversed inasmuch as the tax *per capita* had risen only slightly in the United States and Great Britain, while it had more than doubled in France, and had enormously grown in Germany.[1]

In the above tables it is obvious that the figures are mis-

[1] An elaborate set of comparative figures on this general subject will be found in the League of Nations *Report on the* (Brussels) *International Financial Conference*, 1920, vol. iii, *Statements on the Financial Situation of the Countries represented at the Conference*, and Paper IV, *Public Finance.* The authors of this report are well aware of the difficulties involved and modestly state (page 3, paper iv) that "The bases are so uncertain that little importance can be attached to the results of direct comparison." Yet their conclusions have been widely copied.

The pertinent statistics of the report are given herewith:

	Pre-War revenue per head	*1920 Revenue per head*
United States	$7 = $7	$ 56½
United Kingdom	£4½ = $22	$ 120
France	fr. 129 = $25	$ 47¾
Germany	mk. 50 = $12	$ 12½

In this table there are two weaknesses. The figures apply only to the respective national governments, to the exclusion of state and local govern-

leading, as evidences of the real tax burden, because of the changes in the value of money. From 1900 to 1913 the difficulty is not serious because, although there was a perceptible rise of prices, the rise was approximately the same in the various countries. From 1913 to 1919, however, the discrepancies are great. The index number of wholesale prices rose from 100 to 260 in the United States, to 235 in the United Kingdom, to 356 in France, and to about the same proportion in Germany. By 1922 the figures had fallen to 141 in the United States, to 159 in the United Kingdom, to 327 in France, and had risen to 34,200 in Germany.

It might be claimed, therefore, that the above tables are of little use because the statistics since the outbreak of the war ought to be reduced to pre-war figures. The first part of this claim is indeed valid; but the reason advanced is not

ments; and secondly, the figures are those of government revenue, not of government taxation. The table is therefore of little use for purposes of the comparison in which we are here interested. The figures, for instance, of the United States and Germany are entirely too low because of the complete neglect of local taxation; and the 1920 figures for France are entirely too high because of the inclusion of non-tax revenues.

Another set of comparative figures will be found in *Taxation and National Income, Research Report, no. 55*, October, 1922, of the National Industrial Conference Board, New York. These were prepared by my former student, Mr. L. Gottlieb. The pertinent figures of *per-capita* taxes (pp. 28-34) are as follows:

In dollars	1903	1913	1918	1921
United States	17.55	22.93	57.59	79.15
United Kingdom	23.55	26.07	75.69	124.84
France	17.02	22.29	30.09	84.32
Germany	11.90	18.69	43.17	243.42

This table is more nearly in accord with the figures in the text. The discrepancies are largely due to the fact that for France the figures do not comprise the monopolies, the revenues from which (apart from the Post Office) ought to be included. On the other hand, the figures include the *taxes municipales*, which, as we have seen (*cf.* above, p. 5), are not taxes at all. For Germany the figures are in large part estimates which do not agree with the later official figures used in this article.

Comparative statistics will also be found in the article by Alpha, "Reparations and the Policy of Repudiation," in *Foreign Affairs*, September 15th, 1923. published by the Council of Foreign Relations, New York. For Great Britain, the author quotes (p. 72), figures from the *London Economist* purporting to show that £793 million were collected in taxes. These are far too low even for state taxation and several hundred millions out of the way because of inattention to local taxes. In fact, as all local taxes are omitted in the article, Alpha's figures are absurdly low for Germany, far too low for Great Britain and somewhat too low for France. His conclusions are, therefore, without much importance.

correct. For no accurate method of reduction to pre-war conditions is feasible.

To take the market value of the foreign currencies in dollars is illicit, not only because the value of the dollar itself has changed, but because of the frequently great discrepancy between foreign exchange and internal prices. To take the internal index number of prices, either retail or wholesale, as given above, is inadequate because of the failure to include both real estate and wages in the index numbers. Even, however, if these difficulties could be overcome and if the statistics could be reduced to the pre-war level, they would in themselves be of little use for our purpose. A little reflection will show that even accurate *per capita* figures are of no real significance in the endeavor to ascertain comparative tax burdens. For the important point is not how many dollars, whether of pre-war or of post-war valuation, are paid, but what proportion of individual or social income is taken in taxes. A small *per capita* tax in a poor country or in a modest stratum of society may be a very much heavier tax burden than a larger *per capita* tax in a richer country or in a wealthier class of community.

It is important, therefore, in the next place, to ascertain the revenue *per capita;* and if the *per capita* income is expressed in the same terms, whether pre-war or post-war, as the *per capita* taxation, it makes no difference whether we use pre-war or post-war conditions.

Such an endeavor, however, to ascertain the *per capita* income is fraught with great difficulty. It requires in the first place an exact estimate of the total national wealth and of the entire social income. Such estimates are difficult to make and are inevitably attended with error. If, however, we use the best available figures as presented by the most competent scientists we should have a table somewhat like the one on the next page.

From this table it appears that the comparison of *per capita* income presents a different picture from that of *per*

COMPARATIVE SOCIAL AND PER CAPITA INCOME [1]

	1900-1901		1913-1914		1918-1919	
	Social income in billions (milliards)	income per capita	Social income in billions (milliards)	income per capita	Social income in billions (milliards)	income per capita
United States...	$18=$18.	$234	$33.5=$33.5	$343	$66.8=$66.8	$637
United Kingdom	£1.75= $8.52	$203	£2.35=$10.96	$238	£3.80=$18.54	$403
France	fr. 26= $5.02	$129	fr. 36= $6.94	$178	fr. 50= $9.65	$247
Germany	mk. 28= $6.66	$115	mk. 43=$10.23	$152	mk. 65=$15.47	$256

[1] The figures of income for the United States are taken from W. I. King, *The Wealth and Income of the People of the United States* (1918); and from *Income in the United States, Its Amount and Distribution 1909-1919*. By the National Bureau of Economic Research, New York, 1922.

The figures for the United Kingdom are taken from Sir Robert Giffen, *Essays in Finance*, 2d ed., 1880, and *The Growth of Capital*, 1889; Sir L. Chiozza-Money, *Riches and Poverty*, 1905, and *The National Wealth Will it Endure?*, 1914; B. Mallett, "A Method of Estimating Capital Wealth from the Estate Duty," *Journal of the Royal Statistical Society*, vol. 71 (1908), p. 65; Mallett and Strutt, "The Multiplier and Capital Wealth," *ibid.*, vol. 78 (1915), p. 555; A. L. Bowley, *The Change in Distribution of the National Income, 1880-1913*, 1920, p. 16, and his *Product of Industry: The Analysis of National Income before the War*, 1919; Sir Josiah Stamp, *Wealth and Taxable Capacity*, 1921, p. 75.

The earlier figures for France are taken from de Lavergne et Henry, *La Richesse de la France*, 1908; E. Théry, *La fortune publique de la France* (1911); R. Pupin, *La richesse de la France devant la guerre*, 1916, and *Richesse privée et finances publiques de l'avant-guerre à l'après-guerre*, 1919; and C. Colson, *Cours d'économie politique*, éd. défin., iii (1918), ch. iv. The figures in the last column are the estimate of the present writer.

The figures for Germany are taken from K. Helfferich, *Deutschlands Volkswohlstand*, 7th ed., 1917; and H. Behnsen und W. Genzmer, *Die Folgen der Marktentwertung für uns und die Anderen*, 1921. The latter put the social income in 1920 at 24.4 milliards gold. Moulton and McGuire, *Germany's Capacity to Pay*, 1923, p. 196, put the *per-capita* income at about $100.

Comparative figures are found in Edgar Crammond, "The Economic Relations of the British and German Empires," *Journal of the Royal Statistical Society*, vol. 77 (1914), p. 777; Sir Josiah Stamp, "The Wealth and Income of the Chief Powers," *ibid.*, vol. 82 (1919), p. 441; and the League of Nations *Report* mentioned above, p. 35, note 1.

The League of Nations' estimate, converted into $ at the *current* rate of exchange, for social income per head in 1920 is as follows:

United States	$700 = $700	France	fr. 3,200 = $265
United Kingdom ..	£112½ = $445	Germany	mk. 3,900 = $103

These figures compare reasonably well with those given in the text, when allowance is made for the great drop in the mark. In the final report, vol. iv, pt. ii, p. 21, somewhat different figures are given.

The comparative estimate of national wealth compiled for the Washing-

capita taxation, Germany and France creeping up on the United Kingdom until 1913 but losing thereafter.

Possessing then the *per capita* figures of both income and taxation, it is obvious that we shall reach a closer approximation to the estimates of relative tax burdens in the various countries by comparing the *per capita* taxation with the *per capita* income. If we attempt to compute from the above tables such a ratio of taxation to income, *per capita,* the result expressed in percentages would be as follows:

	1900-1901	*1913-1914*	*1918-1919*
United States	7.76	6.68	10.03
United Kingdom	9.99	11.29	23.93
France	14.96	14.11	12.44
Germany	7.99	10.51	17.42

From this it would appear that at the beginning of the century the average individual tax burden, measured in the ratio of taxes paid to income received, was greatest in France and smallest in the United States; that at the outbreak of the war the disparity between France and the United Kingdom was less, the relative burden having diminished in France but increased in the United Kingdom, while the burden had become heavier in Germany and still lighter in the United States; and that in 1919, several months after the close of the war, the tax burden was heaviest in the United Kingdom where it had a little more than doubled, considerably less in Germany where it had increased about two-thirds, much lighter in France where it was actually less than at any preceding period since the beginning of the century, and lowest in the United States despite an increase of about one-half in the burden.

These figures, however, do not present an accurate picture of the true situation. For in estimating comparative tax burdens attention must be paid to the difference between direct and indirect taxes. Where the major share of the tax

ton Conference on Limitation of Armaments and found in W. R. Ingall's *Wealth and Income of the American People* (1922), p. 310, is obviously inadequate.

revenues is derived from indirect taxes most of which reflect themselves in an increased price level, the burden on the lower incomes is relatively great because the rise in wages proverbially lags behind that of prices; while the tax burden upon those in receipt of larger incomes and who are therefore better able to pay is relatively slight. In countries, on the contrary, where the great mass of revenues is derived from direct taxes, the burden on the lower incomes is relatively small, not only because of the graduated income tax but also because of the property taxes, capital levies and inheritance taxes from which are exempted the more moderate tax payers who are able to amass little if any capital; while the burden on the richer classes and the wealthier business men is relatively great. The social effects of excessive taxation, in retarding business enterprise and the accumulation of capital, are therefore especially marked in countries with a preponderance of direct taxation. On the other hand, it is to be noted that the same percentage of income taken by taxation involves a relatively greater burden in countries of lower *per capita* taxes.

Taking all these points into consideration, it is accordingly questionable whether France with its preponderance of indirect taxes should really enjoy the dubious distinction of having suffered the heaviest tax burden in 1900 and 1913; and there seems to be no doubt that in 1919 the real tax burden was lower in France than in the United Kingdom and Germany and perhaps lower than in the United States.

In the succeeding years the situation changed considerably. A progressive depreciation of the money unit on the stupendous scale in which it occurred in Germany is equivalent to the heaviest kind of taxation. It is also the worst form of taxation, because while excessive taxation is ordinarily a drain upon individual or social revenues, the gigantic inflation of prices which occurred in Germany in 1922-1923 meant a wiping-out not only of incomes but of capital wealth. While it may be true that certain business men may have made paper fortunes through speculation, it is beyond all peradventure of doubt that the German people became impoverished and suffered through this catastrophic inflation a burden of taxation out of all comparison with that in any other country. It has in fact been reliably estimated that the national wealth of Germany was approximately cut in half, and that the earning capacity of the people was greatly lessened by the reduction in the standard of life and the increase of disease and destitution. So far as other countries are concerned, some interest is attached to the table below:

	1922-1923			1923-1924		
	Tax revenues in millions	Population in millions	Tax per capita	Tax revenues in millions	Population in millions	Tax per capita
United States....	$7,554=$7,554	111	$68.05	$7,830=$7,830	112	$69.91
United Kingdom.	£954=$4,636	48	96.58	£970=$4,724	49	98.13
France	fr. 21,307=$4,112	39	105.44	fr. 23,807=$4,571	39	117.19

The complete figures, if available, would probably show the next heaviest tax burden (after Germany) in Great Britain with a somewhat slighter burden in France and a much lower burden in the United States. For although the *per capita* taxation in France was increasing, while that in Great Britain was gradually falling, the disparity dating from the war had not yet been completely overcome; and while the *per capita* income was greater in Great Britain, considerably more of the French tax revenues were still being derived from indirect taxation. As a consequence the real tax burden in France probably continued to be somewhat lower than in Great Britain, and far lower than in Germany.[1]

[1] The actual figures for 1924-25 bear out the forecast in the text. The statistics of tax revenues are as follows:

An accurate comparison of the tax burdens for the future when the currency situation will have again returned to

Great Britain
April 1924-1925
(in £, 000 omitted)

Customs	99,344
Excise	135,128
Motor duty	16,164
Death duties	59,450
Stamps	22,850
Land tax / House duty	1,450
Income duty	336,516
Excise profits	700
Corporation duty	18,100
Total	689,702

Germany
April 1924-1925
(in mk., 000,000 omitted)

Income tax	2,211
Corporation tax	314
Property tax	499
Stock exchange tax	112
Sales tax	1,915
Tax on transportation	313
Other direct taxes	316
Non-recurring taxes	79
Customs	356
Tobacco	513
Beer	196
Sugar	217
Spirits monopoly	141
Miscellaneous	8
Total	7,312

France
1924
(in fr., 000,000 omitted)

Direct taxes	5,285
Registry and stamp taxes	5,655
Securities tax	1,704
Sales tax	4,160
Customs	1,609
Indirect taxes	4,510
Monopolies	2,275
Miscellaneous	1,443
Public domain	400
War profits tax	1,331
Total	28,912

United States
July 1, 1924-1925
(in $, 000 omitted)

Customs	547,561
Income tax	1,760,538
Miscellaneous internal revenue	828,638
Total, ordinary	3,780,149

In Great Britain the local rates may be estimated at £275 millions, making a total tax revenue of £965 millions. In France where the taxes proper, calculated as before, in the national budget amounted to fr. 27,069 millions, the local taxes may be estimated at 3 billions (milliards), making a total of 30,069 billions. In Germany, the above figures as reported by the Agent General for Reparations include mks. 2,745 millions paid over by the *Reich* to the states, but do not comprise the separately levied state and local taxes. These may be estimated at 2½ billions (milliards), making a total tax revenue of 9.812 millions of marks. In the United States there must be added to the above figures about 8 millions, representing the bank taxes and the head tax, and almost $4,600 millions of state and local taxes, making a total tax revenue of $7,744 millions.

The figures for the social income are less exact because they rest largely on estimates. The social income in Great Britain remained at about £3,9 billions, representing the same purchasing power as in 1913-14. That of France has been computed at about fr. 112 billions (milliards) in 1923 and at from 125 to 165 billions (milliards) in 1924. 150 milliards would probably be a more accurate figure—a social income nominally a little larger than just before the war, but representing a considerably smaller purchasing power, thus reflecting the ravages of the conflict. In Germany the estimates vary greatly—from 26 to 40 billion (milliard) gold marks with a mean of 32

normal, will depend not only upon the preceding considerations, but also upon the effectiveness with which the tax laws are actually enforced and upon the degree to which the various strata of society are subject to actual taxation. It would be necessary, for instance, to compare not only the success of the income tax in reaching the wealthier classes in the different countries but also the actual proportion of individual incomes paid by the poor, the moderately rich, and the wealthy. There are, unfortunately, no statistics available for such investigations. Until they become available, a comparative study of tax burdens will have to content itself with the inadequate and largely approximate figures here presented.

billions (milliards), or just about one half the income before the war. For the United States the best available estimate is about 70 million dollars.

Combining these figures; and, inasmuch as Great Britain and Germany are now on a gold basis, taking the franc at its present (1925) value of 4.75 cents, we should have the following table for the fiscal year 1924-1925:

	Social income in billions (milliards)	Population in millions	Income *per capita*	Total tax in billions (milliards)	Tax *per capita*	Ratio of tax to income *per capita*
United States	\$70 = \$70	112	\$625	\$7,744 = \$7,744	\$69.14	11.06
United Kingdom	£3.9 = \$18.99	49	\$387	£965 = \$4,699	\$95.89	24.77
France	fr. 150 = \$ 7.12	39	\$183	fr. 30,069 = \$1,428	\$36.62	20.01
Germany	mk. 33 = \$ 7.91	64	\$124	mk. 9.81 = \$2,325	\$36.32	29.21

In other words, while the tax burden in France was rapidly increasing so as to be almost double that existing at the close of the war, it was still somewhat lower than in Great Britain; and while both the *per capita* tax and the total social income in France were almost exactly the same as in Germany, the *per capita* income in France was so much greater that the tax burden was considerably smaller. The tax burden in Germany was in fact far and away the highest in any of the four countries. The tax burden in the United States remained relatively insignificant and, because of the decrease in taxation coupled with the increase in the *per capita* income, was fast being reduced to that existing at the beginning of the century.

The far higher taxation in France carried through in 1925 and the gradual reduction in Great Britain will probably soon reverse the relative position of the two countries; and it is not unlikely that in the near future the most severe tax burdens in Europe will be suffered almost equally by France and Germany—nominally the victor and the victim of the great international tragedy. This is an illuminating commentary on the fiscal consequences of modern warfare.

CHAPTER TWO

THE ALLIED DEBTS

[This was originally published in the *New York Times,* Nov. 5, 1922, and in *International Conciliation,* No. 181, 1922.]

In a speech at Toledo on Oct. 16th, Secretary Hoover, a member of the Allied Debt Commission, gave his views, which presumably represent the policy of the commission as well as of the government. There is no doubt, however, that there is a growing sentiment in the country which is not in harmony with the views of Mr. Hoover—a sentiment which is entertained by an increasing number not only of business men, but also of farmers and labor leaders. Mr. Hoover's views, moreover, are contrary to those expressed by leading financiers like Mr. Lamont and Mr. Krech at the recent Bankers' Convention in New York.

It may be worth while, therefore, to pass in review the arguments adduced by Mr. Hoover, and to attempt a constructive criticism of a public servant who stands so deservedly high in the affections of the community. In the discussion of the allied debt there are three fundamental points. The first is the character of the obligations; the second refers to the ability of the debtors to pay, and the third has to deal with the desirability on our part of insisting on immediate or early settlement. Let us take these points in order:

I. *Is the Allied Debt a Just Debt?*

Mr. Hoover starts with the following statement: "These loans were made at the urgent request of the borrowers and under their solemn assurances of repayment. They have no relation to other nations or other debts. The American taxpayer did not participate in reparations and acquired no territory or any other benefits under the treaty, as did our debtors. There is no doubt as to the moral or contractual obligation. The repudiation of these loans would undermine the whole fabric of international good faith. I do not believe any public official, either of the United States or any other country, could or should approve their cancellation."

As to the contractual obligation, there can, of course, be no question. The money was borrowed at the request of the Allies; it was loaned in good faith, and it indubitably constitutes a valid debt. But is the question of moral obligation the same?

In the first place, contrary to widespread opinion, the loans to the Allies were to an overwhelming extent made during the war itself. Although private individuals loaned money to the belligerents, not a cent was advanced by the Government until we entered the war. And while it is true that comparatively small amounts were loaned after the conclusion of peace, those loans were made almost entirely for expenses contracted during the war.

Of the total amount of about ten billions, there was loaned to Belgium after the signing of the treaty of peace in June, 1919, up to Nov. 15, 1919, only three millions, and up to Nov. 15, 1920, another ten millions. To France about $250,000,000 was loaned from the date of the signing of the treaty to Nov. 15, 1919, and another $110,000,000 in the next year. To Italy between the signing of the treaty and Nov. 15, 1919, the total advances were a little under sixty millions, and another fifty millions between that date and Nov. 15, 1920. To Great Britain nothing at all was loaned in either period. Thus, substantially, the entire amount was advanced during the war.

Now, what was the object of these loans? As Secretary McAdoo has told us in his report for the fiscal year ended

June 30, 1919: "It is difficult to exaggerate the great purposes served and the great results accomplished by these advances to foreign Governments. In the most critical stage of the war they immeasurably assisted America's gallant associates in obtaining the munitions, supplies and equipment that were so imperatively needed to meet the enemy's offensives or to carry the fighting into his territory, and probably of equal importance was the fact that they served to hearten the allied armies and peoples by the knowledge that the vast credit resources of the United States were being shared with them for the effective prosecution of a common cause. Conversely, it is not difficult to estimate the disheartening effect that these loans of billions and willingness of America to lend for the prosecution of the war as much more as was needed, to the limit of her ability must have had upon the spirit and morale of the peoples and armies of the enemy. * * * * *The service of these loans in assisting to hold the battlefronts of Europe until the might of our heroic army could be felt effectively*, made possible, beyond the shadow of a doubt, the ending of the war in the Fall of 1918. Without this aid to the allied Governments the war unquestionably would have been prolonged, if not lost, with the resultant great additional cost in life and treasure."

In other words, as the sentence italicized by me shows, most of the money was loaned and the proceeds used to carry on a joint enterprise during a time when our aid in the shape of actual combatants was insignificant. If the war was a joint enterprise, carried on for a common purpose, is there any more reason to separate the financial contribution than the human contribution? When we finally put our army under the orders of Foch we fused our efforts with those of our allies and gave an indelible stamp to our common efforts. If we are to charge France and Italy for the wheat that kept their forces alive, for the uniforms that kept their soldiers warm while they held the battlefront, we might as well charge so much per man for the American Army when it finally arrived.

What actually happened was that the Allies furnished a huge armed force which only with difficulty withstood the onset of the enemy. In this huge force the human element was represented primarily by France and Italy; the materials were furnished largely by Great Britain; and the food was contributed chiefly by the United States. All three elements were indispensable to the winning of the war; the absence of any of them would have spelled disaster. The mere fact that our chief contribution was rendered in the shape of book credits must not be permitted to obscure the facts.

It is true that we entered the contest with clean hands and with clean hearts; we poured out lavishly our treasures and the lives of our soldiers; we had nothing material to gain from victory and we sedulously refrained from even advancing any claim to the division of the spoils. So far, so good. But consider the other side for a moment.

Mr. Hoover tells us that America did not participate in reparations and acquired no other benefits under the treaty. It is indeed true that we acquired no benefits under the treaty, but is it true that we acquired no benefits from the war? Is not the reverse the fact? While all Europe was in a death grapple we, as the most important neutral, remained aloof and earned incalculable sums.

At the very outset of the war Europe sent us millions of gold to pay for our supplies, and within a short time the flood of materials which we sent abroad created such a prodigious European indebtedness that it changed the United States from the chief debtor nation of the world to the chief creditor nation. The fortunes made in this country were stupendous; wages rose precipitately, and while Europe was in the throes of convulsions we reached the dizzy heights of untold prosperity. Is it, then, fair to urge that we made nothing out of the war?

On the contrary, this country has been the greatest beneficiary of the war. We received, indeed, no ships to ruin our shipping trade, as was the case in Great Britain; we received no colonies which would have been burdens rather than assets; but we heaped up wealth, while all other countries lost it.

The revolution which converted us from a debtor to a creditor nation, and which made us at a blow the economic arbiter of the world, is due to the fact that we received these enormous profits. Had we been in the war from the beginning we also should now have been hovering on the brink of bankruptcy. Instead of being able to count the ten billions as assets, our Government probably would have been in the position of owing ten times ten billions as our share of the cost of the war.

And, now, after having escaped all these dangers, after having made enormous profits out of the contest, after having emerged as the real beneficiary of the war, we have the hardihood to say that our relatively insignificant cash contribution,—all of which, incidentally, was expended in this country and went to enrich our people,—constitutes a debt which we have the moral right to exact from those who fought by our side and who suffered for the common cause —that is, for our cause—sacrifices incalculably greater than our own!

How are we to explain the almost simultaneous appearance of war-profits taxes in every country if not on the ground of conviction that it is illicit for an individual to make profits out of the blood and misery of his fellow countrymen in so fearful a crisis? But if it is indefensible for a private individual to retain all or even a large part of such profits, why is not the same rule applicable to a nation? What moral right have we to retain the profits that have been gained indeed, but not really earned, in such warfare?

Is the allied debt, then, a just debt? We advanced the

money, indeed, in the form of loans, and legally our position is impregnable. What we actually did, however, was to defray our share of a common burden which, if it were to be adjusted on a truly equitable basis, would make us not the creditor but the debtor of the allied group. To insist now on our pound of flesh is to take the part of a Shylock standing on his legal rights, not of a high-minded partner in a joint common enterprise.

When Mr. Hoover tells us that the Allies gave us their solemn assurance of repayment, he is undoubtedly correct. When a man borrows money he always avers his intention to repay. But it may be questioned whether any of the Allies seriously thought at that time of repayment. It may even be questioned whether any one in our Government seriously contemplated repayment. The situation was so urgent and the crisis so profound that if the Allies had asked for gifts or contributions instead of loans they would have been given the funds just as readily. We know now that England had come absolutely to the end of her tether. Washington knew it then. When we sent our millions of boys to fight, we did not stop to dicker whether this was to be a gift or a loan. What was true of the lives of our soldiers would have been equally true of the guns, the airplanes and the uniforms which they so sorely needed. We made the loans because the Allies asked for loans; had they asked for gifts, we should have been equally ready to comply.

Finally, when Mr. Hoover says he does not believe that the public officials of any country approve the cancellation of the debts, he must be sorely misinformed as to the point of view of nearly every prominent European statesman. It is true that Great Britain has been goaded by our ungenerous attitude into the position where she declares her intention to repay every penny; for, like every proud debtor, Great Britain cannot endure the thought of being twitted with an unpaid debt. But let us not forget that Great

Britain loaned to her Allies almost twice as much as she borrowed from us, and that every responsible statesman in Great Britain would be only too glad of a comprehensive plan whereby she could be relieved of her debt to us and thus be put in position to forego the still larger debts due to her by the other Allies.

From the point of view of the equities of the case, therefore, can the debt of the Allies be called a just debt? We have every legal right to demand it, but from the higher point of view have we a moral right? We emerged from the stupendous struggle with clean hands, indeed, but with full hands. We are the one nation in the world which has profited by the war. Is it not almost like adding insult to injury to ask those who suffered the most and who bore the brunt of a common enterprise to suffer still more in order to enrich us further?

II. *Can Europe Pay?*

Inasmuch, however, as the debt is undoubtedly a legal obligation, the question arises as to the ability of the debtors to pay. Here we must not deceive ourselves. Technically, we are confronted by one solvent debtor and by a number of embarrassed debtors. Practically, however, our real debtors are all of them in the second category; for our real debtors are France, Italy, Belgium and a dozen or more of the other countries. Almost one-half of the principal of the ten billions, is, indeed, owing to us by Great Britain; but while Great Britain was borrowing from us, she was lending still more to France, Italy, Russia and the other Allies. She was able to make these loans because of the advances made by us. In effect Great Britain served simply as a channel through which we made loans to the Continental Allies; the ten billions went to the Continent, although part of it went there through an indirect and devious route *via* Great Britain. The question, therefore, resolves itself into this: Can the Continental countries pay the debts? Are they in any position to do so?

Mr. Hoover tells us that the interest and amortization charges upon the debts amount to only from 2 to 12 per cent. of their annual income. But if what has just been stated is true, and if our insistence on payment of Great Britain puts her into the unfortunate position of demanding payment from the other Allies, Mr. Hoover's figures must be at least doubled. The Allies will be called upon to pay not from 2 to 12 per cent. of their annual income, but from 4 to 24 per cent. And 24 per cent. cannot be considered a negligible sum, especially when it is the last straw that breaks the camel's back.

In the next place, Mr. Hoover attempts to controvert the proposition that countries must pay their debts primarily through an exportable surplus, that is, through the exportation of raw materials or manufactured goods. I have the highest regard for Mr. Hoover as a statesman and administrator, but I respectfully submit that his economics in this respect are not sound. A far better analysis of the situation is to be found in the address of Mr. McKenna. Let us consider more closely how international debts can be paid.

First, of course, they can be paid in cash, i. e., in gold. This method of disposing of the allied debts can, however, be eliminated because the Continental nations have no gold to speak of. The great mass of the world's gold supply is in the United States.

The second possible method of paying a nation's debts is by turning over domestic property to the foreign creditor. Where the creditor is the government, which of course cannot retain the property that may come into its possession but must dispose of it to private individuals, it is clear that if the lands, railroads, or factories abroad were turned over to our government in payment of the debt, the government would have to dispose of them to individual investors. But why should American citizens invest in European lands, railroads, or factories under the present conditions, with the prospects of endlessly increased taxation and decreasing incomes staring them in the face?

The political impossibility of the situation, moreover, is obvious. No self-respecting nation would allow absentee ownership of all its land and industries; and, on the other hand, no nation would look with favor on the investment by its own citizens in an immense amount of property abroad, which would make them waver in their allegiance because of their economic interests. Politically as well as economically, the attempt to pay debts by the transfer of one nation's property to another is excluded.

We come, in the third place, to the so-called "invisible items" on which Mr. Hoover lays so much stress. That these items exist is undoubted. In all international financial relations we have to deal with the money in the possession of, or remitted by, immigrants; with sums expended by tourists; with profits on shipping; with bankers' commissions; with insurance premiums, and with interest on investments. Every elementary textbook of economics makes allowance for these. Ever since the time of Cairnes we have made the distinction between the balance of trade and what is known as the equilibrium of commerce. The balance of trade which refers only to imports and exports of commodities is a familiar concept. Exports must offset imports, imports must offset exports. If there is a surplus of exports over imports, we speak of a favorable balance of trade. But the equilibrium of commerce is a different matter.

Because of the existence of the so-called invisible items, the debits and credits between any two countries generally stand at an equilibrium when there is a definite excess either of exports or of imports. Great Britain before the war, for instance, received such immense sums as interest, freight, bankers' commissions, insurance premiums, etc., that its commorce with foreign countries as a whole was in equilibrium when she imported several hundred million dollars more than she exported. Her debits and credits in international trade were equilibrated through an excess of imports. Her imports were paid for by her exports plus her profits. The excess of imports was due to profits consisting of these invisible items.

It is clear, therefore, that the existence of these invisible items does not disclose any added capacity on the part of a country to pay debts. If we start with a commercial equilibrium which includes these invisible items, the only way to pay a debt is to export more goods or more securities.

How was France enabled to pay her debt to Germany in 1870? First, of course, she had a large stock of gold which she turned over. Then she issued a great internal loan, the proceeds of which she remitted through the medium of bills of exchange. But the most effective method of payment was by immensely increasing her exports. The equilibrium of commerce between France and the outside world for the period prior to 1870 was, as in England, attained at a point where the imports exceeded the exports, the excess of imports representing profits on foreign investments. After 1870, however, the equilibrium of commerce stood at a point where the excess of imports was converted into a large excess of exports. France was able to pay the debt because her productive powers enabled her to convert an excess of imports into an excess of exports and to apply this excess to her indebtedness. Mr. Hoover's treatment of so-called "invisible items" fails to make this distinction between the normal balance of trade and the new equilibrium of commerce.

What is the situation in the Continental countries of Europe? They have no gold to remit. They cannot send us their land, railroads or factories. They have no more securities of foreign countries to turn over, as England did during the war. There is no likelihood of any substantial increase in the invisible items which they could transfer to us. On the contrary, in the present economic situation there is slight probability of their receiving additional sums on foreign investments or profits on a larger merchant marine, or gains through developing banks or insurance companies; and the sums yielded by a possible increase in American travelers abroad or in the sums remitted by immigrants to this country would be only a drop in the bucket.

It remains true, therefore, despite Mr. Hoover's statement, that the only way in which a foreign debt of any magnitude can be paid is through an exportable surplus. This means that there is a surplus of social income; and that the surplus take the form of exports.

In the present situation in Europe, however, there is no surplus of social income, and is not apt to be for a long time. People are prone to forget the gigantic ravages of war; never before in history has there been such prodigious waste of man-power and of capital. Despite the slight improvement that is visible now, Europe has on the whole been steadily going down hill. Even in Great Britain the most competent thinkers maintain that Great Britain is living on her capital, or at least is not forging ahead. Certainly the Continent of Europe as a whole is, economically speaking, bankrupt, and it will be some time before the social income and outgo balance each other. And, in the second place, even when there is again a social surplus, the possibility of putting this surplus into exports will depend on unpredictable competitive conditions.

On one point, indeed, we may thoroughly agree with Mr. Hoover. Until Europe takes energetically in hand the question of expenditures, both government and individual, there is little hope. This means the stoppage of waste and the substitution of thrift for the riotous profligacy which has been the inevitable concomitant of war. It means, in Government finance, a drastic reduction of expenditures and the substitution of international coöperation for the sharp lines of extreme nationalism that have been drawn all over the Continent.

But the accomplishment of this task depends on political forces. There is no hope of great decrease of armaments until a sense of security replaces the present feeling of suspicion. Again, it comes with especially bad grace from us in the United States, who have enacted one of the most extreme protective tariffs in our history, to preach free trade and international amity to Europe. Certainly, insistence by us on the immediate payment of debts will make matters worse than they now are. Can we blame France for saying that, if the United States and Great Britain demand payment in full of the indebtedness, she will certainly not be overgenerous in her demands for reparations from Germany? Reparations and allied debt payment are for the present inextricably intertwined.

The truth is that our debtors are virtually bankrupt. With the exception of Great Britain, they cannot pay now, and will not be able to pay in any near future. I have found no prominent business man or banker here or abroad who believes that there is any possibility of Continental Europe paying the debts at present. You cannot extract water from a stone.

III. *Will it Benefit Us to be Paid?*

But even if the Allies could pay, the question arises: Should we demand that they pay now and forthwith? If they have the ability to pay, have we the capacity to receive?

Mr. Hoover seeks to answer this question in the affirmative by telling us of the three-cornered trade; of the fact, familiar to every tyro, that a nation in international trade may acquit its obligations to another country by transferring the debits to a third country, which stands in an opposite relation. Mr. Hoover endeavors to quiet our fears about the danger of European countries exporting to us a surplus of manufactured goods, which would stop the wheels of our industry, by saying that this surplus may come in the shape of raw materials which we need—rubber, silk, coffee, cocoa, or what not.

Is this true? Will Europe be able to send more to the tropics unless she has an exportable surplus? And how will an increase of European exports create an augmentation in the capacity of the tropics to supply, or in the readiness of the United States to demand, more raw materials? Let us concede, however, that the tropical countries will send us more rubber, tin, silk or coffee, and that the European debtors will send their manufactured goods to the tropics instead of to the United States. What will then happen to our exports to China, South America and Africa? If the rubber and coffee are sent out by them to pay for more goods received from Europe, what will there be left with which to buy goods from the United States? It makes little difference to us whether the wheels of industry are stopped here because of the plethora of exports from Europe into the United States or because of the inability of the United States to send its wares to the tropics. In both cases there will be a falling-off in the demand for our products.

No explanation can obscure the fact that, despite the three-cornered trade, a nation's commerce must be envisaged as a totality. If the rest of the world pays a debt by exporting more goods, whether to us or to another country, it makes it harder for us to export the usual quantity of goods in return. The reason why, under normal conditions, exports are mutually profitable, is that the exporting country is thereby enabled to secure imports, that is, to buy commodities. It is a matter of give and take. But when, in order to pay an immense debt, the rest of the world has to increase its exports to us, there is nothing to call for imports in return; and with this cessation of our exports to foreign countries our factories will close, our industries will languish and a period of depression will set in.

The most striking example of this state of affairs in international trade is the recent transfer of the German merchant marine to Great Britain. The average man thought that that would be a great thing for Great Britain, since she was getting something for nothing. But what was the result? First, there was such a drop in freight rates that stagnation was brought into the shipping business. Secondly, shipbuilding in England fell off to such an extent as to lead to a crisis in the industry, with a wave of unemployment sweeping over the country. Instead of being a blessing, it proved to be a disaster.

What is the real trouble in the United States, with wheat at a little over $1 a bushel and with depression in our industry? How long will it be before the American farmer realizes that our debtors are also our customers, and that we cannot expect any permanent prosperity unless there is a market in which to sell our wares? Even if it were possible to compel our Allies to pay their debts, it would make the situation here still worse. In business life the best way to deal with a bankrupt creditor is to set him on his feet again. But there is a difference between public and private business. In private business, even if the bankrupt is not put on his feet, the creditor can at least find new customers and continue to dispose of his output elsewhere. In public business and finance, as in the present situation, it is different: we must either convert these bankrupt nations into good customers or have no customers at all. By saving them we save ourselves.

The trouble with the Debt-Commission law is that the hands of the commission are tied. It was a concession to the ignorance and the prejudice of the average voter. While I am sure that Mr. Hoover is entirely sincere in his belief, I suspect that he is largely, even if unconsciously, influenced by the politics of the situation and what he believes to be the general sentiment of the country. The situation here is analogous to that in France, where the business men and the economists will tell you privately that they do not at all agree with the views enunciated by the politicians who fear to brave the popular wrath. What we need in this country is a more thorough study of what Mr. Hoover concedes to be the complex elements in the problem. When that study is made, it will in my judgment lead the American people to the conclusion that they cannot afford to press for an immediate repayment of the debt, or even for such a refunding as is contemplated in the law.

It may indeed be just as well to keep the debt on the books for a time. We have ample precedent for this, as in the case of the Turkish debt owing to Russia before the war. It may be good politics occasionally to remind our debtors politely of the fact that there is a debt. But would it not be both generous and wise for us to coöperate with our debtors in some project which would look to the utilization of those debts as a means of the reconstruction of a shattered world?

The debt cannot be paid now, and if it could be paid at once it would harm us more than our debtors. As a matter not simply of equity, but of good business, let us study the matter further. We must not harbor the delusion that we can any longer be sufficient unto ourselves alone. More and more we shall have to depend on our exports, whether of raw materials or of manufactured products. Let us not, in the excess of our zeal, kill with one stone two birds each of which we should seek to keep alive—the one, the hope of European regeneration in the interests of a broad humanity; the other, our own prosperity, which will surely be imperiled by the ruin or the ill-will of our best customers.

[*Note.* The recent failure in Oct., 1925, to come to an agreement with France reinforces the lesson of this chapter. What France is unable to do, Italy, with a relatively greater tax burden, will be still less able to do. If any arrangement at all is effected, it can be only at the cost of great concessions. The United States is still living in a fool's paradise.]

CHAPTER THREE

INCOME TAXES AND THE PRICE LEVEL

[This was originally an address before the Academy of Political Science in the City of New York at its meeting on "Wealth and Taxation," April, 1924, and appeared in the *Papers and Proceedings,* vol. xi (1924).]

The connection between taxes and prices has long engaged the attention of scholars and the solicitude of statesmen. Whereas in former times the practical controversy turned about the tariff, of recent years it has come to the forefront of discussion in connection with the sales tax and now with the income tax. The problem is a subtle and difficult one, and there are perhaps few questions on which there exists a greater divergence of opinion, if not among scientists, at least among business men. It is the endeavor of the following paper to probe this question to its foundation, so far as the income tax is concerned.

I. *Are All Taxes Shifted?*

The most obvious way in which the influence of a tax on prices manifests itself is through the process of shifting. For if a tax is shifted or rolled off from the producer to the consumer, the price to the consumer will naturally be increased by the amount of the tax. By the shifting of the tax we mean its transfer from the original taxpayer to some other person; and as the latter ultimately bears the burden of the tax we may call him the tax-bearer. In order that the tax may be shifted there must, of course, be some economic transaction as between the two parties. In the great mass of cases these transactions take the form of an exchange or a transfer of economic rights—generally through purchase or sale, or through rent or lease; and the question resolves itself into one of a change of price as between the two parties to the exchange.

There is, however, another way in which prices may be affected, apart from the immediate shifting from the original taxpayer to the tax-bearer. The payment of a tax may so modify the position of the taxpayer as to influence his future actions. It may, for instance, cause him not only to change the price, but to alter the output of the commodities or services in question, and it may affect his desire to save or to spend or to invest or to do other things of economic importance. Any such change in his economic attitude may have a reaction upon other classes and may ultimately modify the prices of goods or services which are only indirectly connected with the original taxpayer. In other words, a tax which affects the situation of the original taxpayer may alter the equilibrium of economic forces subsisting between him and his neighbors and may have widespread consequences upon the community, comparable to the ultimate effects that may be produced by any other change in the relative prices of goods or services.

It is obvious, however, that such a consequence depends upon the existence of further relations between the original taxpayer and other individuals. It is necessary here again to hold in mind the distinction between the direct relations which make possible a shifting of the tax and the indirect relations which depend on the ultimate effects of the tax. This distinction is neglected by those who believe that all taxes are shifted to the consumer in the shape of higher prices—the so-called doctrine of the diffusion of taxation. Over a century ago a Frenchman by the name of Canard contended that the imposition of a tax was like the injection of a drop of liquid into the veins of a human being; although introduced at a single point, it will at once be carried throughout the body by the circulation of the blood. Economic transactions in the community are like the circulation of blood in the individual.

In this widely held opinion there are two fallacies. In the first place there are some taxes which do not involve any further direct relations. A poll tax or an inheritance tax, for instance, is not necessarily concerned with anything that the individual produces or sells; it is difficult to see how such a tax can be shifted when the tax involves no further direct economic relation between the taxpayer and other individuals. It is only in a very indirect way that a poll tax, by affecting the general purchasing power of the individual, may modify his demand for economic goods or services in general, or that a high inheritance tax, affecting the readiness of the testator to accumulate wealth, may exert a subtle influence upon the entire economic process. But such indirect effects are very different from the rise of prices traceable to the imposition of the tax. There can, in other words, be no shifting of the tax in such cases, because there is no further immediate economic transaction between the taxpayer and other individuals.

The second fallacy in the general-diffusion theory consists in the fact that even where there are such further relations between the taxpayer and other individuals, economic forces may prevent any shifting of the tax. Take, for example, a tax imposed upon the net profits of a monopolist or upon the rent of a piece of unimproved land. In the case of a monopolist, like the owner of a patented process, the price of the article produced will always be fixed at the highest point consistent with the greatest sales; this is the point of maximum monopoly revenue. If the monopolist were to try to raise the price beyond that point, his sales would fall off to such an extent as to reduce his net profits. If a tax is imposed upon the output or the gross profits of the monopolist, it may indeed lead him to revise his price schedule, because the point of maximum monopoly revenue will now have been altered as a consequence of the tax upon his output or cost. That is, although he may now sell less units than before, his net profits may be greater because of the new margin between cost and price. But if the tax is imposed upon his net profits, it will not lead him to increase the price; for, if he could do this without cutting down his sales, he would have done it before the tax was imposed. What the consumer is willing to give is unaffected by what the producer is compelled to take. In the case of a tax on output he may find it to his interest to sell a little less at a higher price, because the less he sells, the smaller his tax; but in a tax on net profits his tax is reduced not by the falling off in output but by the falling off in profits: and if he increased the price he would suffer a double loss, namely in his lower profits as well as in the payment of the tax. He will therefore prefer to maintain his profits and to pay the tax, that is, he will not shift the tax to the consumer.[1]

[1] We venture to repeat here, with some changes, the illustration found in the volume mentioned in the next note. Let it be assumed that a monopolist can sell, at the price of $5 each, 1000 units of a particular article. Let it be further assumed that the cost of each unit is $2. His gross receipts will then be $5000, and his net profits ($5 — 2) × 1000 or $3000. If he charged more, the sales would fall off; if he charged less, the receipts would be smaller. In either case his net profits would diminish. Let it be assumed that, if he charged $6 a unit, the sale would fall off to 700 units. His gross receipts would then be $6 × 700 or $4200, and his net profits ($6 — 2) × 700 or $2,800, or less than before. If, on the contrary, he charged only $4 a unit, his sales would increase, let us say, to 1200 units, his gross receipts would be $4800, and his net profits ($4 — 2) × 1200 = $2400. He will therefore under the conditions always prefer the price $5, which marks the point of maximum monopoly revenue.

If the government now imposes a tax of $1 a unit, what will be the result? The net return on each unit is reduced to $2, the total net profits to $2000. If the monopolist attempts to add the whole tax to the price, he will sell only 700 units; and since the cost per unit has been increased by the tax to $3, his net profits will be 700 × ($6—3) = $2100. Granting that this is the highest net return that the new conditions admit, the monopolist will increase the price from $5 (which gives him $2000 profits) to $6 (which gives him $2100 profits.) The entire tax will be shifted to the consumer.

But suppose on the other hand that instead of a tax which, as in the above example, amounts to 50% of the cost per unit, or 20% of the original selling price per unit, a tax of 40% is imposed on net profits. Taking the same figures, with no change in price or output, the monopolist must pay 40% of $3000 or $1200, and his remaining surplus will be $1800. If he attempts to add the tax to the price and raises the price to $6, his taxable net profits will be, as above, $2800, his tax $1120 and his surplus

The same thing is true, although in an entirely different way, with a piece of unimproved land. Its price depends upon the amount of similar available land and the demand of those who desire to use the land. A tax upon the land owner does not of itself affect either the one or the other. The amount of land is not influenced by a tax on the land, differing in this respect from a tax on the house which stands upon the land. A house is a piece of capital; and unless house-builders secure the usual return from the investment of their capital, they will not build houses; and the consequent shortage of houses will raise rents. In a tax on land on the contrary, the supply is unaffected by the tax; and there is nothing to compel the user of the land to pay more than he did before the imposition of the tax. The result of a new tax upon the land, therefore, will be to bring about a lowering of the value of the land in the hands of its present owner; for a new purchaser of the land, who will have to pay the annual tax, will make allowance for this in the purchase price. But a tax on land cannot, as in the case of a tax on a house, lead to an increase of price to the person who uses the land.

We have thus seen that the doctrine of the general diffusion or shifting of taxes is a fallacy, first, because some taxes, like the poll tax and the inheritance tax, do not give rise to any further direct transactions; and second, because even where there are such direct transactions, conditions may cause the taxpayer to assume the tax either voluntarily, as in the case of a monopoly, or unwillingly, as in the case of land. In other words, some, but not all, taxes are incapable of being shifted.

$1680, instead of $1800. He will therefore refrain from adding the tax to the price. His final profits are indeed less than before in both cases—but it will be clear why he prefers the tax per unit of product or sales to a tax on income. It is also clear why, with the particular figures here selected, an income tax is for the community as a whole preferable to a tax on product or on sales. For while the producer suffers more under the income tax than under the tax on sales, the difference is more than compensated by the extra loss imposed on the consumer by the tax on product or the sales tax.

We have mentioned some taxes that cannot be shifted. About some taxes that are generally shifted, there is also no dispute. In a tax on commodities such as the ordinary excise or customs duty everyone agrees that the tax tends to be shifted from producer to consumer in the shape of higher prices. The only question at issue is first as to the exact proportion of the tax which is shifted and secondly as to the possible ulterior consequences. Into the niceties of this argument it is impossible to go here. Those who are interested in this particular problem may be referred to a volume that has been written on the subject.[1] It may suffice to say that the proportion of the tax which is shifted, depends partly upon the elasticity of the demand and partly upon the elasticity of the supply. In everyday language, the degree to which the producer will find it profitable to raise his price depends partly upon the probable falling off in sales and partly upon the change in cost per unit which may attend the diminution of his output. As regards ulterior consequences, it will suffice to say that even where it is possible for the producer to shift only part of the tax to the consumer it may affect the various producers in different ways and, by changing the conditions of the market, may confer an advantage on the larger producers which in some cases will even tend to produce a monopoly. Again, even though it is true that the tariff is a tax, the indirect effects of the tax may—not to say, as claimed by the protectionists, must—confer such advantages on the domestic producer, especially in young industries, as ultimately to compensate for the increased burden on the consumer. But in all these cases there is no dissent from the opinion that the original taxpayer shifts the tax, in whole or in greater part.

In a sales tax the same is true: the only point at issue

[1] Seligman, *The Shifting and Incidence of Taxation*, 4th ed., 1921. The subject has also been more recently treated by H. G. Brown, *The Economics of Taxation*, 1924.

here is as to whether the consumer suffers by more than the amount of the tax, or, in other words, whether there is a so-called pyramiding of the tax, whereby not only the tax but a sum over and above the tax is taken from the ultimate consumer. The problem to which we shall now address ourselves is whether the income tax is like the poll tax, the inheritance tax, and the land tax, in not being susceptible of transfer in the shape of higher prices: or whether it resembles a tax on commodities or a sales tax or the tariff, in being usually shifted to the consumer.

The ordinary business man finds but little difficulty in answering this question. He is accustomed to include all taxes in his outlays or cost of operation; and when he considers the price at which he shall offer his goods, he is apt, in the case of a tax, to add it to the cost of his raw materials and his overhead and then, after figuring a reasonable profit on this cost, to fix his price accordingly. But when we come to study the actual results of the operation, the situation is by no means so simple. It needs, in fact, a rather careful analysis of the various complicated elements in the problem.

II. *The Shifting of Special Taxes on Income*

In the first place we must distinguish between a uniform or general tax on all incomes and a partial or special or exclusive tax on certain forms of income. Where the income is derived from property, the latter kind of income tax would be tantamount to a special tax on particular kinds of property. Examples of this are very common. In the case of property, we may have a special tax on land or a special tax on moneyed capital or a special tax on mortgages and the like. In the case of an income tax an interesting illustration is afforded by France. The French income tax is composed of two parts. One consists of a general tax upon the entire income, as is the case with our federal tax. Another part, however, consists of taxes on the separate constituents of income, such as income from land, from professions, from moneyed capital, from business and the like. Each of these taxes on the constituent kinds of income is or has been levied at a different rate. Where such taxes apply to the income from property, there is but little difference between them and the customary property taxes, provided the latter permit, as is not always the case, a deduction of debts. Where, as in some of the American states, indebtedness is not deductible from property, as for instance in the case of real estate in New York, the tax is tantamount to the impersonal taxes or taxes on the yield or product of property, as they are still found in Europe. But where debts are deducted and the tax is imposed on net assets or net property, it makes little difference whether we call it a tax on property or a tax on the income from property; for the selling value of property tends to be equal to the capitalized value of the income to be derived therefrom.

Where we have a series of special taxes on income, it is necessary to consider each class by itself. If we are dealing with ordinary competitive conditions, many such special income taxes will be shifted. If a tax, for instance, is imposed on the profits of a particular class of business, the tax will usually be shifted. The argument is analogous to that in the case of a special tax on the income of houses or on the income of moneyed capital loaned at interest. Why should the individual continue to keep his capital in a particular kind of business, subject to a special tax if, by transferring his capital to some other field not subject to taxation, he can increase his net returns? Such special taxes, therefore, tend to be shifted; for otherwise the individual will withdraw his capital from that class of enterprises and the consequent diminution of supply will inevitably lead to an increase of price.

The same argument applies, with certain reservations, to income from personal exertions like wages and professional salaries. In the case of ordinary unskilled labor, if wages are near the minimum of subsistence, a special tax on wages (which in modern times is not found because of the individual and family exemptions in the general income tax) will be apt to be shifted in first instance to the employer in the shape of higher wages; and he in turn may be able to pass the tax on to the consumer in the shape of higher prices. Where wages are above the minimum of subsistence and enable the laborer to enjoy a higher standard of life, the question as to whether he will be able to shift the tax to the employer in the shape of higher wages, or whether he will have to bear the tax himself and thus suffer a reduction in his standard of life, depends upon many conditions which can be summed up under the head of the relative resisting powers of both parties. Under actual conditions where the standard of life is tenaciously maintained, as in the United States, a tax even on the higher class of laborers will tend to be shifted. The same would be likely to be true of the earnings of the professional classes, like physicians, lawyers, architects, engineers and the like. For, in the long run, if such classes were subject to an exclusive tax, it would, under conditions of free competition, lead to a gradual exodus to other occupations not subject to tax; and this decrease in the supply would naturally lead to an increase of the remuneration of those that remained. There are, indeed, exceptional cases where high professional earnings represent either monopoly returns or incomes that are fixed by custom rather than competition; and in such instances, like railway presidents and great surgeons, it is not at all impossible that, having already charged all that the traffic will bear, they would refrain from adding the tax to their charges or salaries. In the great run of cases, however, a special tax on professional incomes, like a tax on wages where the workmen are well organized, is apt to be passed on.

While special income taxes are thus ordinarily shifted,

this result does not apply in all cases. For, as was pointed out above, a tax on the income of a monopolist, whether he be a business man or a professional man, cannot be shifted. Monopoly price is always at the point of maximum monopoly revenue: the monopolist will always charge what the traffic will bear, and a tax will not enable him to charge more. In the same way, as we have seen above, a tax on land, exclusive of improvements, cannot be shifted, because there cannot be, as in the case of houses or other forms of capital, a change in the supply. An exclusive tax on land, however, like an exclusive tax on the dividends or stock of some particular class of corporations, even if it cannot be shifted, will be capitalized into a lower selling value of the property so that the new owner or purchaser will not bear the tax. There will be a change of price, and the new taxpayer will thus suffer no burden.

III. *The Shifting of a General Income Tax*

In the main, then, a special tax on the income of particular classes, with the exceptions just noted, will lead to changed prices,—either higher prices as in the ordinary case of shifting, or lower prices as in the case of land or of securities where the tax is capitalized rather than shifted. Inasmuch as the individual business man ordinarily thinks of himself in the light of one who is subject to special taxation, it is natural that he should generalize the above conclusion and hold that income taxes, like so many other taxes, are shifted to the purchaser in the form of higher prices.

As a matter of fact, however, the situation is different when we deal with a general income tax such as our federal income tax.[1] If everyone is taxable upon his income, from whatever source derived, there is no taxless field to which

[1] The only point which militates against the acceptance of the federal tax as a general income tax is the 12½% rate on corporations with individual credit for dividends. But as this credit for dividends applies only to the normal tax of 4-8%, it is really of minor importance.

he can repair. If he pays the tax in the first instance, he cannot improve his position by transferring his capital and his energies to some other business or occupation; for he would meet in the new enterprise precisely the same conditions, so far as the tax is concerned, as in the old one. How then can such a change in the relations of demand and supply be brought about as to render possible a shifting of the tax or an increase of price? If the tax is on professional earnings there will be no exodus from the profession because there will be no resulting improvements to the taxpayer. The recipient of income from houses or from interest on capital will not be led to diminish his investments, because in whatever new fields he might be tempted to invest, he would suffer the same burden. The business man subject to a general income tax would also be in precisely the same predicament. So that in case of a general income tax there is no difference, as before, between conditions of monopoly and conditions of competition.

But how shall we meet the objection of the ordinary business man who tells us that he adds the income tax, like the tax on product or on sales, to his cost and thus to his price? It is obvious, however, that there is a fallacy in this contention, at all events when we deal with a graduated income tax. For the larger sum paid as a surtax is measured by profits, not by sales. Let us grant, for the moment, that the smaller taxpayer, subject only to the normal tax, will add the tax to the price of the commodities. Then, if the high profits of his fortunate competitor, subject to large surtaxes, are due not to greater sales but to lower cost or more efficient management, it is clear that the addition per unit made to the price by this fortunate individual must be considerably greater than the addition to price made by the competitor who pays only normal taxes. If the surtax-payer attempts such an excessive rise of price per unit, his sales will fall off, his market will be captured by the competitor subject only to normal tax, and his profits will disappear. He will accordingly refrain from adding the high tax to the price. It is clear therefore that in the above case only the normal tax, and not the surtaxes can be added to the price.

Suppose, however, that the higher profits are due to greater sales, so that the surtax-payer will distribute his tax among a larger number of units than his competitor. Even then, however, the addition which he would make to the price would turn out to be the same as that made by his smaller competitor only in the very exceptional case where the amount of his sales before and after the change of price would bear the same proportion to the amount of his competitor's sales as would the relative ratio of their taxes. For only in that way would the graduation in the amount of sales keep exact pace with the graduation in the amount of taxes.

Barring this highly exceptional case, it therefore remains true that the surtaxes will not be shifted to the consumer in the shape of higher prices. Even if the normal tax or an amount equal to the tax paid by the least heavily assessed individual is shifted, the excess above that amount in the shape of a surtax or super-tax cannot be shifted. The belief so widely prevalent among business men that income taxes are added to the price thus turns out to be fallacious, at least so far as the surtaxes are concerned.

But it can now be shown that the same is true of the normal tax. Despite the widely held belief to the contrary, even a proportional income tax cannot be shifted. In order to prove this, however, it is necessary to discuss somewhat more fully the conditions which fix prices.

How are prices fixed? It is obvious that while prices are affected by the conditions of demand and supply, the normal point around which the market prices oscillate is in close relation to the cost of production. Some commodities oscillate around a hundred dollars a unit; others around one dollar a unit. But when we say cost of production, we have at once to inquire: whose cost of production? Producers obviously differ in ability and in opportunity. It is true that at any given time all similar units in the supply of a given commodity must sell in the market at the same price. If prices differ, it is because of differences in the brand or in the quality or in the speed with which the order can be filled or some analogous reason. But while there is only one price for exactly similar units of the same commodity in the market at any given time, there are under conditions of competition always differences in cost. Some producers have more ability; some factories are more favorably situated; some employers get better results from their labor force; some individuals are able to reduce their overhead or to organize more successfully their advertising or selling campaigns. In short, some have relatively high costs and some relatively low costs of production. At any given time the normal price will tend to equal the highest cost of production. As long as the demand at any particular time is sufficient to take off the total supply of commodities produced at different costs, the price at which the whole supply will be sold tends to be fixed at the point of greatest cost. Inasmuch as the price is fixed at the cost of producing the most expensive portion of the supply that is actually sold, the difference between the lowest cost and the actual price—that is, the difference between the cost of producing the article and bringing it to market under the most disadvantageous circumstances and that of producing it under the more favorable conditions, constitutes the producers' surplus or profits. Profits are the result of the industrial process; they represent not cost, but surplus over cost.

The next obvious point is that in actual life, under competitive conditions, the situation is continually changing. The more efficient producer or perhaps some newcomer in the field with more capital, or with improved machinery, or with better facilities for marketing the product, or with more ability to cut down his overhead, will endeavor to capture a part of the market by putting out an increased supply at a lower cost of production. The fact of this increased supply will tend to lower the price; and, although his percentage of profits may be smaller than it would have been at the old price, the more fortunate producer expects larger total profits because of his ability to sell more. This increase of supply, at a lower price, must manifestly injure the less efficient producer at the margin of profitable production. In every business there are always some producers who are able only just to make both ends meet; their machinery is antiquated, their capital is depleted, their private expenses are too great, their business activity and knowledge are no longer what they should be, and as a consequence their former profits tend to vanish. They may decide for a time to continue the struggle, hoping against hope; they may live on their capital; or they may deceive themselves by a fallacious system of bookkeeping, and figure out a nominal profit. But sooner or later such producers will find that they are getting no return or no adequate return on their industrial capital. They will abandon the business and their place will be taken by a more efficient individual.

All industrial progress consists of such a change at the top and the bottom of the line of producers. Fresh capital is continually coming in; the discouraged are continually stepping out. Under such conditions of change, normal price tends in the direction of the cost of production under the most favorable, not under the least favorable, conditions; it tends toward lowest cost, not toward highest cost. The actual price in the market at any given time is indeed always fixed at the point of highest cost; for at any given moment there is always some unlucky producer who furnishes a part of the supply at cost. But next year he will be crowded out and his place will be taken by someone who can produce at lower cost.

What is the bearing of this analysis upon the problem of taxation? It resolves itself into the question of how the marginal producer, the producer at the margin, is affected. A tax on a commodity per unit affects the cost of the marginal producer as well as of every other producer and therefore tends to be added to the price, because whatever increases marginal cost must ultimately increase price. But a tax on income is a tax on net profits; and net profits are not cost, but the surplus over cost. A tax on profits cannot reach the man who makes no profits. But the man at the margin who makes no profits, or who makes only the minimum profits which correspond to wages of management or recompense for the risk, pays no tax because he makes no profits or pays only a negligible tax upon these minimum profits. If the man at the margin who at any particular time fixes the price for the entire supply of commodities that is sold in the market pays no tax, how can the income tax be added to the price? The tax on profits is paid only by the man who makes profits, that is by the intra-marginal producer, not by the marginal producer. But the tax paid by the intra-marginal producer cannot affect the price which is fixed by the marginal producer who pays no tax.

IV. *The Business Man's Theory*

The ordinary business man who thinks that he is adding the tax to the price is in reality not doing so. Whether he can get the price which he has set depends not upon himself, but upon market conditions. If his competitor who pays a smaller tax because of smaller anticipated profits, or who perhaps pays no tax at all, marks his goods at a lower price because of the smaller tax, all the others will have to follow suit whether their taxes are high or low. Where a man has added the tax to the price, the inability to dispose of his goods at this higher price will lead him quickly to mark down his goods; with the result that his anticipated profits may not materialize. There is many a slip 'twixt cup and lip. The profits of a business man at the end of the year depend upon a multiplicity of perhaps very insignificant factors; he can never tell at the beginning what his profits are going to be at the end. The mere fact that he adds his anticipated taxes to the asking price will not by any means enable him always to get the price that he asks. The profits upon which he pays taxes come at the end, and not at the beginning, of the period. If every man could fix his profits at will by charging increased prices because of anticipated increased taxes, the making of profits would be a very simple proposition. Unfortunately, however, business life does not work that way.

It might indeed be claimed that, if the business man were correct in his opinion, it would be stupid for him to object to high income taxes. For, if the business man really adds the income tax to his cost and then charges proportionate profits on this increased cost, why, it might be asked, would not high income taxes increase his profits?

This argument, however, is really invalid.[1] For the producer does not necessarily remain scatheless even if his taxes are shifted. He may be able, under a tax on product or on sales, to increase the price of his commodities; but the increase in price will almost surely lead to a falling off in consumption and will therefore tend to restrict his profits. This is the reason why the business man does not welcome taxes on his product, even if the tax is passed on. In the same way, even though the producer should be able to add the income tax to the price of his goods and thus increase his profits per unit of output, he would, in all probability, sell so many less units as to diminish his total net profits. The business man, therefore, is quite justified in objecting to high taxes on business profits, even if he thinks that he is able to shift them to the consumer.

As a matter of fact, however, as we have seen, the business man is not able to do this. The chances are that if he did not increase the price by his anticipated income taxes, his actual profits at the end of the year would probably be

[1] It has nevertheless been advanced by some writers.

the same. For in the first place it is not at all sure that he can hold to the higher prices in the face of the lower taxes imposed on some of his competitors; and, secondly, even if he should be able to hold to the higher prices for a time, he would find his sales falling off to such an extent as to lead to a new and lower price schedule. In other words, business profits are a result of business operations: they are a consequence of price, not a cause of price. A tax on business profits is not a part of cost as is a tax on business products. The latter can be shifted; the former cannot be shifted.

It might be claimed by some that the above reasoning is defective. Producers, it might be said, will not permanently remain in business unless they secure the usual returns, which in the ordinary run of cases can be fixed at, say, six per cent. Not only the producer below cost, but the producer at cost or with profits of less than six per cent will be continually stepping out, and the real marginal class, it might be claimed, is the six per cent class. Even a normal income tax will then, so the argument runs, be shifted because otherwise it would reduce their profits to say, five per cent, with the result that their falling out of the race will reduce the supply and thus increase the price.

This objection, however, is doubly defective. In the first place, it does not follow that the fall of profits to five per cent will lead to an exodus of the previous-six-per-cent producers. For there will now be no other field of business to which they can repair. If the tax is a general tax, the entire level of profits will be reduced from six to five per cent, and the producer will have to content himself with the smaller profits. It is only when the normal tax is so excessively high as to reduce the general rate of profits to a figure where all business enterprise will be checked, that prices can be affected. But, as we shall see below, even this means not a shifting of the tax in the shape of higher prices, but a prevention of what would otherwise be a tendency to lower prices.

In the second place, if the price of the commodity is raised as a result of the addition of the tax made by the six-per-cent producers, all of the lower-profit or no-profit producers—whether we call them marginal or sub-marginal—who pay small taxes or no taxes at all will now also be able to charge the higher price. They will consequently be in a position to increase their output, with the result that their more effective competition will soon lead to an abandonment of the higher price by the six-per-cent producers. For even five-per-cent profits are preferable to the still lower profits which would ensue on a loss of the market.

Thus the analysis stands: a normal income tax cannot be shifted, any more than can a surtax.

There is only one possible weakness in the above analysis. In a period of rapidly rising prices, we may have what is commonly called a sellers' market. Everyone is then anxious to buy; every producer is turning out goods at the maximum rate, and stocks are being depleted almost more rapidly than they can be replenished. Even the producer with the highest cost—the old marginal producer—will now find that he is making money, because the price of his goods is considerably higher than his cost. Being in a position to market his entire output, there will be no inducement for him to cut prices in order to secure a still larger proportion of the total sales. Under such circumstances, indeed, the imposition of a tax of any kind, whether on income or anything else, will afford the producer an excuse for asking a still higher price, and the conditions of the market may enable him to hold to that price. But after all, the tax will then be an excuse for, rather than a cause of, the higher prices which he would probably have been led to demand in any event. And at best, such business conditions can be only temporary. For the large profits due to a sellers' market will speedily lead to a fresh investment of capital and an increased output on the part of some competitors; and as soon as this condition shows itself, the heyday of the old producers is gone. As a matter of fact, the sellers' market is before long apt to be succeeded by a buyers' market, when all the advantages will be on the side of the purchasers, and when the producers will slash prices, tax or no tax, in order to dispose of their accumulated stocks. Just as everyone makes money in good times, so everyone loses money in poor times; and what the consumer has suffered in the first case by high prices, he will now gain by low prices.

Under normal conditions, however, when there is neither a business boom nor a business depression, when there is neither a sellers' market nor a buyers' market, but just an ordinary, normal, average market, the producer will not even have an excuse for adding an income tax to the price. For, as we have pointed out above, prices will tend, under normal conditions, to be fixed at the cost of production of the marginal competitor who pays no taxes because he finds at the end of the year that he has made no profits.[1]

[1] The above conclusions as to the shifting of the income tax are in harmony with the doctrine of Ricardo. His statement is as follows: "To me, however, it appears convincingly certain that neither the income tax, the assessed taxes, nor many others, do in the least affect the prices of commodities. . . . The income tax, were it fairly imposed, would leave every member of the community in the same relative situation in which it found him. Each man's expenses must be diminished to the amount of his tax; and if the seller would wish to relieve himself from the burthen of the tax by raising the price of his commodity the buyer for the same reason would wish to buy cheaper. These contending interests would so exactly counteract each other, that prices would undergo no alteration. The same observations are applicable to the assessed taxes, and to all other taxes which are not levied on commodities. But, if the tax should in its operation be unequal, if it should fall particularly heavy on one class of trade, the profits of that trade would be diminished below the general level of mercantile profits, and those engaged in it would either desert it for one more profitable, or they would raise the price of the commodities in which they dealt, so as to bring it to produce the same rate of profits as other trades.

"Taxes on commodities would certainly raise the price of the commodity taxed to the full amount of the tax. The price for such commodities may be considered as divided into two portions; one portion, its original and natural price, and the other a tax for the liberty of consuming it. If this tax again were laid on a commodity, the consumption of which, by each individual, was in exact proportion to his income, no other commodity would rise but the one taxed; but if it were not in such proportion, those who paid more than their just portion would demand an increased price for the commodity in which they dealt, and, by obtaining it, the society would be put in the same relative situation in which they were before placed." David Ricardo, *Reply to Mr. Bosanquet's Practical Observations*

V. *The Indirect Effects of an Income Tax*

While, then, it is a fact that taxes on business incomes cannot be directly passed on in the shape of higher prices, the question still remains as to what the indirect effects upon prices may be. Here we enter upon the thorny path of the general effects of taxation. It may be said at once that all sorts of ultimate effects are possible. It is conceivable, for instance, that if income taxes are so high as to check the investment of capital, very definite consequences to the entire community may ensue. The continual growth of a country's prosperity depends largely upon the readiness of the able and the venturesome to start new enterprises and to take the risk of the unknown. Where the hazard is great, the profits must be correspondingly great: for in the long run in new and untried fields the profits of some are likely to be counterbalanced by the losses of others. If the government, however, demands too large a percentage of these anticipated profits, the individual may prefer not to subject himself to the risk and may decide to be content with a smaller, but a surer, return. Or, if the income tax is still more excessive, it may decrease the margin above living expenses and thus retard savings and the accumulation of capital. In both cases, whether there is less capital to invest or fewer venturesome individuals to utilize the capital, the result will be the same. The rate of interest will tend to rise, thus to this extent increasing cost and therefore augmenting price. And, on the other hand, the relative slackening of demand for new production will check the increase of employment and the rise of wages that normally go with increased productivity and the growth of capital. This, again, will prevent the gradual fall in the price of the particular commodities subject to the law of increasing productivity. The history of modern capitalism, especially in the

on the Report of the Bullion Committee, 1811, pp. 117-118. In McCulloch's *The Works of David Ricardo*, new ed., 1876, this passage will be found on p. 357.

United States, shows a steady increase in wages and in the laborer's standard of life and a steady decrease in the cost of the manufactured articles which enter into ordinary consumption. To the extent that excessive income taxes actually check accumulation and enterprise, they may therefore have this indirect result of preventing the increase of wages and the rise of the standard of life. But this result will be not so much an increase of price (except in so far as the rate of interest actually rises) as the prevention of a further reduction in the prices of commodities and a further rise in the rate of wages which is itself compatible, under the theory of the economy of high wages, with lower prices.

Whether taxes on business income will engender such indirect consequences depends, however, on a variety of circumstances. It depends first upon whether the taxes are used for fresh expenditure or to pay the interest on an old debt. If the taxes are used for new expenditure, the problem becomes one as to the relative productivity of private and public outlay. The statement so often heard that it is always better for the government to let capital fructify in the hands of the private individual is by no means correct. Certain forms of government expenditure or investment may be far more productive than certain forms of private expenditure or investment. The money spent for new roads or for new schools may be far more productive, in the real sense of the term, than the money invested by private individuals in the manufacture of opium products or of the munitions of war.

There are, of course, considerations on the other side. If the government attempts to run the railroads or to manage the coal mines it is entirely probable that the enterprise will be less productive of wealth than if it were conducted by private individuals. It is undoubtedly true in general that there is apt to be less extravagance and waste under private than under public management. But when the community has entrusted to the government the carrying on of what are everywhere conceded to be proper coöperative functions it does not follow that the results will be injurious. The taxes may be so high as to retard accumulation and investment; but if they are spent for governmental purposes that are acknowledged to be necessary or advisable, the smaller evil may be swallowed up in the larger benefit. The problem is really one of the proper limits of government expenditure, and of the choice between low taxes on the one hand and the accomplishment of desirable governmental purposes in an adequate, albeit economical, fashion on the other.

The problem differs when we deal with taxes imposed to pay the interest on an old debt. This is the situation in the greater part of the world today. In the United States a large part of our present high taxes is devoted to the debt service. It is immaterial whether we consider the war expenses productive or unproductive of wealth or of welfare: the money has been spent, the debt has been contracted, and taxes must be imposed to pay the interest and to provide for amortization. The chief consideration now is the rapidity of debt payment. If the taxes are excessive, it may be better to go slow in discharging the debt rather than further to retard capital investment and enterprise. But if a definite policy of taxation for debt service has been decided upon, the next consideration is whether the debt is a foreign or a domestic debt. If the debt is held largely or exclusively abroad, there can be no advantages to compensate for the excessive burdens upon the domestic producer. If the debt is a domestic debt, the funds taken from the taxpayer are handed over to the bondholder. The capital still remains in the country and is presumably available for investment by someone.

A further analysis discloses the fact that conditions may here be very different. If the bonds are held largely by the small man who will now increase his personal or family expenditures because of the money received from government, there are no advantages to the community as a whole which will compensate for the burden of taxation. But if the bonds are held by the wealthier classes who now have more money to invest, or by people in more moderate circumstances who put the interest into the bank, rather than spend it upon themselves, there may indeed be compensating advantages. It is true that the business man who pays the high taxes will have less capital to plough back into his business; but to the extent that he is also a bondholder, the deficiency will be made good. That is doubtless the reason why, despite the high income taxes in the United States during the past few years, the volume of accumulated investment has suffered no perceptible reduction.

Even with this qualification, however, it still remains true that excessive income taxes may discourage enterprise and thus prevent a reduction of price. For while the old capitalist may find that his bond interest will reimburse him for his taxes, the venturesome individual who would otherwise embark upon a new and untried course may still be prevented from devoting his energies and abilities to the hazardous enterprise if the excessive rate of taxation threatens to reduce his profits below what he considers an adequate return. To the extent—but only to the extent—that progress depends upon the entrance of the new man into the industrial field does the argument as to this ultimate effect of income taxes upon prices remain true.

We have limited ourselves to a discussion of what is apt to be the effect of income taxes upon prices. We have not discussed the more important problem of government policy. It is conceivable, for instance, that a tax system might be so arranged as to prevent any ulterior effects upon prices and nevertheless be entirely unacceptable. An aristocratic or plutocratic government might conceivably raise its entire revenue from a tax on the poor or the moderately well-to-do consumer and wholly exempt large business. Such a policy would indeed not produce any of the injurious effects on enterprise and investment that have been mentioned above.

But it would so obviously contravene the principle of equality and of ability to pay as to be wholly inadmissible. A democracy which is educated both economically and morally will seek in its tax system to preserve the proper balance between the principle of ability to pay on the one hand and the principle of what might be called innocuity, i.e. harmlessness of taxation on the other. Into this field of discussion, however, we are not called upon to enter.

In conclusion then we may sum up as follows: Taxes upon the separate classes of income will or will not be shifted according to the particular category or the particular circumstances. A general or universal tax on all income, if actually enforced, cannot be shifted directly. But in so far as taxation brings about a new equilibrium of economic forces, even a general income tax may ultimately and indirectly affect prices, either by leading to a readjustment of interest rates, or by preventing an increase of productivity with its usual concomitants of higher wages and lower prices. For the greater the productivity in any field of enterprise, the lower will be the prices of the products in that field, despite the rise of wages. An excessive income tax may accordingly interfere with an otherwise to be anticipated fall in prices as well as rise of wages, thus standing directly athwart the interests of the consumer as well as of the laborer. Even if an income tax cannot be shifted, it may, if excessive, disadvantageously affect the position of other classes besides the immediate taxpayer.

CHAPTER FOUR

TAXATION AND PRICES

[This was originally an address before the Academy of Political Science in the City of New York at its meeting in November, 1924, and appeared in the *Papers and Proceedings*, vol. xi, 1925.]

The problem of the general price level is everywhere attracting the greatest interest. For this there exist two reasons. First, of course, is the world situation as the aftermath of the war. No great war can take place without a cataclysmic influence on prices. By some this is ascribed to the loan policy in the fiscal prosecution of the war, and it is alleged that under a tax policy there would be no inflation. A broader view of the problem, however, has led to the conclusion that the change in the price level is due primarily to the dislocation in the conditions of production and consumption. While exaggerated loans, and especially the issue of paper money, may accentuate the trouble, excessive taxation may have an effect similar in kind, even if less in degree.[1] Even if a moderate and well-balanced tax-loan policy is pursued a great war will none the less be attended with a rise in prices. In a certain sense, indeed, both loans and taxes may be considered as the consequences, rather than the causes, of such price perturbations. For inasmuch as the expenditures necessarily grow, with the higher prices that must be paid for the munitions of war, the amounts to be raised by either loans or taxes must be proportionately augmented. On the other hand, while war taxation may be so excessive as to check production and raise prices, the post-war taxation connected with the payment and the amortization of the war debt may, by engendering a better budgetary balance, play its part in

[1] *Cf.* the chapter "Loans versus Taxes in War Finance" in Seligman, *Essays in Taxation*, 10th ed., 1925.

bringing about a return to the ante-bellum lower price level. But whether taxation raises or lowers the price level, it is of relatively minor importance, except in so far as it serves either to augment or to diminish the disparity between production and consumption.

The second reason why we are all so much interested in the price level is the growing comprehension of the business cycle, with its period of rising and falling prices. Here again, taxation is of relatively minor importance; for the changes in taxation are not apt to be so dramatic as those in the conditions of production and consumption which are ultimately responsible for the alternation of high and low prices.

The problem of taxation is of such consequence at present chiefly because of the fortuitous conjuncture of these two facts—the weight of a war burden combined with the depression of a business cycle. What would ordinarily be borne with comparative equanimity arouses universal discontent today.

There is, however, another point of view from which we can regard the connection between taxation and the price level. Irrespective of the post-bellum situation and of the ups and downs of business there is room for a study of the relation between taxation and prices under normal conditions. Inasmuch as this is the more difficult part of the problem it may be well in this chapter to limit ourselves to a consideration of this topic.

There are here two basic problems. The first is the effect of the constituent elements of a tax system upon prices in particular; and the second is the effect of taxation as a whole on the general price level.

I. *The Effect of Taxes on Particular Prices*

If we consider first the influence of special categories of taxation upon prices we find a great variety of results. Some taxes increase prices proportionately; some taxes increase prices disproportionately; some taxes do not increase prices at all; some taxes do not increase prices directly, but affect them indirectly; and some taxes decrease prices. Let us pass in review each of these phenomena.

A familiar example of the proportional influence of tax upon price is afforded by the ordinary imposts on commodities. While in a careful scientific study attention would have to be given to the modifications attributable to the relative elasticity of demand and the relative elasticity of supply as well as to the prevalence of constant, of diminishing and of increasing returns, it may suffice as a first broad approximation to state that, other things being equal, a tax upon a commodity increases the price of the commodity by the amount of the tax. When we say that other things are equal, we assume that the tax is imposed upon all the commodities in a given class and that, inasmuch as the tax reaches the marginal commodities, it will affect marginal costs and thus produce its influence upon market price. Ordinary taxes on commodities, therefore, tend to increase the price of the commodities by the amount of the tax.

It is immaterial, from this point of view, whether the tax is imposed upon the commodity in the hands of the producer or in the hands of the consumer: there is in this respect little difference between so-called taxes on production and taxes on consumption. When we deal with business taxes, however, we must be careful to distinguish on the one hand between a tax on output or unit of production or on gross product, and a tax on business profits or business earnings on the other. The line of cleavage is to be sought in the fact of marginal cost or marginal production. Where a business tax or a property tax on merchants' stock in trade or a license tax or a corporation tax virtually amounts to a tax on product, it is equivalent, from this point of view, to a tax on commodities. The price of the product rises, other things being equal, in proportion to the amount of the tax.

We do not desire here to enter into the question as to whether this higher price is temporary or permanent in character. It may happen that the increase of prices so affects the relation between demand and supply and the conditions of the market as to modify the facts of competition. Under such circumstances there may be a stimulus to competitive effort which will ultimately lead to a lower level of cost that may compensate, or even more than compensate, the effect of the tax. Thus, while we know the familiar adage that the tariff is a tax, the argument of the protectionists from the time of Alexander Hamilton and Friedrich List to the present, as found in the young-industry argument, is to the effect that the temporary rise of prices will be offset by the consequences of the augmented competition and increased production which will ultimately lead to lower prices. Without entering upon this controverted position here, we may accept the statement that, in its immediate consequences at least, a tax on commodities increases price by the amount of the tax.

A second class of taxes is represented by those where the increase in the price results in an augmentation of the price by more than the amount of the tax. We do not now refer to the older theory whereby this consequence was predicated of all so-called indirect taxes. For this older theory of the indefinite cumulation or pyramiding of taxes rests upon a somewhat dubious theory of business profits which is no longer widely held. What we have in mind, on the contrary, is, e.g., a tax on sales where the tax is not simply imposed once on the commodity in the hands of either the producer or the consumer but where it is paid every time that the commodity changes hands. In such a case it goes without saying that the price will be continually augmented as the commodity goes from hand to hand, inasmuch as the price to every successive owner of the commodity will include the additional tax imposed upon his predecessor. There is here no question of discrepancy between the amount taken from the individual and the sum accruing to the government. The question is only that of the progressive augmentation of the price due to the tax. It is because of this fact that any attempt to introduce general sales taxes is apt in a democracy to meet with vigorous resistance on the part of those who realize that there is always a lag between the higher price of commodities and the higher wage level. A sales tax augments this discrepancy, and is, therefore, always unpopular with the great mass of wage receivers.

The third class of cases comprises those where prices are not affected at all. A poll tax, for instance, which influences the personal situation of the individual has no effect on the price of any particular commodity. It may conceivably, if excessive, somewhat influence the general purchasing power of the individual. But in general, it is likely to exert only an infinitesimal effect on the price level, and its influence on the price of any particular commodity is quite unpredictable. In the same way, an inheritance tax cannot well exert any assignable influence on the prices of the commodities forming part of the estate and can have only the most remote effect on the price level in general.

We come, fourthly, to those taxes where the influence on prices is indirect rather than direct. Outstanding in this category are taxes on income or on excess profits. Inasmuch as this particular topic has been more fully treated in the preceding chapter it will suffice to recall the conclusions there elaborated. Since profits are a result and not a cause of price, differing in this respect from interest and wages, and since a tax on business income, whether or not called a tax on excess profits, is a tax on surplus, not reaching the marginal producer, such a tax cannot directly affect prices which are normally fixed at the point of marginal cost. It is here that a tax on net earnings differs from a tax on output or production. There is no direct influence on prices. To the extent, however, that so-called business taxes reach the interest on invested capital rather than pure economic profit the result indeed may be somewhat different.

But while a tax on income or net earnings does not directly affect prices it may indirectly influence prices by so modifying the flow of capital as to affect the conditions of production through the lessening of investment and enterprise. Moreover, an extravagant tax on incomes may affect not only the capacity to save or to produce, but the ability to spend; and in the latter case it may substantially reduce the consuming powers of the community or the general demand for commodities. Thus in both scales of the economic balance or equilibrium, an excessive income tax or a high property tax, so far as it is paid out of income, may affect either the supply of, or the demand for, commodities and thus influence price.

The final category of taxes comprises those which are attended by a decrease rather than an increase of price. This paradox does not refer to the older theory, discussed since the time of Hume, that taxes in general tend to increase incentive and ingenuity and thus reduce cost. Without wishing to dwell here upon this disputable proposition, we desire to point out an entirely different idea, namely that when we are dealing with certain classes of permanent wealth, a tax may, through the process of capitalization, be amortized into a lower selling value of the commodity. A real estate tax in cities, for instance, is composed of a tax on the land and a tax on the building. A tax on the building will as in the case of all taxes on commodities increase the cost of building, and will under normal circumstances be shifted to the tenant in the shape of higher rent or to a new purchaser in the shape of higher price. On the other hand, the tax on the land cannot be shifted, as there is no question here of any cost of production. A land tax reduces the earnings from the land or the economic rent; and in proportion as the rent declines, the capital value of the land will correspondingly fall. In the same way a tax on a bond which reduces the net income from the bond will cause its market value to diminish in proportion. In other words, in commodities of a more permanent character, like land and securities, where the tax is not shifted, but capitalized, the result of the tax will be a lower price, not a higher price.

If we sum up this part of the discussion we realize that the influence of taxation on prices depends upon the kind of tax and the amount of taxation. Where the tax system is composed primarily of indirect taxes on production or consumption, as was once the universal custom and as is still common in Latin-American countries, the direct relation between taxation and prices is close. Where the system is composed largely of income taxes, or of property taxes paid out of income rather than out of property, the influence of taxation on price is much less direct. Where taxes are excessive and modify in an important measure the ability either to spend or to invest, the effect of taxation upon prices is slower but none the less sure. Where the tax system is composed largely of land taxes or of special taxes on corporate securities, taxes tend to decrease rather than to increase the prices of commodities. The conclusion is that if the purpose is to prevent as far as possible interference with prices, the ideal system will be that of a moderate and carefully selected combination of certain so-called direct taxes. It need, however, not be pointed out that in the elaboration of any tax system, it is important to observe a principle of far greater significance than simply the desire to avoid changes in prices. Finally, it must be remembered that what we have been discussing is the effect of taxation upon particular prices. Other things being equal, a rise in the price of one or more commodities is apt to be attended by a fall in the price of other commodities. It is only when the tax is essentially of a general character, or where it affects the universal disposition to spend or to save, that we can speak of any influence of taxation on the price level, that is, the price of all commodities.

II. *The Effect of Taxes on the General Price Level*

We come in the second place to the more significant and at the same time more controverted subject of the influence of taxation, not in particular but upon prices and values in general. This involves the problem of what might be called the productivity of the government expenditure which is defrayed by taxation. When we consider taxation as a whole the situation is different from that which emerges from a consideration of individual taxation.

In dealing with the nature of tax obligation, i.e., with the fiscal relation of the individual to the government, we have long since advanced beyond the primitive conception of taxation as a price or as an exchange of individual support of the government for governmental protection of the individual. This older doctrine, called by John Stuart Mill the *quid pro quo* theory, is generally acknowledged as untenable today. In the first place, it neglects the more organic concept of the state in modern political theory. In the second place it overlooks the fact that taxation involves compulsion, while in the ordinary price system we have the free choice under the competitive market, or the freedom of substitution under a monopoly. In the third place, the theory which predicates reciprocal benefits to the two parties to the transaction overlooks the fact that in many cases the taxpayer secures no individual benefit at all, as when the bachelor has to pay a school tax for his neighbor with a patriarchal family; and that even where the taxpayer derives some direct or indirect benefit, there is no way of measuring the particular benefit that accrues to him. In the ordinary market the special benefit to the individual is the marginal utility of the commodity or service, which plays so important a rôle in affecting the price: in taxation, the marginal utility, if it exists, is not ascertainable.

But while the exchange theory has been abandoned as an explanation of the fiscal relation of the individual to the state, it is still of significance when we are dealing with the group rather than the individual. Under modern conditions, we no longer contemplate taxation as something extorted from the community in order to minister to the whims of the all-powerful ruler or prince, who regards his subjects as a flock of sheep always to be shorn, occasionally to be flayed. Taxes in the democracies of today are voted by the representatives of the people and are spent by officials who again are ultimately responsible to the people. In other words, the community nowadays votes taxes only because, and to the extent that, it expects to get something in return; and that something is good government. More technically speaking, what is sought is the satisfaction of the public collective wants of the individual—wants that can be satisfied only by the activity of the group of taxpayers as a whole. From this point of view, taxation may indeed be conceived as an exchange, and since in this sense a tax is a price, the influence of taxation upon the price level depends largely upon the conditions of the exchange.

In approaching the problem in this way we meet two considerations of importance. The one is the rather obvious point of economy and efficiency. When the government carries on an enterprise which might be, and often is, left to private initiative, like the management of railways or the provision of water or gas, or the running of busses, the problem is that of productivity in the positive sense. If through poor management, due to slothfulness or to politics or to improper accounting, the enterprise designed to be profitable or at least self-supporting is run at a loss, there can be no doubt as to the unproductive nature of the expenditure. If the commodities or services furnished by the government enterprise are produced at a greater cost than would be the case under private management, it is clear that the price of the commodity or service will be higher. Where taxes, therefore, are levied to an unnecessary extent or are spent uneconomically, inefficiently or unwisely, there is a distinct connection between taxation and the price level. There is but little doubt that in all modern democracies the higher level of prices is in part referable to the wastefulness and inefficiency of government enterprise.

The other side of the problem, however, is more important as it is less obvious. By this we mean the study of the relative, rather than of the absolute, productivity of taxation—a study which involves the connection between high prices and social utility. Let us attempt to clarify our meaning. In former times people were obsessed by what might be called the consumption theory of taxation. It was laid down as a general proposition that government ought to be limited to the narrowest possible activity and that individuals would always accomplish results more cheaply than the government. Inasmuch as, according to this view, everything attempted by the government represents a kind of unproductive consumption, the natural conclusion was that the best system of taxation is that which is least in amount. Whatever expenditures the government incurs are wasteful: *ergo,* cut public expenditures to the bone.

As a reaction against this *laissez faire* theory, there developed in the nineteenth century the opposite doctrine, which may be called the production or reproduction theory of taxation. According to this doctrine, taxation acts very much like the sun's rays in sucking up from a large pond the moisture which is gradually diffused through the atmosphere and is finally precipitated upon the land in the shape of a fertilizing shower, recreating life and engendering prosperity. Taxation would thus be considered as an essentially productive phenomenon, with the conclusion that the more that is spent by government, the better for the community.

It is interesting to observe that whereas the consumption theory of taxation arose in France at the time of the protest against overmuch government, the production or reproduction theory of taxation was developed in Germany at the time of the endeavor to strengthen the basis of the absolute,

God-given monarchy. Each doctrine, it is clear, represents an indefensible extreme. Taxation is neither an unwise consumption nor is it necessarily a beneficent production. In some cases it may be the one; in some cases, the other: which it is, depends upon the kind of tax system, upon the kind of government, and upon the kind of public sentiment behind the government.

The scientific attitude toward the problem is represented neither by the reactionary stand-patter who regards every increase of taxation as confiscation, nor by the enthusiastic communist who deifies the group and distorts the lessons of history by neglecting the individual. In the United States we are at present perhaps in greater danger from the former than from the latter extreme. It does not follow that, because our taxes are higher and our expenditures greater, they are really unproductive in the true sense of the term. The taxes may embody themselves in material or in immaterial goods; and in both cases, provided indeed there is no glaring waste, we may have a greater social utility which will ultimately reflect itself in a lower price level. For whatever increases social utility diminishes sacrifice or effort; and whatever decreases cost will ultimately decrease price and increase welfare.

Take, for instance, the prodigious increase of taxation in recent years. So far as federal taxes are concerned, due almost wholly to the war and to the aftermath of the war, we can certainly not speak of any productivity of taxation except indeed in the sense that the prosecution of a successful war, in preventing the loss of national existence or averting the imposition of a huge tribute, may be considered in a certain sense productive. But with the general question of the undoubted waste of war we have no desire to deal in this place. What is more significant is to consider the prodigious increase of state and local taxation during the past decade.

The figures of absolute or *per capita* increase are of very slight significance. Our taxes are higher today largely because of changes in the price level. Higher taxes are from this point of view the result, and not the cause, of the higher price level. But even then the *per capita* figures are of no real importance. What we most desire in discussing the weight of taxation is to ascertain the relative burden: but relative to what? Naturally the best criterion is that of the social income.

A tax burden, individual or social, grows if it takes a constantly larger proportion of the income, individual or social. If now we collate the figures of taxation, as contained in the Census reports, with the figures of social income as worked out by the National Bureau of Economic Research—on the whole the most satisfactory that we have—we find that the proportion of state and local taxes in the United States was in relation to social income actually somewhat less in 1920 than in 1910—and in many states considerably less. It is true that 1920 is not a completely satisfactory year, for it was a year of inflated profits and unusual business prosperity. But even allowing for this fact and for the undoubted increase of taxes in the last three or four years, it still remains true that in relation to social income the burden has not materially augmented.

This point becomes of additional interest when we consider what was done with our state and local taxes. Some of the funds were indeed devoted to purposes connected with the war, like soldier bonuses and the like. But the great mass of increased taxes have gone to education, to improved roads, and to public health and philanthropy in the wider sense. It would be difficult to take the position that taxes levied for such purposes are unproductive. More and more we realize the essential truth in the old statement that government is entitled to do those things that individuals either cannot do or ought not to do. Private individuals obviously cannot provide free roads and free schools; and even where the services afforded are not gratuitous, we are gradually perceiving that certain forms of education and charity ought no longer be left to private initiative, any more than the provision of justice or of protection.

There is one further consideration that deserves attention. It does not follow that, because a government service fails to yield a profit or even to be self-supporting, it is unproductive. A private water company or lighting corporation will naturally fix its charges in some relation to the unit of service, irrespective of the personal situation of the consumer. A government enterprise on the other hand may purposely endeavor, in fixing its price schedule, to consider, as it does in its tax system, the faculty or ability of the individual. As the families of the poorer consumers are ordinarily larger than those of the wealthy consumers, the private water company in apportioning prices to consumption virtually discriminates in favor of the rich: while the government service might conceivably attempt to redress the balance by lowering the unit of charge in the slums. Does anyone doubt as to where the greater social utility, that is, the real productivity, would be found? In the same way, a private railway system will obviously follow the method of charging all that the traffic will bear; whereas a government system may modify its rates by fitting the scale of charges to the national policy of protection or what not. So a private street-car system may refrain from building into the unoccupied suburbs, the development of which may none the less become a matter of high social and municipal importance. It must not be supposed that we are here arguing for the extension of government business, which may of course be undesirable for other reasons. All that we are attempting to emphasize is the fact that the real productivity or social utility of taxation is not necessarily to be measured by the facts that the service fails to be self-supporting.

The conclusion is obvious. Where taxes are unproductive they are apt to raise the price level by increasing cost. Where taxes are productive of wealth either directly, or indirectly through the growth of social utility, they are likely to engender a fall in the price level.

The lessons are clear. If we desire to prevent a disparity between the level of prices and the level of wages we must first of all reduce our expenditures on war and on preparation for war; for these must, from every sound point of view, be declared to be, in the last analysis unproductive. If one-tenth of the energy which is today so abundantly directed to reducing the crushing burden of taxation bequeathed to us by the war were devoted to the strengthening of international coöperation in order to lessen the chances of war, we should really be making a beginning in the right direction. Instead of the futile cry against government extravagance we ought to be waging the fight against government aloofness from world participation. And when that is once accomplished and the way is finally cleared for the promotion of the more enduring and civilized ends of government, we must then steer our way carefully between two extremes; we must not be drunken enthusiasts, reeling from side to side in an intoxication of prodigal expenditure, but we must also take care not to be puritanical ascetics who mistake niggardliness for economy and who thus dry up the real sources of social progress. With the growth of civilization we are bound to devote a continually greater proportion of the social income to taxation. This is not necessarily unproductive. It simply means that with advancing democracy and increasing equality the satisfaction of our collective public wants plays a constantly greater rôle in our economic and social life. Just as the progress of the individual in culture and wealth is marked by the growing ratio of his immaterial to his material wants, so the progress of the community in all that really constitutes civilization is characterized by the increasing importance of the satisfaction of collective over individual wants. If only we learn not to let the legitimate demands of a peace economy be confused with, and swallowed up, in the burdens of war; if we insist on a budgetary and administrative reform which will yield efficiency and reasonable economy; if in other words we emphasize the necessity of getting a dollar's worth for every dollar spent, we need have little fear of the growing burden of taxation, and we can confidently anticipate a relation between taxation and the price level which will facilitate and not impede the path of progress.

CHAPTER FIVE

ARE STOCK DIVIDENDS INCOME?

[This was originally a memorandum submitted to the Supreme Court of the United States in the case of Eisner vs. Macomber, 252 U. S. 289 (1919) in which the decision accepted the conclusions here set forth. It was published in the *American Economic Review,* vol. ix, 1919.]

Among the difficult problems raised by our income tax is that of the nature of stock dividends. Under the act of 1913 they were held to be income by an interpretation placed on the law by the Department of Internal Revenue. In the act of 1916 they were made specifically taxable as income. Some time after the enactment of this law the Supreme Court decided that the administrative interpretation of the act of 1913 was erroneous,[1] and that the word income as used in that act did not include stock dividends. The question now arises whether the act of 1916 is constitutional in declaring stock dividends to be income. It is being hotly disputed in a case now pending. We have accordingly deemed it wise to consider the problem purely from the economic point of view, especially as the subject has hitherto received comparatively little attention.[2]

[1] *Towne* v. *Eisner, 255* U. S., 418.

[2] The only discussion of the topic is the short colloquy between Professor F. R. Fairchild and Mr. H. H. Bond in the *Bulletin of the National Tax Association,* vol. iii, pp. 161-3 and 237-243. Professor Davenport has also contributed a brief note in the same *Bulletin,* vol. iv, p. 53. Professor Irving Fisher does not deal with the problem in *The Nature of Capital and Income.*

[Since this article was written the subject has aroused considerable interest. The chief contribution has been made by Professor R. M. Haig in chap. i, of *The Federal Income Tax, Columbia University Lectures,* 1921. *Cf.* the discussion in *Papers and Proceedings of the Thirty-third Annual Meeting of the American Economic Association, Dec.,* 1920, pp. 148-170.

The broader concept of income was first formulated by G. Schanz, "Der Einkommensbegriff und die Einkommensteuergesetze," *Finanz Archiv,* vol. xiii, 1896, which has not met with favor among his countrymen.]

In order to prepare the way for the discussion we must travel over more or less familiar ground; but it will, we hope, soon appear that the subject deserves a considerably closer analysis than it has yet received. We shall therefore start out with the concepts of income and of capital.

I. *What are Income and Capital?*

The most natural definition of income is all wealth that comes in. This, however, is obviously much too vague. The things that come in are fundamentally utilities and services. We desire things, at bottom, because of their utility. They can impart this utility only in the shape of pleasurable sensations or satisfactions. These alone constitute true income. If the satisfaction comes from a human effort we speak of a service; if it comes from material things or relations we speak of a use or utility. The satisfactions are afforded by the services of human beings and by the utilities of material things or relations. Income is the inflow of satisfactions from services and utilities. Income is therefore fundamentally pleasure or benefit income.

When these services or utility-affording commodities are restricted in quantity, and cost some effort to procure, they acquire a value. Since we must economize in their enjoyment and use, we speak of them as economic goods and services. Economic value or value in economic life is therefore to be distinguished from other forms of value like aesthetic or moral value. In civilized society this value has come to be estimated in terms of money. Income is accordingly now used to denote the inflow or revenue in money. Speaking more broadly, however, it may be said that in a society based on money transactions income denotes any inflow of satisfactions which can be parted with for money. It may not be money income, but it must be capable of being transmuted into money income.

The second characteristic of income is that it denotes

a flow or succession of such satisfactions, expressed in money or money's worth, during a period of time. If there is only a single utility or a unique service, we speak of an accession, rather than of a succession, of satisfactions. But whether there be one or many, we think of their coming in during a period of time. The quality of periodicity is essential. Thus, income must be either annual, or monthly, or daily income, or income for some other period of time.

Thus far the ordinary analysis has gone. There still remain, however, other criteria of income.

Since the real wealth of an individual or a community consists of this inflow of satisfactions which we call income, it is clear that the satisfaction must be realized before we can predicate of it the quality of income. The satisfaction may come from the repair of a broken stove, from the occupation of a house, from a foal born to a broodmare. The plumber affords a service, the house yields an immaterial benefit, the mare produces a commodity. The employer or owner can sell the services of the plumber, rent the house, or dispose of the foal. In each case he secures a money income. He is able to do this because the other party receives a corresponding income in the shape of satisfaction. The stove owner has a good fire, the tenant enjoys shelter, the purchaser of the foal acquires a saddle horse. The first party's money income is correlative to the second party's pleasure income which, if not money, is money's worth.

If now the plumber falls ill, if the house is unrented or untenanted, if the foal is stillborn, there is no income to the employer or owner, because nothing is realized. The plumber continues, perhaps, to be paid by the month, the house still commands a market price, the broodmare is still worth a definite amount, because in each case a steady income is anticipated. It is only when the failure of the income is repeated that the wages of the plumber and the value of the house or the price of the mare will fall. On the other hand, the repair to the stove may be so badly made that the stove is worthless; the house may turn out to be so leaky as to be uninhabitable; the foal may be so defective as to be unusable. The gain which it was thought would be enjoyed has not been realized. There is in truth no income. And under a proper legal system it is possible to recover what has been paid so that the employer, landlord, or horse-trader likewise loses his income. The net result is that an unrealized or imaginary income is not an income at all. Just as a true satisfaction is realized satisfaction, so true income is realized income. In order to constitute income, the anticipated or putative gain must be not only realizable, but realized. If it is not realized, there is no income. Realization is a necessary attribute of income.

The next characteristic of income is that it is something distinct and separate from the person or thing that affords the income. Where the income consists of concrete objects, this is quite obvious. Each foal is separate from the mare and cannot possibly be confused with its mother. The succession of separate foals constitute the income and perhaps the only income from the mare. The mare is, so to speak, a bundle of inchoate or unborn foals. When the foal is actually born and separated from its mother, it constitutes the income from the mother; just as the fruit separated from the tree is the income from the tree. The same thing is true, however, in the other cases. The income of the house is really separate from the house itself. The house is to all intents and purposes a bundle of inchoate utilities: it will afford these utilities from year to year. The owner may during any given period dispose of the utility while retaining the title to the house. The rental that he receives by separating the actual utility from the bundle of inchoate utilities that we call the house constitutes his income from the house. Separation is of the essence of the enjoyment. The same finally is true of the plumber. His skill is indeed a part of him; but in order to secure the income that we call wages he must transmute his skill into something outside of, and separate from, himself. At a particular period he may render a service in repairing the stove; the service is then something separate from the man. If he disposes of the service, he enjoys an income. But he cannot secure the income without performing—that is, divesting himself of—this service. Separation, again, is of the nature of the transaction.

Thus in every case, whether we are dealing with human services, immaterial utilities or concrete objects, there can be no income unless there is a separation from the individual or the thing that affords the service or the utility. Separation, like realization, is a necessary attribute of income.

As against the income, which, as we have seen, is the satisfaction afforded by services or utilities, is the capital. When we buy anything, we buy the right of securing such a satisfaction or stream of satisfactions from the commodity which embodies the utilities. Every commodity is a store of such future or inchoate satisfactions. Since human beings are no longer bought and sold, and since wealth exists for man rather than man for wealth, we can no longer buy the source of human services, although we buy the services themselves. We can only buy things or the source of non-human utilities. The process of valuation through which we assign a capital value to this complex of future anticipated income values, and through which the flow of satisfactions is transmuted into a fund, is called capitalization. At a given time the object or relation which affords the utilities or the income is called the capital. The capital possesses a value which reflects our estimate of the succession of anticipated utilities or income. Nothing would have any capital value if it possessed no income value.

Common usage distinguishes between a particular piece of capital (technically known as a capital good) like a house or a machine, and the fund of capital which represents the translation into money of the value of the particular pieces of capital. These may wear out and disappear; but, if they are replaced by others, the fund remains intact. As has been so well said, the fund of capital is like a mill pond: the drops of water flow in at one end and out at the other. But the pond itself, although continually changing, remains at a level, with the same volume of contents. The fund of capital is the mill pond: the particular pieces of capital are the drops that are continually flowing in and out of the pond. Capital, in the sense of a fund, is used to designate the *caput* or principal sum of money from which a revenue is expected.

Income is spoken of as a result of the capital. In reality, capital or capital value is a result of the income or income value. Capital, again, is spoken of as the source of income. In reality, the income or income value is the source of capital or capital value. Physically, the fruit is a product of the tree; economically, the tree has a value only because the fruit has a value. To all intents and purposes it is correct to say that capital produces an income; strictly speaking, however, the capital is produced by the income, or at least the capital value depends on the income value.

The real distinction between income and capital as the embodiment or the measurement of wealth, therefore, is that income represents a flow or stream of utilities or money, and capital represents a fund or stock of utilities or money. The flow or stream is periodic; it represents a succession of utilities or money during a period of time. The fund or stock is the accumulation of such utilities or income at an instant of time. Income is expressed in terms of a flow; capital in terms of a stock. The capital value of anything at any instant of time is primarily the result of adding together the present worth of each and all of the anticipated successive income values. The income is primary; the capital is secondary.

II. *The Relation between Capital and Income*

We are now in a position to study some of the relations of capital and income.

In some cases there seems to be no distinction between the two. This is of course not ordinarily true. The value of anything is, as we have seen, ultimately derived from the satisfactions or uses which it affords. Some things, like a city lot, are permanent and afford a use in perpetuity. The capital or selling value of the lot, however, is not a summation of all future income or rental values from the lot. By the very constitution of human nature we lay more stress on present than on future enjoyments; our present estimate of future uses becomes fainter as the use recedes into the future, until the present value of a very distant use vanishes entirely. The selling or capital value of a lot is accordingly only twenty or twenty-five times the rental or income value. Land is worth, as we say, about twenty-five years' purchase. Other commodities are less permanent, and are gradually worn out by use. The distinction between the capital value and the income value is then considerably less, as in the case of an automobile. The man who rents out an automobile must secure in the first year as income perhaps one-third or one-half of its capital value.

Finally, there are commodities which afford only a single use; the use of an ordinary article of food consists in its consumption. In this case the distinction between capital and income disappears. Capital, as we have seen, is a capitalization of incomes, a summation of our present estimates of the value of all future anticipated uses. But if there is only a single use, there can be no summation of successive uses. There can be no capitalization of a single use. Since, however, we speak of capital as a stock of wealth existing at an instant of time, while income is the flow of wealth during a period of time, the apple which affords only a single income is popularly regarded as capital. Yet its price, although ordinarily called a selling price, might equally well be called a rental price. In charging for its use, we charge for the apple itself. The capital and the income coalesce.

In this case, therefore, we must qualify the statement made above that separation is of the essence of income. If there is no difference between capital and income, we cannot separate the two. In all other cases however, that is, in the great mass of wealth (except that destined for immediate and total consumption), the distinction holds good. Income is something separate from capital; and if capital be regarded as the stock which yields the income, the enjoyment or money's worth in the shape of gain must, in order to constitute income, be separated from the capital.

It follows from this that if the income is separated from the capital and if we desire a continuance of the income, the capital must remain intact. In any particular piece of capital, this does not, of course, happen of itself. If the commodity is permanent, like a city plot, the capital indeed remains unimpaired. But in the great mass of cases the commodity gradually disappears through use. Some things are consumed in a short time, others last a longer time; but in almost all cases there is a wear and tear which, if allowed to go unchecked, finally renders the commodity useless so that it will cease yielding an income. There will be no net revenue because the cost of repairs will ultimately equal the gross returns. In actual life we sometimes guard against the results of such depreciation by instituting a sinking fund. Instead of spending all the earnings, we set aside an annual sum which will exactly counterbalance the depreciation, so that at the end of the period the accumulated fund will sink or offset the outlay incurred to replace the commodity.

In order to estimate the real net income from a piece of

capital we must therefore deduct from the earnings the amount of the annual depreciation charge, which will vary with the durability or permanence of the commodity in question. Otherwise, in separating the income from the capital we should be depleting the capital. Income in the true sense of net income is that which is separated from the capital, while leaving the capital intact. As it has elsewhere been defined:

"Income as contrasted with capital denotes that amount of wealth which flows in during a definite period and which is at the disposal of the owner for purposes of consumption, so that in consuming it, his capital remains unimpaired."[1]

III. *Income and Accretion to Capital*

We are now prepared to consider a more difficult problem. If my income increases, there is undeniably an increase in my wealth, or a net gain. This increase of wealth or gain, however, may also show itself in a change of my capital or my assets. In that case we speak of an accretion to capital or a capital increment. How, now, are we to determine whether a particular gain is income or accretion to capital. This question needs a more careful analysis than it has hitherto received.

In the case of a concrete commodity the capital or selling value may change for three reasons.

In the first place the income may be not consumed, but saved and added to the capital. There is indeed a difference here between money and money's worth, between a fund of capital and piece of capital. If I have a fund of capital, as $100, and decide to save the income of $5, I shall have at the end of the year $105, and with each ensuing year correspondingly more capital. This accretion to capital is clearly nothing but accumulated or reconverted income. The income has been realized and separated from the principal. While indeed it is now again merged with

[1] Seligman, *The Income Tax*, 2nd ed., 1914, p. 19.

the principal, it is easy to keep the two sums separate and distinct. No one can question the fact that the gain, even though added to the capital, is pure income.

In the case of money's worth or utilities the matter is a little more complex. The income of many things is not embodied in an object, but consists of utilities that are incapable of being accumulated and that must be enjoyed or consumed at once. A house is of use only for habitation. We cannot make the house more valuable by postponing or deferring its use. We cannot reconvert the use or income into capital. If the use is not enjoyed, it is lost. There can therefore be no capital increment through a postponement or accumulation of income.

Where the income consists, however, of material objects capable of preservation, the matter is simple. The farmer's crop is his income. If he elects to add his crop of cotton to his previously existing stock (which he may be holding for a rise), this increment of capital is undeniably income. The new crop is something separate from the old stock. In the same way, the owner of a herd of cattle may decide not to sell his yearlings. Although they may be merged with the herd, however, they are none the less separate; for it makes no difference whether he keeps them in a distinct enclosure or lets them pasture with their mothers. The increment in the value of the herd is income, because it is both realized and separated.

Finally, there are cases where the income, if not originally separated, cannot be kept separated. The best example of this is a growing forest. The income of a forest is the annual yield of timber. The trees of a certain size may be cut yearly, leaving the forest intact. With proper forestry there will be a steady and regular cut of timber, what is lumbered in any year being made good by the growth of the remaining and oncoming trees. If, however, the trees are not cut, the forest becomes more valuable—up to a certain point at least. What would have been income has been converted into capital increment. But this capital increment is not income, because it has not been separated and because it is not capable of separation if uncut. When the trees are ultimately cut, the gain undoubtedly becomes income. Up to that time, however, the increase in the value of the forest is only inchoate income. What is done with the particular trees therefore determines whether they are income or capital. To the owner of the forest there is an increment of wealth in each case; but from the economic point of view there is a distinction between the increase in the form of income and the increase in the form of capital. If the income is immediately enjoyed or dissipated, the increase of wealth disappears in the enjoyment; if the enjoyment of the income is postponed or deferred, the increase of wealth is not dissipated. In the one case we have spending, in the other saving. Capital can be increased only by postponement of enjoyment. Modern life with its mastery of science over nature enables the community not only to spend more for the conveniences and luxuries of life, but also to save more and thus to accumulate capital.

We see thus that if the income has been actually realized and separated and then again added to, or reconverted into, the capital, it remains none the less income although called capital increment. But if the income is simply unconsumed or postponed, without being actually realized and separated, the resulting capital increment is not income. What we are dealing with in such a case is inchoate, not real, income. Realizability is not realization; separability is not separation. The gain in the form of accretion to capital is income only when it is the result of adding actually received (*i.e.*, realized and separated) income to the capital. Otherwise the gain is inchoate income, to become real income only when it is actually realized.

The second case of a change in the value of capital referred to above on page 106 is that due to a change in the income from the capital. The demand for the particular satisfaction or commodity may decline: ostrich feathers may go out of fashion; Sicilian oranges may no longer command a market in New York in competition with Florida fruit. This diminution in income will be at once reflected or amortized in a reduction of the value of the capital. If ostriches are raised primarily for feathers, their value will fall; if the Sicilian lands are of little use for other crops they will decrease in value, as indeed has actually happened. On the contrary, an increase in the income will be capitalized into an enhancement of the capital. If dry farming or irrigation causes two blades to grow in place of one, not only is the income from the land greater, but the land itself will rise in value. Capital is capitalized income. In such cases, therefore, there is no difficulty. We are in presence of two separate phenomena—an increase of income and an increase of capital. The one is the result of the other, but there is no danger of their confusion. The owner of the commodity enjoys two increments or gains—a capital gain and an income gain. The gain in the value of the capital is not income, because it is not separated and realized.

When, instead of a particular commodity or capital good, we deal with a fund of capital, the same is true. If the dividends of a stock increase, the market price of the stock will rise. Both capital and income are enhanced in value. But the augmented value of the stock is not income as long as the stock is not sold, *i. e.*, as long as there is neither realization nor separation.

In the third place a change in capital may supervene without any change in the income. A plot of land may rent at the same figure as before, but a speculative move in the market may enhance its selling price. A stock may become valuable for purposes of control, even though the dividend rate remains unchanged; and its market value will quickly rise. In all these cases we have a capital increment with no change in income.

In reality, however, the discrepancy in many such cases is less than it seems. The present income, it is true, remains the same, but there is an expectation of greater income in the future. The boom in real estate is based on the idea that the rental value of the land will rise. The control of the stock is sought in the hope ultimately of securing a gain through the augmented returns. Capital is a capitalization not simply of present or actual income but of the present worth of all future anticipated incomes. There can be no permanent change in the value of the capital unless there is at least an anticipated change in future income.

It remains true, nevertheless, that there may be temporary and ephemeral fluctuations of market price in complete disregard of future or anticipated incomes, and where the particular commodity or security is desired for other purposes than the income immediately to be derived therefrom. It is equally true that no small part of business profits is due to such fluctuations of price. Here again, however, there is no danger of confusing capital increment with income. For, as in the preceding case, the gain derived from such fluctuations becomes income only when the attributes of separation and realization are present. If the house appreciates in value because some one desires it for a particular purpose, the increase is income if I sell the house. But if I do not dispose of the house, the gain is only an inchoate gain, not a realized gain. Since there is no separation and no realization, the capital increment does not constitute income.

Thus all cases of appreciation of capital may be resolved into three types:

1) The capital increment is the accumulation of past income.

2) The capital increment is the result of augmented present and future income.

3) The capital increment is independent of change in the income.

In the first case the capital increment is undoubtedly income. In the two other cases it becomes income only when actually realized and separated from the principal. Until then it remains inchoate income, not actual income; a paper gain, not an actual gain. Thus in all three cases realization and separation constitute the true criteria of income.

IV. *What is Taxable Income?*

When income taxes were first introduced, economic science was only in its infancy and a satisfactory analysis of the relations between capital and income had not yet been worked out. We therefore find considerable confusion and diversity in the earlier income tax laws of various states, some survivals of which have persisted even to this day.

In the first place, income was commonly limited to money income. Difficulties, however, soon arose in the case of farmers consuming their own produce and of individuals residing in their own houses. The truer conception of income as benefit income was only slowly adopted. If I own my house and receive no money income, I am not taxed under the present law in the United States: if I sell the house and devote the income of the proceeds to renting another house of precisely the same character, I am compelled to pay the income tax. Yet the economic situation is essentially the same, and the similarity was recognized in the Civil War income taxes.[1] In the case of farmers' produce our present law occupies a middle position: crops consumed by the farmer or his family are held not to be income, but the expenses involved in raising the crop cannot be deducted. These inconsistencies, which are no doubt retained in the law partly for administrative reasons, would

[1] *Cf.* Seligman, *The Income Tax*, 2nd ed., 1914, pp. 443-445.

disappear if it were recognized that income is not only money, but money's worth.

Secondly, we find in the original conception of income the idea of regularity. Only those incomings or net money receipts which were regularly received in the course of economic activity were considered income. Thus for a long time occasional earnings from gambling were not considered income, as was the case also with chance finds or gains. If, however, these finds, as *e.g.*, of precious metal, were the result of continued and regular effort they were held to be taxable income.

This idea of regularity gradually disappeared as the true nature of income came to be recognized. But the survivals of the old idea are still occasionally to be found. Inheritances, for instance, are today scarcely anywhere deemed to be taxable income. From the point of view of the individual, however, they constitute income, even though it be accidental and not regular income. As a consequence they are now almost everywhere separately taxed, although not under an income tax law. For the real economic justification of the inheritance tax on the share going to the recipient (as distinguished from the tax on the estate of the decedent) is that it constitutes accidental income and thus augments his ability to pay. Again, in many income tax laws, like our own, gifts are held to be capital or corpus and not income, evidently on the theory that they do not constitute regularly accruing gains. If the gift, however, were made periodically, an interesting question would arise.[1]

In general, then, it may be said that the element of regularity as an essential constituent of the concept of income has well-nigh disappeared. If I receive a thousand dollars for particular services this year and nothing in previous or subsequent years, it is none the less held to be income, even

[1] [Since the above was written gifts have become taxable, but not under the income tax law as a constituent element of income.]

though it be irregular. The old conception of regularity, however, as we have seen, still survives in part.

In the third place, the original conception of income was limited to the usufruct of a commodity, without allowing for a gain derived from the disposal of the commodity itself. Later the conception was broadened, but only in part. In England, for instance, the decision was influenced by the idea of regularity, just discussed. That is, gains derived from the sale of property are even today considered income only if made in the ordinary course of business. If an individual, not in the real estate business, sells a particular piece of land, the gain would not be taxable as income because it constitutes only an occasional or unique transaction. In England such an irregular gain would be considered accretion to capital, not income. In the United States, however, as in many other places where the broader concept of income has come to be recognized, gains derived from sales, whether occasional or not, are held to be taxable income. To this procedure there is no objection from the modern economic point of view.

Thus the newer conception of income comprises not alone money, but money's worth; not alone regular, but irregular receipts; not alone gains from a usufruct, but gains from the disposal of the thing that yields the usufruct. It is simply a survival of old errors, fortified no doubt by the desire to avoid practical administrative difficulties, that in England the gain from the sale of an isolated piece of property is held to be accretion to capital and that in both England and the United States the rental value of a house is held not to be income and that the reception of an inheritance is regarded as a capital increment.

In one point, however, almost all modern income tax laws are agreed. While there is still, as we have seen, a difference of attitude in the treatment of gains derived from sales, there is but little difference in the treatment of other gains. The distinction here is the one adverted to above between realized and unrealized gains. As we have seen, unrealized gains are inchoate gains, and inchoate gains are not income.

If I own a plot of land and secure no tenant for it, I receive no income and am nowhere subject to income tax. In some countries land is indeed taxable on its rental value; but rental value is not income. Since there is no gain at all, it is not subject to income tax. If, however, in the same year the value of the land rose, the owner would undoubtedly feel that he was wealthier. But would this appreciation in the value of the land constitute income? The answer everywhere is in the negative; and properly so, because we are in the presence of an unrealized gain. The land may have apprciated in value by the tax date; but it may equally well depreciate immediately thereafter. If the appreciation is realized through the sale of the property, there is of course a realized gain which is correctly held to be taxable income in the United States (although not in England). Again, if I sell the land and invest the proceeds in something else which then falls in value during the same taxable year, I am permitted to set off my loss against my profit. In that case there is no net gain and therefore no taxable income. The reason why a mere unrealized increase in the value of the land does not constitute income is primarily because of the uncertainty as to whether this particular consequence may not happen. In the same way, if I own securities which rise in value, there is a realized gain or taxable income only when the securities are sold.

We may put the conclusions briefly as follows:

> Capital increment is a gain only when realized.
> A realized capital increment is income in the wider sense.
> An unrealized capital increment is not income, but a mere appreciation of capital.

As indicated above, the real point is the separation of the increment from the capital. This separation is necessary in order to constitute income. The increment when separated is income; the increment unseparated remains capital. Separation and realization are of the essence of the transmutation of capital into income. The capital as such remains intact: the increment or capital gain when actually realized and separated constitutes income.

V. *The Economic Nature of Stock Dividends*

We are now prepared for an analysis of the economic nature of stock dividends. This can be best introduced by taking an assumed case of a corporation with a capital of $100,000 divided into 1,000 shares, each worth par, and owned by ten stockholders, each of whom owns ten shares of stock worth $10,000.

During the taxable year the corporation has net earnings of $50,000, on which it is of course subject to income tax. On the last day of the year, December 31st, the stockholders hold a meeting in order to decide what to do with the $50,000. Three courses are open to them:

A) They may declare a cash dividend.
B) They may turn the earnings into surplus.
C) They may declare a stock dividend.

What happens in each of these cases?

A) After a cash dividend of $50 is declared on each share, the capital remains at $100,000, the number of shares is still 1,000, and the stock is still worth par, other things being the same, while the $50,000 is distributed to the stockholders in dividends, each of the stockholders receiving $5,000 as his dividend or income.

B) When the earnings are turned into surplus, the capital is now $150,000, the shares are still 1,000 in number, but each share is now worth $150. Each of the ten stockholders who continues to own ten shares now has property worth $15,000.

C) If a stock dividend of $50 is declared in additional shares to each owner of $100 worth of shares, the capital is now $150,000; the number of shares is now 1,500 instead of 1,000, and the value of each share is still $100. Each of the ten stockholders now possesses fifteen shares, instead of ten, and his investment is worth $15,000.

There are now two possibilities. Either (a) the earnings have been gradually accumulated during the year, with periodical statements open to the public, or (b) the knowledge of the increased earnings is kept secret from everyone until December 31st when action is taken.

What now will be the relative economic situation in these three cases?

A, a) The case of a cash dividend where the earnings have been known to accumulate during the year. Here the stock will gradually rise until, with the expectation of a $50 dividend, it will be worth on December 31st, $150. Immediately after the declaration of the cash dividend, the stock will again fall to par. In actual life, indeed, there may be an interference with this normal result. As a matter of fact, each share may be worth a little less or a little more than $150, depending upon the market estimate of future prospects. Additions to surplus are often not expected to earn quite as much as the original investment, in which case the price will be less than $150; on the other hand, if continued large earnings are anticipated, the price may be above $150. Apart from these countervailing influences of the market, however, the situation as reflected in the statement at the beginning of this paragraph may be accepted as the normal one. In the same way the declaration of an extra cash dividend may lead to an expectation of continued earnings on the same scale, so that the price of the stock will not finally fall quite to par. But for purposes of simplicity this hypothesis may be eliminated, and the situation as described above may be considered the typical one.

A, b) If the earnings are unknown and unsuspected, the stock will naturally remain at par and the declaration of the cash dividend will not change the value of the stock (except in the same eventuality as before).

B, a) The case of addition to surplus, where the earnings have been accumulated throughout the year and have been well known to everybody. The stock will accordingly rise gradually until on December 31st it will reach $150. After the addition to the surplus the stock will remain at that figure.

B, b) If, on the other hand, the earnings have been unknown and unsuspected, the stock will remain at par until December 31st, when it will jump to $150 and remain there, with the same practical qualifications as above.

C, a) In the case of the stock dividend, where the earnings have been accumulated during the year and their existence known to all, the stock will as before rise to $150 by December 30th. After the declaration of the stock dividend, the stock will on December 31st fall to par, just as in the case of the cash dividend.

C, b) If, before the declaration of the stock dividend, the earnings have been unknown and unsuspected, the value of each share will, precisely as in the case of the cash dividend, remain at par.

What now is the economic consequence of all this?

In A, the cash dividend, we are undoubtedly in the presence of actual income accruing to the stockholder. The cash paid to the stockholder is separated from the assets of the corporation; the gain, accruing to the stockholder, is actually realized by him. Both realization and separation are present.

In B, the addition to surplus, there is an appreciation of capital either (a) before or (b) after December 31st. But this manifestly does not constitute any income to the shareholder. For, in the first place, there is no separation of the gain. It is merged into, and coalesces with, the surplus.

And, secondly, there is no realized gain to the shareholder. His investment is worth more; but it has not been realized. It is like the appreciation in value of a house or a piece of land. There is no income because there is neither realization nor separation. It would be mere folly to attempt to tax the shareholder because of an increase in the surplus of the corporation. The increase is indeed income to the corporation, or rather it represents the disposition of the corporate income; but it is not income to the stockholder.[1]

In C, the stock dividend, we again have an appreciation of capital; but each share either (a) falls in value before December 31st or (b) remains at the old figure after that

[1] The one striking example of this error is the case of the Civil War tax of 1864, which provided (in Sec. 117) that "the gains and profits of all companies whether incorporated or partnership, other than the companies specified in this section, shall be included in estimating the annual gains, profits or income of any person entitled to the same, whether divided or otherwise." Under this section the Supreme Court held in *Collector* vs. *Hubbard* (12 Wall. 17) that the wording of the act justified the taxation to the individual of his share in the undivided corporate profits.

In extenuation of this law, however, the following facts must be borne in mind. The act of 1864 did not differentiate, as do our modern laws, between a corporate income tax and an individual income tax. The act of 1864 taxed only a few classes of corporations, like certain financial and transportation companies. (For a list see Seligman, *The Income Tax*, p. 444.) In no other case was there a corporate income tax. The provision, declaring the profits of all corporations (except those specifically mentioned), to be a part of the income of the stockholder, was only a crude attempt to reach the corporate income and to prevent the evasion of the tax. Since that time, however, progress has been made in the theory of the income tax and of the corporate or business tax. We now have in every country, including our own, a corporate income tax side by side with the individual income tax. There is therefore no justification for a continuance of the clumsy method of the Civil War tax. No country today thinks of characterizing as income the undivided share of the stockholder in the surplus of a corporation. The Hubbard case, therefore, has no application to present conditions, and from the economic point of view it was irrelevant for the government to cite it (Eisner *vs.* Macumber, *Brief for the United States*, p. 11).

The law of 1864 endeavored to tax the corporate income to the individual shareholder, because no attempt was made to tax it to the corporation. But under the present law the corporate income *is* taxed to the corporation, and there is accordingly no justification for taxing it to the individual. For a tax on undivided profits would then tax the same income twice. This, of course, does not mean that our present practice of levying, in addition to the corporate income tax, a separate tax on the stockholder when he actually realizes his own income is theoretically or practically indefensible. For in this case there are two separate incomes, one to the corporation and one to the individual. Whereas in the contemplation of the act of 1864 there was only one income—that of the corporation, taxable to the individual solely because it seemed inexpedient to tax it to the corporation.

date. Since each shareholder, however, now owns more shares than he did, the net result is precisely as in the case of B, the increase of surplus. There is no separation of anything. There are indeed more paper certificates; but this does not change the essential nature of the transaction. There is no more separation of the assets than in B, the addition to surplus. There is no separation of the assets as in A, the cash dividend. The assets remain an undivided whole, whether they nominally consist of surplus or of any other item. Nor is there any realization. The gain or capital increment is unrealized gain or inchoate income, precisely as in the case of B, the addition to surplus. There is no income to the shareholder, therefore, because there is neither realization nor separation.

It might be objected that in C, the stock dividend, the owner of 100 shares which previously were worth $10,000 may take his 50 new shares and sell them for $5,000, leaving his original capital of $10,000 unimpaired. This, it might he said, puts C, the stock dividend, on a plane with A, the cash dividend. For the owner in the latter case will obviously sell his dividends for $5,000, leaving his original capital of $10,000 unimpaired.

It is a mistake, however, to think that this creates an analogy between C and A, that is, between the stock dividend and the cash dividend. For, in the case of B, the addition to surplus, the stockholder could have done precisely the same thing. That is, he could have taken 33 1/3 shares, sold them at $150, netted $5,000, and still have remaining his 66 2/3 shares worth, at $150, the sum of $10,000.

In this respect, then, there is no difference between A, B and C. If the stockholder cashes in his gains, all three cases are on a par. In none of these cases would there be any difference between income from capital and accretion to capital. For, when the gains are cashed in, the accretion to the capital is separated from the capital, leaving the capital unimpaired. Furthermore, if the stockholder sells all his stock, he will get in every case $15,000, and there will be in every case a gain or taxable income of $5,000. A capital gain cannot be realized without being separated; and when we have both separation and realization, capital increment has all the earmarks of income. If the stockholder sells his stock dividend the proceeds are undoubtedly income.

The question at issue, however, is entirely different: namely, what is the situation if the stockholder does *not* sell the stock? Here the real difference is between A, the cash dividend, on the one hand, and both B and C, the increase of surplus and the stock dividend, on the other.

In A, the cash dividend, the realized gain is income; in B, the increase in surplus, the unrealized gain is not income; in C, the stock dividend, the unrealized gain is not income.

Or, to put it in other words: A, the cash dividend, is indisputably income; B, the addition to surplus, is simply accretion to capital; C, the stock dividend, is equally nothing but accretion to capital. C then is like B and not like A; and in neither B nor C is the capital accretion income, because in neither case is the gain separated or realized. The stock dividend is like an increased surplus; it is not like a cash dividend. In fact, a stock dividend is not a dividend at all, in the sense in which a cash dividend is a dividend. The entire confusion really arises from a misnomer. For a dividend implies an actually realized increase of wealth; whereas, in a stock dividend there is no actually realized increase of wealth. As a matter of fact: in C, a (the stock dividend where the earnings have been slowly and openly accumulated) the stockholder is certainly no richer after December 31st than he was on December 30th. And while in C, b (the stock dividend where the earnings have been unknown and unsuspected) the stockholder is in a certain sense richer on December 31st than on December 30th, the gain is an unrealized increase of wealth, a mere paper increment. What is most important, above all, is that he is no richer than he would have been if there had been no stock dividend at all but a simple distribution to surplus. The income tax, it must be remembered, is not a tax on every increase of wealth actual or imaginary; it is a tax only on income; and capital increment constitutes income, as we have seen, only when invested with the attributes of separation and realization.

A final objection might be raised as to the result of a fourth possibility in addition to the three alternatives mentioned on page 115. The directors of the corporation might decide to invest the $50,000 earnings in the securities of another corporation and then declare a dividend in kind. This is often done nowadays. But, if a distribution in "other stock" is income, it is triumphantly asked, why is a distribution of its own stock not likewise income? This objection has confused many thinkers. Yet the answer to the question is very simple. For in the one case there are both separation and realization; in the other, there is neither separation nor realization.

In the one case, the directors actually take the $50,000 and separate them from the assets. Whether they turn over to the stockholders the $50,000 in cash or buy commodities like copper and wool, or securities like stocks and bonds, and then turn them over to the stockholders is immaterial. In every case there is a separation of earnings from the assets and in every case the earnings when separated from the assets and turned over to the stockholder constitute his income. Whether the stockholder gets cash, or commodities in the shape of copper or wool, or the securities of the other corporation is immaterial to him. In every case he gets something which is the result of a separation from the principal. But if he gets a stock dividend, *i.e.*, the securities of his own corporation, he does not get anything which has been separated from the principal. He gets only an additional evidence of his share in the undivided and unseparated assets. In the one case there is separation; in the other there is no separation.

Nor can we say that the acquisition of a share of stock in another corporation is unrealized gain. On the contrary, it is realized in the true economic sense of the term. If, instead of a cash dividend, the stockholder receives some copper or wool, we should not say that it is unrealized gain, and that too, whether he keeps or sells the copper or wool. If, however, he receives instead of the copper or wool a share of stock in some other corporation, we should again not say the gain was unrealized and, that too, whether he keeps or sells the stock. For in every case where the acquisition is the result of a distinct separation of assets—a separation of earnings from the principal—there is realization; and where there is realization there is income. It is beside the point to claim that this share in a new corporation might fall in value before he sold it: the copper or wool might equally depreciate before he disposed of it; and the bank in which he deposited the cash dividend or the individual to whom he loaned the cash might equally well fail, so that he would possibly receive during the taxable year only a part of the original sum. The cash dividend is indisputably income even if the proceeds are subsequently lost. Whatever be the policy of the law toward deduction for losses, and irrespective of whether the taxpayer is permitted to count as a loss the mere depreciation of the copper or wool or "other stock," there can be no doubt that the gain (from which a deduction may or may not be permitted) is realized as soon as there is an acquisition of cash, of copper or wool, or of "other stock." Realization does not mean immunity from loss. Realization occurs as soon as actual separation has been effected.

Thus in all these cases—cash dividend, copper or wool, and "other stock"—there are both separation and realization: in a stock dividend there is neither separation nor realization. The gain from "other stock" is income; the gain from a stock dividend is not income.

The real distinction to be kept continually in mind in

threading one's way through the mazes of the income tax is between the actual receipt of income on the one hand and the unrealized appreciation of capital on the other. A cash dividend is an example of the former; a stock dividend is an example of the latter. In the cash dividend, as in the "other stock," the gain is realized and separated; in the stock dividend, as in the addition to surplus, the gain is unrealized and unseparated. The first is income; the second is capital. A cash dividend is income; a stock dividend is not income.

CHAPTER SIX

THE SALES TAX

[This chapter is a combination of an address entitled "The Sales Tax compared with the Recommendations of the Tax Committee" delivered at the Second National Industrial Tax Conference in New York City October 22, 1920, and of the testimony at the *Hearing before the Committee on Finance, United States Senate, 67th Congress, First Session,* May 27, 1921, Part 16.]

The suggestion of a general sales tax has aroused widespread discussion. None of its advocates has however seemed to be aware of the fact that it is far from being a new proposition; and few have endeavored to present an impartial study of its probable consequences. An attempt to supply the gaps in this discussion may accordingly not be without interest.

I. *History of the Sales Tax*

While there have been many examples of taxes on the sale of particular commodities there have been with few exceptions only sporadic efforts made in any country or at any time to levy a tax on sales in general; and whenever such a tax has been attempted it has met with opposition and consequently with little success.

We hear of a sales tax in ancient Egypt, but do not know much about it. We do know, however, that in Roman times [1] the general sales tax was introduced by Augustus under the name of the *centesima rerum venalium;* that is, one-hundredth of all things sold or a one per cent. tax on sales. It led to such resistance that Augustus was able to maintain it only on the plea that it was necessary for the

[1] Tacitus, *Ann.* i, 78, ii, 42.

maintenance of the army. Even then it engendered such objections that in the year 17 Tiberius reduced it one-half. Later on, however, he restored it to the original rate and subsequently even increased it to two per cent. It was then accordingly called a *ducentesima.* But it aroused such opposition that, according to Suetonius,[1] Caligula after a few years abolished it in Italy. Later on, we find it reintroduced under another name as *vectigal rerum venalium.* But it again proved to be so unpopular and unlucrative that it was abolished after a few years.[2] The experiments with the general sales tax in Rome can there not be called extraordinarily favorable.

In the Middle Ages, when Europe was split up into a number of principalities, the feudal lords often tried these general sales taxes, which always met with great resistance. The first time that it was levied as a national tax was in France, when Louis XI made the experiment in 1465 under the name of *sol par livre* or nickel per dollar, i.e., a five per cent. tax. It was applied at first only to articles sold at wholesale.

It is to be observed that all through the Middle Ages taxes on the sale of particular commodities and especially upon the necessaries of life were common. In France, for instance, beverages were subject to a sales tax known as the *aides,* and salt to a sales tax known as the *gabelle.* These and similar taxes persisted under various names down to the revolution. But when Louis XI levied a general sales tax in 1465, it met with such opposition as almost to create a rebellion, and he accordingly abandoned it after a short time. It was tried again in 1485.[3]

When Henry IV encountered the fiscal difficulties connected with the war, Sully decided to reintroduce the tax in 1597 under the name of *pancarte.* This lasted for only a

[1] Suetonius, *Caligula,* 16.
[2] Humbert, *Essai sur les finances chez les Romains,* i, p. 279.
[3] Clamageran, *Histoire de l'impôt en France,* ii, pp. 29, 36.

few years, being abolished in 1602.[1] It was applied again at various intervals in the seventeenth century, not alone to wholesale but also to retail sales. It always met with great opposition. In fact, when Louis XIV tried it again in 1642 the intendant de Guyenne wrote that "the very name of the general sales tax puts the people into a fury." [2] Accordingly it was abolished after three or four years. Subsequently in 1681, owing to the fact that the French Kings met with such difficulty in making both ends meet, it was tried again, under the name of *subvention du vingtième,* or the five per cent. tax. But each time it was imposed it led to great popular discontent, and even to local riots, until it was soon abolished. The French experience with the general sales tax therefore warrants us in the statement that as an effective method of raising public revenues it proved to be a failure. In fact, when the French Revolution broke out the first thing the convention did was to abolish all the sales taxes, including the *gabelles* and the *aides* on the necessaries of life.

In the Kingdom of Naples the general sales tax was tried once, in the fifteenth century, but was soon abandoned. The only country where it was permanently levied was Spain. Starting in the early Middle Ages in the communes, it was introduced as a national tax in 1342. It included virtually all articles and was levied at first at the rate of one per cent., then at five per cent., and later at ten per cent., on all sales. The *alcavala*, as it was called, led to not a little difficulty, but it was continued by the absolute monarchs who were at their wits' ends to devise some method of balancing the budget. The Spanish economists of the time do not tire of calling attention to the enormities and the unfortunate economic consequences of the *alcavala.*[3]

[1] Clamageran, *op. cit.*, pp. 339, 509.

[2] "Le seul mot de sol pour livre met le peuple en fureur." *Op. cit.*, 543.

[3] *Cf.* The chief critics in the seventeenth century are Dr. Sandro de Moncada, *Restauracion politica de España*, Madrid, 1619 (*Cf.* the fifth discourse, entitled *Mudanza de alcavalas util al rey y a España*) ; and Dr. Diego Josef Dormer, *Discursos historicos-politicos sobre lo que se ofrece*

Isabella as a special mark of royal favor exempted Catalonia and Aragon from the sales tax, and we are told by various writers that the relative prosperity of these two states was due in large part to immunity from the detested and burdensome impost. Other writers have gone so far, although with some exaggeration, as to contend that one of the chief causes of Spain's economic downfall in the later Middle Ages, was the existence of this general sales tax. The consequences of the *alcavala* are explained very fully by the Spanish writers.[1] In those days the large estates were generally entailed and consequently not subject to sale, as were the smaller properties. The tax therefore fell with crushing severity upon the poor every time their land changed hands, and we are even told of peasants being compelled to sacrifice their cattle in order to escape the tax. The *alcavala* in short, has been notorious as an example of misdirected zeal in public finance.

These are the only important examples of general sales taxes. The one possible exception to this statement is the impost closely resembling a general sales tax which was developed in the German Empire in the seventeenth and eighteenth centuries. At that time the richer classes managed to evade their share of the direct taxes, and some of the tax reformers contended that if there could only be a tax on all kinds of consumption, every member of the community would be reached proportionately. Thus there developed the project of the general excise, or a tax on the sale of practically everything. Although introduced as a means of securing equality of taxation, the German *General Accise* led to so many abuses that it was soon abandoned. In England, although frequently discussed, the project of a gen-

tratar en la junta. n. p. 1684. In the eighteenth century the leading critics are: Miguel de Zavala y Auñon, *Representacion al rey . . . que distribuidos los tributos proporcialmente, sea menos la paga de sus vasallos,* etc., Madrid, 1732; and Don Miguel Caxa de Leruelos, *Restauracion de la abundancia de España,* Madrid, 1732.

[1] *Cf.* M. Colmeiro, *Historia de la economía política en España,* 1863, i, p. 472.

eral excise never had any chance of being adopted, partly because England was always suspicious of continental devices.

In the nineteenth century the nearest approach to the sales tax was that developed in England by Pitt under the stress of the war with France. According to this system, wellnigh every commodity was taxed; sometimes when it was sold, but more frequently when it was produced. Gladstone, when he came to the front in the forties addressed himself to that problem, and always considered it his chief title to fame that he reduced the multiplicity of these taxes on everything, as some one expressed it "that a man eats, feels, smells, or hears." Gladstone substituted a system of concentrated taxes, i. e. taxes on non-necessities of wide consumption where the administrative difficulties were minimized and the yield was greater. Just as Peel brought about a change in the tariff, reducing it from several thousand to a very few items, with a greater total yield, so Gladstone reduced the number of the internal revenue taxes, and secured a larger revenue.

No other important country discussed a general sales tax until the project arose in France after the Franco-Prussian war, as a tax *sur le chiffre d'affaires* or, as we should say, a turnover tax. The leading French economists of the day, like Leroy-Beaulieu and Léon Say, both of whom wrote on the subject, rejected it, although they were not by any means radicals; they were in fact very conservative economists and not at all favorable to what we are accustomed to call social reform. They objected to the general sales tax chiefly on the ground that it would be unequal as between different producers and that it would fail to distinguish between integrated and simple production. While they did not use these particular epithets, they explained that a general turnover tax would yield an unfair advantage to the large dealer or manufacturer as compared to the small man. Their second objection was the administrative difficulty in getting people to keep proper books showing their turnover and the fear lest the tax might be easily evaded. They did not call attention to the point which some of us like primarily to emphasize, viz., the inequality from the point of view of the consumers. But the two objections which they did discuss were sufficient to cause them to withhold their approval from the project and prevented the passage of the bill in the legislature.

The chief modern examples of general sales taxes are the result of the Great War. England discussed it fully and turned it down, not alone for the reasons mentioned by the French writers, but also because of the social aspects involved in the taxation of necessities. Even Italy, which at one time thought of imposing a sales tax, rejected it for similar reasons. The only leading countries that have adopted a general sales tax are Germany and France. Germany, after trying every conceivable resource, in desperation levied a general sales tax, but even then sought to redress the inequality by imposing an additional and much higher tax on the sale of luxuries. France also was led to adopt the tax because she had tried everything else; such as a high income tax, a high excess-profits tax, and a high inheritance tax. In France the results have been far from satisfactory. On the revenue side, it turned out to be defective and the estimate of budgetary receipts had to be revised several times. In other respects also the shortcomings were soon disclosed. To quote one of the French experts:

Never before has France devised a tax which was received so badly by both business firms and the public, the former because of the inquisitorial inspection methods which are necessary to prevent wholesale dissimulation in accounts and the public because of the tendency of the business men to throw the burden, wherever possible, on the purchasers rather than on their own business profits. It is impossible to collect the tax without having Government agents making the closest scrutiny of business records. It is also impossible for the French finances to support such an army of functionaries as this would require; and as the tax therefore is left to the honesty of merchants and producers, who merely sign monthly statements of their sales total and pay to collectors, there is consequently much danger of the records being arranged to suit the taxpayers' purposes.

"The French sales tax has shown itself as exerting a disastrous and paralyzing effect on business in general, and it is only a question of time until it will have to be superseded by a more rational method of raising money.[1]

There is only one other important country where the general sales tax is to be found. We do not speak of Mexico or the Philippines which still cling to the old Spanish traditions. For in many Latin-American countries there has always been a great repugnance to direct taxation, as we understand it in the Anglo-Saxon democracies. The first thing for instance, that the Americans did in Cuba was to abolish the *consumo* tax and to replace it by a property tax. So that the continuance of the sales tax in Mexico as in the Philippines must be regarded as a survival of primitive conditions.

The only Anglo-Saxon community which has seen fit to adopt something akin to the sales tax is Canada. The Canadian tax, however, is not a general sales tax; it is a tax on the sale of some commodities, with a list of exemptions, which includes almost every important article in the workingman's budget. Mr. Drayton, the Canadian minister of finance, explained in his budget speech of 1922 the reasons why he was opposed to the introduction of a general sales or turnover tax:

Many submissions have been received in favor of a sales or turnover tax. The principle of either a sales or turnover tax has been strongly advocated by many boards of trade and commercial bodies. The general turnover tax in particular has been strongly supported. This tax would call for the payment of a tax on every transaction taking place in the country. . . . Theoretically, the general turnover tax on commodities and services has much to commend it. In practical administration, though, in view of the fact that after careful survey it has been established that books are not kept in many retail stores, the cost of administration would be unduly great and the difficulties of collection many. Instead of extending the tax, it is proposed to confine its opera-

[1] Guillaume de Tarde, state counsellor and adviser to the ministry, quoted in a cable despatch in the *New York Herald*, May 28, 1921.

tion to the sales of manufacturers, wholesalers, jobbers, and importers, and to continue a list of special exemptions, which, broadly speaking, will cover foodstuffs in their natural state, all initial sales of farm produce, as well as the first products of the fisheries, mines, and forests.

Finally attention may be directed to the Civil War project for a general sales tax. We had during the war, as is well known, a comprehensive tax on manufactured articles, and it was proposed to supplement this by a general sales tax. David A. Wells, the fiscal adviser to the government, referring to the former tax said:[1]

> Such a system as this violates all the fundamental principles of taxation, inasmuch as the taxes are neither definite in amount, equal in application, nor convenient of collection. While this system prevails, furthermore, it seems useless to talk of reducing prices to anything like their former level. A similar duplication of taxation to this just described must, in our opinion, attend the adoption of a general sales tax, which at present seems to find so much favor throughout the country.

And he closes:

> Local taxes on industrial circulation in every village in the Union would be confessedly calamitous, but they could not be as bad as a frontier drawn around each individual in the nation, over which nothing could pass, in or out, not smitten with the tax repeated at each border.

His advice was taken, and the proposition of a sales tax, so specious and so attractive at first, which seemed to win everyone by its seeming simplicity, was soon abandoned.

II. *The Arguments for and against the Sales Tax*

The conclusion to be drawn from this historical survey is that the general sales tax constitutes the last resort of countries which find themselves in such fiscal difficulties that they must subordinate all other principles of taxation to that of adequacy.

There are four principles of taxation which the statesman must observe in framing a fiscal system. First is the principle of adequacy. If a tax does not yield the desired revenue it is a failure. The paramount consideration in almost

[1] *Report of the U. S. Revenue Commission*, 1866, p. 21.

every tax is that it should raise money. Second, there is the principle of what might be called innocuity, i. e., of doing as little harm as possible to the community. Violation of that principle was the trouble with our excess-profits tax. Its unlooked-for practical results were such that despite certain theoretical advantages it really reduced the national dividend instead of increasing it.

Third, there are the administrative principles laid down by Adam Smith. The tax must not be too complicated; it must be certain; it must be convenient. If the tax does not work administratively, no matter how ideal it is otherwise, it is a poor tax. Finally, we come to the principle of equality. All these other considerations being observed, the object of a statesman must be to frame a system of taxation which will be as nearly equal as possible, not only between the individual taxpayers, but between the various classes in the community.

The sales tax, it is evident, sins against every one of these principles.

First as to adequacy. If the tax were adopted, it is exceedingly probable that the mediæval lesson, as well as the more recent experience of France would be repeated; and that the revenue would be woefully inadequate. There are no means of estimating, with any degree of precision, what such a tax will actually yield. Some of our so-called "experts" tell us that a one per cent. tax will yield six billion dollars; others put the yield as low as half a billion dollars. Where such enormous disparities exist in the estimates, it behooves us to be exceedingly conservative in our expectations. It is not probable that the actual yield of the tax will suffice to realize the cherished plans of its advocates, in replacing some of the existing revenues.

We come next to the question as to the probable effect of the tax upon the community. Several points are to be mentioned here. A controversy has arisen as to who will pay the tax. If the tax is imposed on the commodities in the hands of the purchaser, there is no doubt as to the fact that the consumer will pay, even though the restriction of his purchases may also exert a prejudicial effect on the turnover of the seller. The question is as to what will happen in case the tax is imposed on the seller, rather than the purchaser. The consequences will be almost equally injurious irrespective of the reply to be given to this question. If the tax is shifted to the purchaser, its effect will be doubly baleful. For in the first case, as we shall see in a moment, it will amount to a tax on expenditure and thus invert the principle of ability to pay. In the second place, the tax will be cumulative or to use a common term, pyramided, so that the price of the commodity will in the end be raised by much more than the original rate of the tax. This constitutes the familiar difference between a tax on output, and a tax on turnover or sales. In the former case, the tax being levied at the initial stage of the process, the price will be increased on every subsequent transaction, if at all, only by the interest on the capital involved; while in the latter case, inasmuch as the price will in each case be increased by the profits of the antecedent transaction, the tax will be paid on this continually augmented level of price. As a result, a general sales tax of one per cent. may in the end constitute far more than one per cent. of the original selling price. The tax in other words will be pyramided; it will be cumulative in character.

On the other hand, if the tax is not shifted to the consumer, it is also open to two criticisms. For if the tax remains on the producer, it will be equivalent to a tax on gross receipts. A tax on gross receipts is like the tithe: gross receipts are no indication of the real profitableness of the business. Taxes on output or gross receipts which make no allowance for the expenses constitute a rough and ready system, suitable only for the more primitive stages of economic life. In modern times, just as the tithe has been replaced by the tax on net produce or on the capitalized net produce in the shape of selling value, so the tax on gross receipts is everywhere giving way to the tax on profits or net receipts. Under our present business practice a tax on gross receipts would be exceedingly inequitable as between various classes of business, or as between different individuals in the same class, depending largely on the rapidity of the turnover. Figures that have been compiled tend to show that a tax of one per cent. on gross sales would amount in some cases to five per cent. of the net income and in other cases to as much as thirty per cent. In a business community which is striving more and more to adjust its taxation to the ability of the individual such a reversion to bygone practices would seem to be unwise in the extreme.

In another respect also the sales tax, if it rests on the seller, would be inequitable. It would affect business very differently according as we were dealing with so-called multiple-process organizations or with simple and less integrated enterprises. There is a great difference between so-called single-process business, *i.e.*, those which concentrate on one process, and the larger enterprises which carry on several processes at once. We have not a few textile plants which buy the cotton from the ginning mill, and sell the finished product through their own selling organization to the wholesaler, and even in some cases to the retailer. In the same way the United States Steel Corporation owns mines, railroads and steamboats, as well as open-hearth plants and may in the case of tools supply its products direct to the mail order house. We find in modern times not only vertical but horizontal integration in business plants and enterprises. A general sales tax will obviously afford decided advantages to the organization which is able to dispense with the various stages in the purchase of the products needed in the successive processes. This consideration is a familiar one in fiscal literature, having been emphasized half a century ago by Leroy-Beaulieu. He tells us that:

In order to establish the turnover tax, we do not say with complete justice but without a monstrous and revolting inequality, it would be necessary to make a classification of industries and professions, and to fix a different rate for each. This would land us in well-nigh inextricable difficulties. . . .

Another defect of this tax is that it would be shifted very unequally in the case of identical products. The subdivided industries where the same commodity, before reaching the final stage of readiness for sale, passes through several hands, would have to endure a burden infinitely more heavy than similar industries where all the operations are concentrated in one plant. In this way a kind of privilege would be accorded to the large, as over against the small enterprise.[1]

The adoption of a general sales tax would moreover tend to bring about great changes in business practice, looking toward the elimination of the middleman, even where he had shown his superior economic efficiency. In the attempt to economize in the tax, the best interests of the consumer might be sacrificed.

We come in the third place to a consideration of the administrative objections to the general sales tax. It is questionable whether these have been adequately realized. The administration of ordinary taxes on property or profits is difficult enough, even if we have to deal only with those individuals or businesses that possess the given minimum of property or profits. But in the case of a general sales tax we are dealing with the totality of the community, with every individual—man, woman or child—who buys any commodity that is offered for sale. We are dealing with the small man as well as the big man—with the patron of a five or ten cent store as well as the purchaser of a Rolls-

[1] Pour que la taxe sur le chiffre d'affaires pût être établie, nous ne disons pas avec complête équité, mais sans une monstrueuse et révoltante injustice, il eût donc fallu faire un classement des industries et des professions, admettre pour chacune d'elles un taux d'impôt différent: c'eût été, croyons-nous, presque inextricable.

Un autre défaut de cet impôt sur le chiffre d'affaires c'eût été qu'il se répercuterait d'une manière fort inégale, méme sur les produits identiques; les industries morcelées où un meme objet, avant d'arriver à être prêt pour la vérité, passe par plusieurs mains différentes, eussent supporter une charge infiniment plus lourde que les industries similaires où toutes les opérations sont concentrées dans une même maison. C'eût donc créer une sorte de privilège pour les grandes maisons au depens des petites.—Paul Leroy-Beaulieu, *Traité des finances*, 7ᵉ éd. 1906, i, pp. 504, 505.

Royce or a palatial yacht. What possible devices can be utilized to guard against wholesale fraud and evasion, when it is to the interest of both buyer and seller to avoid the tax. Especially in a democracy like ours, where the administrative system is proverbially weak, the attempt to levy a general sales tax would impose upon our officials an administrative burden for which they are hopelessly unprepared. The defects of our so-called "nuisance taxes" are fairly widely recognized; but they are insignificant when compared to the probable results of a general sales tax with all its complexities and its uncertainties.

Finally if the general sales tax is defective from the point of view of adequacy, of consequences on business prosperity and of good administration, it is above all to be criticized from the point of view of fiscal justice. This brings us to the chief criticism to be urged against a general sales tax: it is a tax on consumption, on expenditure. We do not object to all taxes on consumption; for every well-balanced system of taxation should include indirect as well as direct taxes. But there is consumption and consumption. There are articles of luxurious consumption; there are articles of convenient consumption; there are articles of necessary consumption. The sales taxes that we have in this country today and which are found in other Anglo-Saxon countries as well, are with few exceptions taxes on the sale (and sometimes the production) of articles of luxurious consumption or of the widespread consumption of what cannot really be called necessaries, as for example, tobacco and liquor before the present dispensation. But when we come to a general sales tax, we are dealing primarily with a tax on necessaries, inasmuch as the great mass of commodities consists of articles used by the people in modest circumstances. Therefore, as the French writers in the Middle Ages pointed out, a general sales tax is a sort of inverted income tax. Instead of taxing the man with a higher income more, as we do, you tax the man with the higher income less—not indeed actually less, but relatively less in proportion to his wealth as measured by property or by income. For although the rich man consumes more than the poor man, and will accordingly pay a larger tax, the amount of his consumption or of his purchases will not increase in proportion to his wealth. Above all a general sales tax would render impossible the application of a graduated or progressive scale of taxation. It would in fact amount to an upside-down system of progressive taxation. It is this instinctive reaction of the common man to the proposal of a sales tax which is responsible for the opposition manifested from the time of the Romans through the Middle Ages, down to modern times. At this very moment in this country, the laboring classes and farmers are up in arms against it. And they are right.

It may be true that our present revenue system errs on the side of taxing wealth unduly and consumption not enough. But if we were to abolish the excess-profits tax, reduce the surtaxes on income, and then substitute a general sales tax, the shoe would pinch on the other foot. Instead of deriving most of our revenues from wealth, as we do at present, we should have more than half of the entire revenue coming not only from taxes on consumption, but from taxes on the necessaries of life. That is a situation which can not be contemplated with equanimity.

In their legitimate and comprehensible enthusiasm to reduce the present crushing burden of taxes on income and profits, some of our business men have resuscitated the project of a general sales tax, and some of our political leaders have lent too ready an ear to their demands. These business men and these political leaders are sadly mistaken. They have failed to analyze the true bearings of the system which they recommend; they have omitted to study the consequences upon business life itself; they have been blind to the essential injustice of the project. The general sales tax is a discredited remnant of an outworn system; it is essentially undemocratic in its nature; and it would, if enacted, exaggerate rather than attenuate, the present inequalities of wealth and opportunity.[1]

[1] [The Senate Finance Committee to which this memorandum was submitted, finally decided, notwithstanding the views of Senator Smoot, against the adoption of the tax. In the House it never had much chance of success.]

CHAPTER SEVEN

THE PROBLEM OF TAX-EXEMPT SECURITIES

[This chapter first appeared in part in the *Hearings before the Committee on Ways and Means, House of Representatives, on Tax-exempt Securities,* Jan., 1922, and in part in the *New York Times,* Dec. 31, 1922.]

The recommendation of the President in his recent message to Congress, also found in the report of the Secretary of the Treasury, that we should end the further issue of tax-exempt bonds by an amendment to the constitution brings the matter to the forefront of public discussion. As there seems to be much misunderstanding of the topic, it may be wise to discuss it under five heads:

1. What is the reason for tax exemption?
2. What are the facts?
3. What are the objections to tax exemptions?
4. What are the alleged advantages?
5. What is the solution of the problem?

I. *Why Do We Have Exemptions?*

Exemptions from taxation are as old as taxation itself. In their origin they undoubtedly played a useful rôle. Thus, in mediæval times, a man was subject to a scutage, or "shield money"; but if he went to war and provided his own horse and armor in the feudal array he was exempt from the tax. Exemptions were accorded for public rather than private reasons. Even today—not to speak of growing crops and workingmen's tools—ministers' houses, cemeteries, educational and religious institutions are exempt from taxation. The public at large is willing to bear the higher rate of taxation because the exempted classes or institutions are really performing a function which the government would otherwise be called upon to assume.

The original system of class exemption, however, soon degenerated. In some cases exemption was acquired by classes which enjoyed political power without assuming political responsibility, as notably in France under the ancient regime. In other cases the exemption became individual in character, finally culminating in a system whereby any one could buy himself free of taxation.

As a result of the French Revolution and the growth of modern democracy, individual exemptions have almost everywhere been abolished and class exemptions have been reduced to the narrowest limits. One of these class exemptions which still persists, however, is that with which we have to deal at present, namely, the exemption of government bonds.

The first obvious reason which led to the exemption of government bonds from taxation was war. At the outbreak of war government credit is apt to weaken, and yet it is precisely at this moment that the need for revenues is greatest. What is more natural, then, than that the government should seek to strengthen its credit, that is, to sell its bonds at a higher price or at a lower interest rate, by granting to the holders an exemption from taxation.

The argument originally applied in time of war was soon extended to times of peace. If exemption of government bonds in war means a strengthening of public credit and an increased facility for the marketing of a loan, there seemed to be no reason why governments should not avail themselves of the same advantages in normal times. This was especially true of the state and local governments in the United States, with their desire to borrow money for productive expenditures for good roads and more schools, instead of for the unproductive expenditures of war. The advocates of tax exemption found a ready defense in the argument that the lower rate of interest would mean a reduced cost of the enterprise and a consequent diminution of the burden on the taxpayers, who would ultimately have to meet the loan.

As the result of a long and interesting development in the judicial construction of the constitution, it has been decided that the bonds of the national government are not subject to tax by the states, and that the bonds of the states and local governments are not subject to tax by the federal government. Here, therefore, we have a remarkable situation. The federal government surely has received no benefits from the issue of state and local securities; nor have the state and local governments derived any peculiar benefits from the issue of the national securities. Yet both kinds of government are inhibited, by constitutional interpretation, from taxing their own citizens who happen to possess securities issued by the other class of government. Whatever the federal government might decide to do about its own bonds—and it is quite conceivable that for reasons of weight, as we shall see, the federal government might like to tax its own bonds—it is prevented from applying the same method to the state and local bonds; *vice versâ,* the state and local governments which might decide to tax their own securities would be prevented from taxing the bonds of the federal government in the possession of their own citizens. The fact that the hands of each class of government are tied in dealing with the securities of the other class of government would thus prevent them from attempting a reform—if a reform seemed desirable—with their own securities.

II. *What Are the Facts?*

Bearing in mind, then, the peculiar character of our American problem, let us consider the facts.

When we entered the war the government was much disturbed at the outlook. Although the credit was good, the necessity of marketing such an unheard-of quantity of bonds created a delicate situation. Secretary McAdoo was exceedingly anxious to issue the first Liberty loan at as low an interest rate as possible, and yet he was confronted by a market in which there were outstanding large quantities of state and local tax-exempt securities. Moreover, he was obsessed by the idea that "Wall Street" should not derive any special advantage from the emission, and he believed that a high interest rate would not only accomplish this result but would saddle an undue annual burden upon the country. He therefore decided, contrary to the advice of many economists and some of the leading financiers, to accord a complete tax exemption to the entire issue.

The result of this manœuvre was, however, not entirely satisfactory. When the succeeding issues of Liberty and Victory bonds were made, the tax exemption was accordingly restricted, both in amount and in duration. In some cases a distinction was made between the normal tax and the surtax; in others the maximum amount of exempt principal was fixed at $20,000, $30,000 or $45,000, and the time limit on the exemption was made from two to five years after the Presidential proclamation of peace.

The net result was that of the total new debt of some twenty-two billions there was exempt from taxation in the hands of any individual not only the 3½ per cent. bonds and the 3¾ per cent. notes, but also on all the issues together a maximum of $160,000, if he had properly distributed his purchases among the various classes of obligations. Inasmuch as the richer investors had at their disposal not only this $160,000, but the entire amount of the 3½ per cent. bonds and the 3¾ per cent. notes, and in view of the fact that a not inconsiderable number of smaller investors were in the $160,000 class, it may be asserted with confidence that from the time of issue up to 1922 virtually the entire issue of government war loans of about twenty-two and a half billions was exempt from taxation. To this should be added almost a billion of pre-war bonds and some half billion of government farm loan bonds.

It must be remembered, however, that inasmuch as the Presidential proclamation of peace did not come until June, 1921, the privilege of tax exemption on all the government war loans, except the first, was to cease automatically between 1923 and 1926. The tax exemption of federal bonds must therefore be pronounced in large part an exemption of limited range, designed primarily for war purposes.[1] On the other hand, the exemption of the entire national debt from state and local taxation will continue, irrespective of the provisions of the federal law.

In the case of the state and local issues, however, the exemption is perpetual for all forms of tax, not alone for state and local, but also for federal taxes. The problem of state and local exemption, therefore, is really the more important one. This is all the more true because of the steady increase in the issue of such securities. The latest general statistics available at the time of writing are those of the census of 1913, but even these are not complete. We know, however, how many bonds were outstanding at that time in states and counties, and in incorporated places of over 30,000, and in civil divisions of less than 30,000 including drainage and irrigation districts, school districts and the like. The exact figures are as follows:

States	$364,836,427
Counties	333,236,161
Local:	
Over 30,000	2,489,665,185
3,000 to 30,000	316,695,185
2,500 to 3,000	232,023,319
Under 2,500	111,516,694
Other specified civil divisions	103,068,188
Total	$3,834,807,291

There are also some official figures for 1919. For that year we have two census reports, one affecting states and the other affecting incorporated places of over 30,000. We

[1] The exact facts are given below in the appendix, p. 156.

find that in 1919 the bonds or funded debt of the states had risen from $364,000,000 in 1913 to $625,000,444, or almost double. We also find that in the cities of 30,000 or over the outstanding bonds had risen from $2,489,000,000 to $3,904,-000,000. Applying the same percentage of growth to the counties and civil divisions under 30,000, for which we have no figures, would bring the tax-exempt securities outstanding in 1919 to a little under $6,000,000,000.

With reference to the bonds issued by the states and municipalities alone we are in a little better position, owing to the records kept in Wall Street. The following table discloses the amounts of bonds issued by the states and localities during the last ten years:

	Long Term	Short Term	Total
1912	$399,046,000	$192,450,000	$591,496,000
1913	408,478,000	483,218,000	891,696,000
1914	445,906,000	286,055,000	731,961,000
1915	492,590,000	154,278,000	647,318,000
1916	497,404,000	292,407,000,	789,811,000
1917	444,933,000	392,444,000	837,377,000
1918	262,819,000	473,135,000	735,954,000
1919	770,195,000	450,094,000	1,220,289,000
1920	773,664,000	664,087,000	1,437,751,000
1921	1,304,289,000	716,104,000	2,020,393,000
*1922	1,039,939,000	210,605,000	1,250,544,000

* Nine months.

From these tables two conclusions are apparent. The first is that since the adoption of the federal war income taxes the issue of state and local securities has enormously increased, and that the rate of increase itself is growing from year to year. The second is that in addition to the $6,000,000,000 outstanding in 1919 we have had another $3,500,000,000 up to the end of 1922. We can therefore confidently assert that there were outstanding in 1922 some $10,000,000,000 of State and local bonds, with an annual increase from one to one and a half billions.[1]

[1] [The Census figures, published in 1924, of the gross debt in 1922 are as follows: states, $1,162,651; counties, $1,386,430; incorporated places,

If this rate of increase is maintained, as seems likely, there will be outstanding by the end of 1926, when most of the Federal securities will lose their exemptions, from $14,000,000,000 to $17,000,000,000 of state and local securities, in addition to the several billions of federal bonds and Farm Loan bonds.

In other words, from 1919 to 1926 there will have been outstanding of tax-exempt bonds an amount ranging from $25,000,000,000 to $35,000,000,000, to be reduced in 1926, unless the federal government issues more tax-exempt bonds, to between $18,000,000,000 and $21,000,000,000. These are the salient facts of the situation. Putting it a little differently, the average of tax-exempt bonds from the end of the war to 1926 is about $30,000,000,000, and the average for the period for the few years after 1926 will be about $20,000,000,000. Making a liberal allowance for the bonds held by banks and corporations, we may safely assume that one-half of the entire issue is held by individuals with an income over $2,000. The National Bureau of Economic Research has computed the proportion as over 57 per cent. What we have to deal with practically is therefore a tax exemption in the hands of individuals ranging between $15,000,000,000 up to 1926, and $10,000,000,000 after 1926, increasing thereafter by from one and a half to two billions annually.

III. *The Disadvantages of Tax Exemption*

The first objection to the system of tax exemption is the loss of revenue. It is obvious that if the outstanding bonds, federal, state and local, bear an interest rate of about 4½ per cent. it would mean that the income on an average of $15,000,000,000 would be about $675,000,000. The federal government alone will have lost up to 1926

$5,833,938; specified civil divisions, $1,872,439; total, $10,255,458. *Wealth, Debt and Taxation, 1922. Public Debt, compiled as a part of the Biennial Report on Wealth, Public Debt and Taxation*, Washington, 1924, p. 81. The estimate in the text was accordingly a close one.]

not only the eight per cent. normal tax, but also the surtax, in so far as these securities are held by the richer individuals. If we assume that these bonds are so held that they are subject to an average tax of 40 per cent. we have a loss to the Federal Government of $270,000,000 a year, or 40 per cent. of $675,000,000, which is the interest on $15,000,-000,000. This makes no allowance for the 12½ per cent. tax on the bonds held by corporations, which will bring the figure to at least $300,000,000. This loss of revenue far transcends any possible gain that might accrue to the federal government from the lower rate of interest on the tax-exempt bonds. From the point of view of revenue the issue of tax-exempt bonds has been a losing investment. Instead of being grateful to Secretary McAdoo for the alleged savings which he secured for the government, we should censure him severely for the increased burden that he has imposed on the community as a whole.

If we add to these figures for the federal government the sums lost by the separate states through inability to subject these securities to the State property or income taxes, the loss of annual revenue becomes appalling.

More important, however, than the fiscal side of the problem is the economic and social side.

The second objection to tax exemption is that it creates a gross inequality of burden. To the extent that these bonds form an increased share of the realized property of the nation, tax exemption means the liberation of unearned incomes at the expense of earned incomes. We may not be ready in this country for the principle which has been adopted almost everywhere else, namely, the principle of differentiation of taxation, whereby lower rates are granted to labor or earned incomes than to property or unearned incomes. But it is certainly true that no country has yet seen fit to tax property or unearned incomes at an actually lower rate than earned incomes. Yet that is what we are virtually doing.

In addition to this glaring inequality we have a still worse situation, namely, the escape of the rich man from the burden, which must, accordingly, be borne by the poor man, and by the recipients of moderate incomes. The President has made us familiar with the facts of the situation. With the exceedingly high surtaxes in our present income tax, making the maximum rate until recently 77 per cent., and now 58 per cent. the temptation on the part of the wealthy to invest in the tax-exempt bonds becomes very great. The result is a progressive falling off in the numbers and amounts of taxable incomes in the higher income scales. The following table from the recent report of the Secretary of the Treasury clearly shows the tendency:

	Number of Returns		Net Income	
	All Classes	Over $300,000	All Classes	Over $300,000
1916	437,036	1,296	$6,298,577,620	$992,972,986
1917	3,472,890	1,015	13,652,383,207	731,372,153
1918	4,425,114	627	15,924,639,355	401,107,868
1919	5,332,760	679	19,859,491,448	440,011,589
1920	7,259,944	395	23,735,629,183	246,354,585

"During the same period," says the Treasury report, "the investment income of all classes increased, while in incomes over $300,000 investment income shrank from $706,945,738 in 1916 to $229,052,039 in 1920. This indicates an astounding decline in taxable incomes over $300,000."

While it is true, of course, that in a period of business depression incomes are apt to decrease, and that when business revives we may expect a larger revenue in these brackets it is scarcely open to doubt that the prodigious falling off is in part at least the result of investment in the tax-exempt securities.

Consider, for a moment, what this means. The development of modern democracy has brought about a demand for the wiping out of the old abuses of taxation whereby the wealthy rolled the burden off on the masses. If America has stood for anything, it was the democratization of society and the conferring of equal opportunities upon all. We are the only country in the world which has raised so much of its war revenues from wealth rather than from consumption. Not a few even think we have gone too far in that direction.

Now we are confronted by a situation in which the wealthy gradually stand from under, and make the less fortunate bear the burden. The existence of the tax-exempt securities is honeycombing our entire system of taxation; it is upsetting the system of graduated taxation which we thought we had adopted; it is converting it into its opposite —a degressive tax, or what the French call an "upside-down progressive tax." We are quickly getting back to the system of the Middle Ages, with its noble principle of *le fort portant le faible*, "the strong bearing the burden of the weak," but which, in practice, was turned into the opposite principle of the weak bearing the burdens of the strong.

What a travesty on justice! What an absurdity for a country like the United States! How can we expect social peace and class contentment with such a glaring inequality of taxation? What wonder that we should have a radical "bloc"!

Tax exemption, in the third place, gives an unfair advantage to certain forms of investment, and for that reason disturbs and even imperils general industry. Tax exemption puts government bonds into a preferred condition and artificially restricts the market for other bonds. Thus, large lenders of mortgage bonds tell us that since these immense issues of state and local tax-exempt bonds, the market for farm mortgages has become less attractive, with the result that the farmer has to pay a higher interest rate.

The fourth objection to the system of tax exemption is that it prevents reduction of our tax burden. We have not, indeed, suffered to the extent of England, not to speak of France and Italy. It has been claimed that England is even now burdening her social income to such an extent as actually to trench on her social capital. Nevertheless, with us the cry for a reduction of the tax burden is widespread. Yet, with our present tax exemptions, that process is inevitably attended with difficulties. Nothing would tend more to a diminution of our tax burdens than to put an end to these tax exemptions. A small normal income tax and a moderate surtax would then suffice for all our needs.

The final objection to the system of tax exemptions, especially state and local tax exemptions, is that it is endangering the entire system of federal revenues. We all remember with dismay the fiscal system of our government before the adoption of the present constitution, when the federal government had to depend entirely on largesses, called requisitions, from the separate states. As the outstanding and tangible wealth comes more and more to consist of securities issued by state and local governments, the basis of the federal income tax—our chief source of reliance, present and prospective—will continually contract. More and more we shall be compelled to resort to an undesirable system of indirect taxes, or taxes on consumption, while with the growing and imperious needs of the federal government, we may be compelled to depend again in large measure on the largesses of the states. Such a prospect is uninviting, to say the least.

IV. *The Alleged Advantages of Tax Exemption*

It is sometimes urged that the objections alluded to in the foregoing section are exaggerated, and that the shortcomings of the system of exemptions are by no means so glaring as depicted. One of the criticisms sometimes advanced is that the inequality of taxation is more fanciful than real, for the reason that the purchaser of the tax-exempt bonds has to pay so much more for the bond. He loses, it is alleged, in the premium which he has to pay for the bond, and this loss offsets any advantage supposed to accrue to him from tax exemption.

To a certain extent there is some truth in this, but only to a limited extent. This is due to what is known as the capitalization or amortization of taxation. If a particular bond or class of bonds, hitherto subject to tax with all others of the same class, is suddenly exempted, the market price will rise to an amount equal to the capitalization of the tax. Let us suppose that the market rate of interest is four per cent. and that five per cent. bonds, subject to one per cent. tax, sell at par. That is, if I own a one hundred dollar bond bearing five per cent. interest and pay one dollar tax, the net return is four dollars and the bond will sell at par. If now one bond is exempted from the tax so that the net return is five dollars, the market value of the bond will, of course, rise proportionately, so as to keep the bond on a net four per cent. income basis. The conclusion seems to be that it makes no difference to the new purchaser whether the bond is taxable or tax exempt. In either case he will make only four dollars net.

The fallacy of this argument is due to the fact that it neglects a consideration of the market conditions. It is true that if one bond is now exempt from tax, its market value will rise by the full capitalization of the tax. But in proportion as the privilege of tax exemption is accorded to another bond, then to another and then to an entire class, the advantage of the privilege tends to diminish.

In other words, as the market tends to broaden, the conditions will change. Tax exemption through capitalization is a scarcity privilege. If all securities were exempt the privilege would disappear and there would be no difference in price. With every billion of dollars added to the amount of tax-exempt securities the advantage becomes smaller. But in proportion as the advantage of exemption diminishes, the premium on the tax-exempt bonds will fall. Yet the advantage of remission from taxation remains unimpaired.

In other words, where the amount of tax-exempt securities is expanded by billions, as in this country at present, the benefits of tax exemption accruing to the owners increase. They will have to pay in the shape of premium a continually diminishing sum, and yet they will enjoy the same remission of tax. The disparity in market price between tax-exempt bonds and the taxables tends to efface itself; the disparity in the tax tends to remain the same.

Another and still more important consideration is neglected by those who claim that our criticism is unfounded. This is due to our graduated or progressive income tax. The reason why there is such a phenomenon as the capitalization of taxes, the reason why we have a premium on the market value of tax-exempt bonds, is that the market discounts the tax that has to be paid in future. Where we have a stable income tax, levied at a normal rate, it may be argued that the future purchaser, with his eyes open, will make allowance for this normal rate. But how about the high surtaxes? The bond may get into the hands of the man subject to the fifty per cent. surtax; but it may also get into the hands of the small investor subject only to the six or eight per cent. normal tax.

Would it be reasonable to say the premium will amount to the capitalization of the fifty per cent. rate? Under the conditions at present, with the demand for tax-exempt bonds on the part of the small and modest investor as well, that position is assuredly untenable. The exact amount of the capitalization depends upon the relative supply and the demand coming from successive classes of investors. Under the actual conditions it is safe to say that probably only a little more than the normal tax is capitalized. Inasmuch as so little of the surtax is capitalized, the wealthy investor will pay a slight premium, but will enjoy remission of taxation on the total fifty per cent. of the income.

If we combine these two arguments—on the one hand the scarcity-value argument, and on the other the graduated tax argument, it will be seen that the wealthy investor in tax-exempt securities pays very little for the privilege, and that the objections arising from the inequality of taxation remain unaffected.

The second criticism often urged is that tax exemption is really beneficial, because the benefit is passed on from the creditor to the debtor or borrower. In other words, it is claimed that the taxpayers in state and local governments benefit because the state and local governments pay so much less interest on their bonds. Whatever advantage is seemingly derived by the wealthy investor really, so it is alleged, accrues to the ordinary taxpayer.

This widespread argument is fallacious for the same reason as that just advanced above. While the state and local governments were able at one time to sell their bonds at a higher price because of exemption from state and local taxes, that advantage was gradually dissipated, as the other state and local governments did the same. Every bond broker will tell us that this special advantage to the state and local bonds gradually disappeared. The same is true at present. The state and local issues always enjoy certain advantages due to the security of the principal and to other reasons. This advantage, measured in terms of interest rates, has ranged in the past from one-half per cent. to one per cent.

The situation is just about the same at present. Barring the spurt in 1919, when the states and locals first enjoyed the exemption from suddenly increased surtaxes of the federal government, the situation has gradually returned to normal. At present, in fact, if we compare the premiums on the state and local bonds in the United States with premiums on the similar class of bonds in Canada we find the range about the same, despite the fact that the Canadian bonds enjoy no similar privilege of tax exemption. It is clear, therefore, that there is a fallacy of the current contention that tax exemption affords a great advantage to the public.

The advantages are exaggerated; the objections cannot be exaggerated.

V. *Conclusion*

We ask, in conclusion, why should the present system be perpetuated? Some of our states and cities still cling to the fallacious opinions set forth above. But even if the contentions were true in fact, they would be indefensible in principle. If the state and local bonds were subject to tax in the same way as other property, including federal bonds, they would suffer no disadvantage. The states indeed have the right to demand that the federal government impose no exclusive or differential burden on them. That was the foundation of the decision of the Supreme Court, which declared that the imposition of an unequal tax on the states might subject them to a disadvantage, and, by impairing state credit, attack their sovereignty. To permit the nation to impose a special tax on the agencies of state government is one thing; to ask the nation to confer a special privilege and advantage on the states is quite another matter.

If the federal government should decide after 1926 to tax its own bonds, is there any reason for according a special privilege to the state and local government bonds? Is there anything sacrosanct about state and local credit as compared to federal credit? The states may have the right to demand of the federal government that they be not subjected to disadvantage; they have no right to ask for a special privilege. Tax exemption in theory, at least, affords them a special privilege. As a matter of fact, as we have seen, the advantage is much slighter than they think.

Moreover, it must not be forgotten that, with the change now taking place in the state and local fiscal systems, even this slight advantage will be far more than outweighed. Twelve states now have an income tax, and many others are discussing it. When the state income taxes will be unable to reach the holders of federal and other state bonds the states will stand to lose far more in the deficit of revenue than the little they gain by partial capitalization of the tax and by the slightly increased price at which they are able to market the securities.

With every year the situation in the states will become more and more analogous to the situation in the federal government. Not only will they lose absolutely in dollars and cents, but the growing inequality between social classes, as between the rich and the moderately wealthy in town and country, will be continually accentuated.

For several years Secretary of the Treasury Mellon has based his chief argument for a reduction of the high income surtaxes on the existence of tax-exempt securities, claiming that the temptation to invest in tax-exempts would be much reduced if the surtax rates were lessened. While we also believe in the desirability of reducing the surtaxes, it must be said that this particular argument does not seem to be very cogent. For, in the first place, if an individual can save even ten or twenty per cent. in his taxes by a shift in his investments, he will be likely to do so. Secondly, since the increasing billions of tax-exempt securities must be bought by some purchasers—whether they pay high or low surtaxes, or none at all—they tend to create a privileged class and to divide the community into opposing sections with dangerously conflicting interests. A mere reduction of the surtaxes, whatever may be its other merits, will not do away with the evils of tax exemption.

What we need is a constitutional amendment providing reciprocity as between state and nation. The nation should have the right to subject state and local bonds to the same tax as it assesses on its own bonds; the state and local governments should have the right to subject federal bonds to the same burdens as they impose on their own bonds. This is no attack on the sovereignty of the states.

It simply removes an unjust and originally unintended privilege. When the people of the states come to understand the problem, they will learn that the privilege really amounts to very little, and that is, moreover, purchased at the cost of a grievous inequality among social classes. In the long run their selfishness will not avail them: they will lose, rather than gain, by the continuance of the tax exemption.

Equality between state and nation; equality between local and federal bonds; equality between economic classes; equality between earned and unearned income; equality between rich and poor—that is the equality which we desire to achieve. The problem of tax exemption is the problem of fiscal equality; it is the problem of social justice.

Appendix

Exemptions of United States war obligations from federal income surtaxes.

(All are exempt from "normal" federal tax. Besides the fully exempt 3½ per cent bonds and 3¾ per cent notes, a maximum amount of $160,000 may, if properly distributed among the various classes of obligations, be held free from surtaxes and profits taxes.)

Class of obligation	Maximum amount of principal, interest on which is exempt	Time limit on exemption	Conditions
Bonds:			
First	Unlimited	Until maturity...	No conditions.
Second (1)....	$5,000	....do	Joint exemption for second, third, and fourth bonds, certificates of indebtedness, and war savings certificates. May be applied to any one of these classes or may be divided among them.
Second (2)....	$30,000	After Jan. 1, 1919, until 5 years after presidential proclamation of peace.	Joint exemption for second, third, and fourth bonds. May be applied to any of these classes or may be divided among them.
Second (3)....	$45,000	2 years after presidential proclamation of peace.	While the maximum amount of this exemption is $45,000, it may not exceed 1½ times amount of fourth bonds subscribed for and still held at time of tax return. May be applied either to second or third bonds or may be divided between them.
Second (4)....	$20,000	After Jan. 1, 1919, for 3 or 4 years; that is, while Victory notes may be held....	While the maximum amount of this exemption is $20,000, it may not exceed 3 times amount of Victory notes subscribed for and still held at time of tax return. May be applied either to second, third, or fourth bonds or may be divided among them.
Third	Identical with exemptions (1), (2), (4) of second bonds	....	
Fourth (1)....	....do	....	
Fourth (2)....	$30,000	2 years after presidential proclamation of peace.	No conditions.
First converted into fourth[1] **(1)**	Identical with exemptions (1), (2), (4) of second bonds	....	
First converted into fourth[1] **(2)**	$30,000	2 years after presidential proclamation of peace.	Do.
Certificates of indebtedness	Identical with exemption (1) of second bonds...	....	
War-savings certificates	....do	....	
3¾ per cent notes	Unlimited	Until maturity...	Do.
4¾ per cent notes	No exemption....	....	

[1] Converted bonds are included with the class of bonds into which they have been converted, with the exception of first bonds converted into fourth bonds, which are separately listed because of special exemption.

CHAPTER EIGHT

DEATH TAXES, STATE OR NATIONAL?

[This was originally an address at the National Inheritance Tax Conference at Washington, D.C., Feb. 19, 1925. It was published in the *Proceedings,* and also appeared in the *National Income Tax Magazine* for March and April, 1925.]

We have heard so much about the difficulties and the evils of the inheritance tax as to lead some to the conclusion that the only escape lies in the abolition of the tax itself. But while all suggestions for the abolition of taxation are welcome, it is, we fear, too late in the day to expect any such suggestion to prevail. The inheritance tax in modern society has come to stay. It is found in every democratic community and it is everywhere becoming of increasing fiscal and social importance. The peculiar conditions of investment in Italy have indeed there led to the restriction of the tax in the direct line; but this defection is more than compensated by the rapid growth of the inheritance tax in every other part of the world. In the face of this overwhelming trend toward the spread of highly graduated death duties or death taxes, as they are sometimes called, it seems needless to indulge in any theoretical argument in its defense; the statesmanship as well as the scholarship of the world has long since passed beyond that point.

I. *The Theory of Death Taxes*

We may, however, be pardoned if we allude to the old objection which has recently been advanced by several representatives of our Federal Treasury department—that the inheritance tax should be abandoned because it is a tax on capital. As to this contention it is only necessary to remember that a tax on capital is not in itself any more reprehensible than a tax on income. Both are taxes on wealth, and if not carefully chosen, and administered, may destroy wealth. A tax on capital indeed diminishes capital, but so does a tax on income diminish income; and in both cases if the tax does not take away the entire income, the surplus will be capitalized and will prevent any net decrease of capital.

Furthermore it is to be remembered that if the taxes are used for productive purposes, they represent not destruction, but simply the shifting, of capital wealth. If the tax is devoted to building a school house or a subway, the capital subtracted from the inheritance is reconstituted in another form. A tax on capital in such a case will not destroy capital; it may even increase capital if the funds now devoted to a school house, when left in the hands of the successor to the estate, would be squandered. The real question is not whether a tax is imposed on capital, but whether the proceeds are well employed or wasted. And in this respect the inheritance tax does not differ from other taxes. Moreover, the critics of an inheritance tax on the score that it is a tax on capital would have considerable difficulty in defending the traditional and most widespread tax that exists in this country—the general property tax; for this is also a tax on capital. If the inheritance tax is to be abolished because it is a levy on capital, the property tax must also be abolished. If the rejoinder is made that the inheritance tax is a different kind of capital tax, because the general property tax, although levied on capital, is really paid out of the income of the property, the answer is a double one: first, the general property tax is often levied on capital which yields no income, as in the case of unimproved city land or non-dividend-paying stocks; while on the other hand the inheritance tax is in many cases paid out of the income of the estate that has accumulated since the death of the owner.

Moreover, if we regard the social rather than the individual situation, the case is still stronger. With capital values in this country of some 320 billions of dollars, according to the last census, and with a social income of between 55 and 70 billions, of which at least one-third is the income of capital, he would indeed have some hardihood to assert that an inheritance tax, federal and state, of less than 200 millions, is not paid out of the income of the capital. In fact the statistics of the estate tax bear out this contention. In the calendar year 1922 the gross estates amounted to 2,937 millions; the net taxable estates to 1,673 millions; and the tax to 119 millions. If we reckon interest at the moderate rate of 5 per cent., the gross estates would have earned in the very first year 147 millions or far more than the tax; and even the net estates would have earned enough to pay the tax within 1½ years. For 1923 the figures are still more convincing on this point: gross estates 2,525 millions; net taxable estates 1,374 millions; tax 69 millions. A capital of 2½ billions will surely yield more than 69 millions of income. Even if we make allowance for the non-productive part of the estates, these conclusions would not be materially altered. And if, in any particular estate, the earnings may not be adequate to prevent the necessity of selling some of the assets at forced prices, this risk can be averted by the rapidly growing custom of insurance against the shrinkage of the estate due to cost of administration, taxation, and other charges. A still simpler method of overcoming this particular objection would be to introduce the device, that has been utilized in other cases of a lump-sum payment, as in the capital levy in Europe or in the special assessments in the United States—namely the privilege of payment in instalments through several years. In this way the annual tax will almost never take more than the income of the estate.

It follows from these considerations that we need not fear any progressive diminution of the capital wealth of the community. And in the very country of Great Britain, to which some of the lugubrious calculations of our worthy Treasury representatives have been applied, the figures show a continuous increase not only in the capital wealth of the community but also in the yield of the death duties. Inasmuch as the old "capital" criticism, resuscitated from a hoary past, is the only objection that has been raised, it really seems unnecessary to attempt any general defense of a tax which has undoubtedly come to stay, and which is bound to play an increasing rôle in every democratic community.

A second preliminary question, the important bearing of which on our present situation will soon be apparent, is as to what kind of an inheritance tax we should have. There are, as is well known, two entirely distinct categories: we may tax the inheritance as a whole by what is known as an estate tax; or we may tax the separate shares going to the recipients of the inheritance by what is variously known, but which can best be termed the share tax. In the United States as in England and in many other countries we find both systems. With us, the federal government limits itself to the estate tax, while most of the states levy only a share tax, although in a few states including Massachusetts and New York we find both—known as the tax respectively on the right to transfer, and on the right to receive the transfer.

The underlying theories of these two categories of the inheritance tax are quite different, although practical statesmanship, which has never bothered much about theories, has proceeded with the elaboration of both. The defense of the share tax is now wellnigh everywhere conceded to be the accidental-income argument.[1] So far as the re-

[1] [For a fuller statement see the chapter on "The Inheritance Tax" in Seligman, *Essays in Taxation*, 10th ed., 1925. A more elaborate discussion will be found in the two works on *The Inheritance Tax* by my students, the earlier one by Max West, 2nd ed., 1898; the later and much fuller one by W. J. Schultz, to be published in 1926.]

cipient of an inheritance is concerned, the accretion to his capital wealth through an inheritance is just as much income, in the broadest sense of the term, as that which comes from gifts or capital gains or other irregular or aleatory sources. Yet for practical reasons the inheritance is not included in the taxable income, but is taxed separately; just as in some countries gifts are taxed separately by a gift tax and capital gains are taxed separately by a capital-increment tax. The fact that in some of our states accidental incomes in the shape of inheritances are taxed, while regular incomes are not yet taxed, is a proof of the belated and incomplete development of fiscal equity with us.

The defense of an estate tax, however, is quite different. Many would, and with reason, uphold it on the privilege-of-inheritance idea, developing the argument promulgated by Bentham, that the conception of the right of bequest involves a social privilege, for which some compensation is rightfully demanded. Others would stress the co-partnership-of-the-state idea, as forcefully upheld by Mr. Andrew Carnegie. There is little doubt that the great mass of the American people agree with Mr. Carnegie when he said, after describing the growth of the large fortunes of the country: "Now who made that growth? The growth of the American public—that is where that wealth came from and that is the partner in every enterprise where money is made honorably; it is the people of the United States. * * * I say the community fails in its duty and our legislators fail in their duties if they do not exact a tremendous share, a progressive share."

In other words, while the share tax rests upon the idea of individual obligation, the estate tax rests upon the idea of social obligation. In the share tax we think of the duty of the recipient; in the estate tax we think of the relation of the estate as a whole to the society which helped to make it possible. The defense in both cases as in that of every direct tax, is ability to pay, or fiscal capacity. But whereas in the share tax the ability is conceived of as an individual matter, in the case of the estate tax it is conceived of as a social matter. In a well-rounded system of inheritance taxes or death duties we need both the individual and the social element: that is, we need both the share tax and the estate tax.

II. *Lack of Uniformity*

With these preliminaries we come to the special subject under consideration. Forty-six of the forty-eight states of the American union levy at present an inheritance tax—almost all of them a share tax, a few of them also an estate tax. The continuing need of revenue from this source is undoubted: the glaring evils arising from the conflicts of tax jurisdiction are daily becoming more unbearable. What practical methods of dealing with this situation are in sight?

The most obvious suggestion is the development of a harmonious system through interstate agreements. This is a consummation devoutly to be wished. But the difficulties of mutual adjustment are enormous. In the first place there is the multiplicity of numbers. If each of the forty-eight states were to make agreements with each of the others we should have several hundreds of separate conventions. This in itself is staggering enough. While the embarrassment would be somewhat relieved by the adoption of reciprocal arrangements, this presupposes that the interests of all the states are identical. Unfortunately, however, entirely apart from interstate rivalry of which we have had not a few recent examples among states where there might be presumed to be an identity of interests, we cannot close our eyes to the existence of divergent economic interests. The problem of a suitable criterion to serve as the basis of attempts to avoid double or multiple taxation is therefore a difficult one. It is easy to suggest, as has often been done here and abroad, that we should adopt as the criterion the principle of situs in the case of real estate and that of domicile in the case of personal property. But the experience of Europe shows that the situation is by no means so simple and that particular conditions in countries or groups of countries may require special adjustment. In the United States, for instance, there is still a marked difference of interest between the creditor states and the debtor states. Especially with the widespread existence of absentee ownership in this country, it is almost hopeless to expect the voluntary acceptance by all states of a single uniform criterion, whether that of domicile or that of situs.

If a comprehensive universal system of interstate comity thus seems to be at present largely a counsel of perfection, might it not be wise to attempt a first step in the right direction by a system of regional or sectional agreements? The economic interests of the Middle Atlantic states or of the Mountain states are fairly homogeneous. Would it not be possible to start the ball rolling, at least, by seeking agreements between the members of each group, in the hope that the beneficial results of such an accommodation would gradually spread to other groups as well? If half a loaf is better than no bread and if the adoption by all the states of an identical method seems to be at present fraught with insurmountable difficulties, is it premature to suggest as the first practical step the endeavor to secure regional or sectional agreements designed to avoid interstate double taxation?

But suppose that our success in this direction turns out to be no greater than in the broader and more comprehensive field. If the states will not of themselves solve the problem, what alternative avenues of escape from the present unbearable evils are open? This brings us to the heart of the subject, namely, the possibility of federal assistance in the solution of the problem. If the states cannot or will not help themselves, can the federal government do anything to better the situation?

There are three possible ways in which this help could be afforded. While none of them is perhaps immediately practicable or desirable, it is nevertheless worth while to consider them in detail, partly for purposes of education, partly for the sake of inducing those states that are intolerant of federal interference to make that interference unnecessary.

The first of the three alternatives, although it is found in some federal countries, is not very promising. It consists in the passage of a federal law designed to regulate the conditions of uniformity under which the separate states shall be permitted to levy inheritance taxes. Such a method of uniformity through legislative regulation would probably encounter constitutional obstacles here; and the prospects of removing these obstacles through constitutional amendment would not be very bright. Uniformity through compulsory national regulation may therefore be eliminated at the present time.

Fortunately, however, there are other methods of achieving uniformity than by the exercise of legislative compulsion. We refer to the decisions of the Supreme Court. The Supreme Court of the United States makes law no less than does congress; and in the special field of fiscal legislation the pressure exerted by the Supreme Court has in not a few instances brought about a large measure of uniformity of state action. Why is this not possible in the inheritance tax? If the victim of some peculiarly glaring attempt to impose multiple taxation upon an inheritance were to contest its constitutionality, and if the Supreme Court should declare the legislation of a particular state invalid from this point of view, might it not be possible for the court to enunciate the principles of an economic and fiscal character by which it had been guided? We have many cases of constitutional importance where the court decisions have been swayed by economic arguments. Take the stock-dividend case as an example. If the Supreme Court were to formulate such a set of economic principles and, what is perhaps more difficult, were to follow these principles consistently for a series of years, it is not at all improbable that the states would gradually conform their legislation to these principles and thus effect a uniformity, somewhat akin to that which until recently existed as a result of the court decisions in National Bank taxation.

While the method of uniformity through judicial decision, which is also found in certain federal states, is undoubtedly superior to the uniformity through legislative regulation and while it is free from constitutional objections, it nevertheless encounters the difficulty of the elaboration of a proper set of criteria which might be uniformly applicable throughout the country. For the court also would be confronted in its decisions by the divergence, and perhaps even the opposition, between the economic interests of the states to which attention has been called above. Moreover, the attainment of the goal in this way would probably involve a protracted delay. Finally, the Supreme Court is not in the habit of making broad generalizations, except in the form of *obiter dicta.* It decides the particular case on its merits, but does not like to mortgage the future.

If then the achievement of uniformity by either judicial or compulsory regulation seems to be unacceptable or of doubtful probability, what remains?

There remains only the third alternative. This consists in the frank recognition of the fact that, if every other expedient fails, only a federal system of taxation can bring about the desired uniformity; and that the legitimate fiscal demands of the states must be met by some adjustment to this federal system. What we have in mind, in other words, is a comprehensive federal inheritance tax, with a division of the yield between the nation and the state, so that the fiscal needs of each will be satisfied and the crying evils of the present be eliminated.

In the discussion of this plan, precedents for which can

also be found abroad, a number of problems present themselves. Of these four are of first-rate importance:

1. Why have a federal inheritance tax at all?
2. What kind of a federal inheritance tax should there be?
3. According to what principle should the proceeds of the tax be divided among the states? and
4. How should any infringement on the reserved rights of the states be avoided?

III. *Why a Federal Tax?*

First then: why should there be any federal inheritance tax at all? This raises the problem of the comparative fiscal needs of the nation and of the commonwealths. If it could be shown that the inheritance tax is not needed for revenue purposes by the nation but is urgently needed by the states, it would be difficult to base the argument for a national inheritance tax solely on the ground of securing uniformity among the states. Inasmuch as the chief purpose of taxation is undoubtedly the securing of an adequate revenue, the argument in favor of a national inheritance tax would be seriously weakened by the contention that no such revenue is needed. Is that contention correct?

If we review our fiscal history, we shall find that in time of peace we have gone through several stages. For over a century, we followed the principle of strict separation or segregation of source. The federal government contented itself with indirect taxes; the states relied on direct taxes. In fact, barring the decade during which Hamilton endeavored to utilize federal taxation for political rather than for purely fiscal purposes, and which may be called the first stage—that of the utilization of the tariff and a few internal taxes—the federal government long found an entirely adequate revenue in the customs duties alone. This sole reliance on the tariff constitutes the second stage in our fiscal history. It was not until after the Civil War that the growing revenue needs of the federal government brought about a reversion to the Hamiltonian plan, thus initiating the third stage where to the tariff there was now added a substantial internal revenue derived almost entirely from liquors and tobacco. During these three stages which lasted to the beginning of the present century, the state governments relied almost exclusively on direct taxation. In fact during the first two stages we find virtually exclusive dependence on the general property tax; while during the third stage, when the property tax began to disclose its defects and its fiscal inadequacy, the states gradually added first the corporation tax and then the inheritance tax. But this still denoted reliance on direct taxation, for the states trespassed in only a very few cases upon the field of indirect taxation, which was commonly considered as reserved to the federal government.

A great change took place, however, a few decades ago. While the fiscal needs of our local governments increased by leaps and bounds, the necessities of the states grew but slowly, as compared with those of the federal government. The consequence was that the latter was compelled to supplement its resources and, in the face of a growing popular opposition to any marked extension of the tariff or of other indirect taxes, the nation was led gradually to enter the field which had been supposed, up to that time, to be reserved to the states. First came the federal corporation tax, next the federal income tax, and then, finally, the federal inheritance tax. For this, although first imposed for war purposes, had nevertheless, as will be remembered, been proposed by the President a few years before, in time of peace, as a means ot warding off the projected income tax. Thus we have entered upon the fourth stage, that of the utilization by the federal government of both direct and indirect taxation.

What has been called the encroachment of the federal government upon the sphere of the states is moreover a world-wide phenomenon. In wellnigh every federal state similar economic and fiscal conditions have brought about analogous results. In Austria, in Germany, in Australia—everywhere we find the emergence of a federal corporation tax, of a federal income tax, of a federal inheritance tax. The principle of separation of sources which is still such an article of faith among some of us—direct taxes to the states, indirect taxes to the nation—may therefore be said to have disappeared everywhere, as a result of overmastering economic forces. When taxation was light and the needs of both state and nation were slight, it was a simple matter to delimit the fiscal field of each. But with the economic transition which has taken place in modern times, the emphasis has been shifted. Whatever may be the traditional arguments in favor of state sovereignty or local government—and their force is still strong with us—there is no doubt that the modern industrial system is daily augmenting the importance of our national economic life, and is accordingly tending with us, as everywhere else in the world, to an inevitable increase of federal fiscal needs as over against those of the states. Interstate commerce and business are growing apace at the expense of intrastate commerce and business: the fiscal systems must adjust themselves to these revolutionary economic changes.

As a matter of fact, national needs are increasing more rapidly than those of the states and localities combined. This was indeed to have been expected during the war; but even now, with conditions almost normal, the same tendency is observable, as appears from the following table:

(In Millions)	Federal Taxes	State and Local Taxes	Total	Federal Percentage of Total
1913	$ 661	$1,529	$2,180	30%
1924	3,352	4,600	7,952	41%

These figures do not quite disclose the actual facts because they include in state and local taxes special assessments, fees and permits, which in 1922 alone amounted to over 600 millions. Even allowing therefore for a possible further reduction of a few hundred millions in federal taxes, it still remains true that they constitute a relatively larger share of the total than a decade ago.

Before 1914, moreover, the revenue from state inheritance taxes was insignificant in the extreme,—apart from New York, in fact completely negligible. If then death taxes may be considered as a virtually new source of revenue for the states and if the federal tax needs are increasing faster than those of the states and the localities, it follows that we should not lightly eliminate the federal revenues from this source.

Let us next contrast the respective resources of the states and the nation. Although the customs duties can be utilized only by the nation, it is unlikely that the tariff will yield much more than it does at present, namely, a half-billion dollars, or about one-eighth of the entire revenue, as compared with the pre-war period when the tariff formed the sole source of federal taxation. Moreover, the federal government is virtually inhibited from securing any revenue from direct property taxes, which constitute the chief reliance of the separate states. We know that as a result of our last experience the so-called direct tax was repaid to the states. While the field of internal indirect taxes will remain open to the federal government, there is a marked movement on the part of the states to encroach upon that field, as notably, in the gasoline and severance taxes. But even where the state governments do not enter upon what has hitherto been considered to be the federal field, it is unlikely that the American people will consent in time of peace to any large measure of indirect internal revenue. Especially in view of the fact that we have voluntarily abandoned, through the eighteenth amendment, a federal revenue which could easily have reached without hardship the sum of a billion or a billion and a half dollars, it is probable that our federal indirect internal revenue system will in the future be limited largely to the tobacco tax, to a few stamp duties, and to a very restricted number of excises. The chief reliance of the future in meeting the several billions of federal expenditures will have to be on direct taxes.

As to this there is, indeed, no doubt that the income tax, both individual and business, will continue to play the chief rôle here. But in view of the growing demand for a reduction of high income-tax rates, is it safe to assume that we shall not have to rely to a far greater extent than at present upon the revenue from inheritance taxes? It is true that our present estate tax yields only an insignificant revenue: in 1924 only 103 millions, in 1925 about 105 millions, plus whatever may be expected from the gift tax, or say between 110-115 millions in all. But if we had the right kind of a tax, administered in the right way, it would not be difficult to secure a revenue of at least several hundred millions from this source alone—a revenue which would bear a fairly respectable relation to the future revenue from the income tax. It must not be forgotten that in Great Britain the death duties before the war yielded considerably more than half as much as the income tax: in fact the percentage was nearer sixty per cent. The figures for a number of years are appended herewith:

In millions of pounds	1911-12	1912-13	1913-14
Income tax	44.8	44.8	47.2
Death duties	25.4	25.2	27.4
Per cent of income tax....	56.7	56.3	58.0

In France, in fact, despite the high war-income tax, the inheritance tax even at present forms a still larger share of the total. In 1923 the inheritance tax yielded 2,770 million francs as against 3,790 millions from the income tax, i. e., the yield of the inheritance tax was 72.8 per cent. of that of the income tax, or almost three-quarters as much. These figures show what fiscal potentialities are contained in the inheritance tax.

Compare them with our American statistics. In 1924 the inheritance tax yielded $103 millions and the income tax $1,842 millions, i.e. the inheritance tax yielded only 5½ per cent. of the sum yielded by the income tax. Even in Great Britain, at the present time, with the very high income tax, the inheritance tax yields 17½ per cent. of the income tax—the figures for 1923-24 being £57.8 millions and £329.9 millions respectively. With the gradual and impending reduction in the income tax rates, the inheritance tax will yield a growing percentage, even if it does not reach the pre-war figures. And while our American ratio of 5½ per cent. may not attain the 60 per cent. of Great Britain or the 70 per cent. of France, it can surely be made to reach from 25 per cent. to 50 per cent. In other words, the inheritance tax yield of the future can, under proper management, amount to from one-quarter to one-third of the yield of the future income tax. At all events from the point of view of fiscal needs and fiscal achievements it is probable that a federal inheritance tax will be increasingly important in this country. Upon the retention of the inheritance tax depends the possibility of reducing the income tax rate to a manageable figure. Even the average business man, when confronted by the choice between high surtaxes with no estate tax, and low surtaxes with a moderate inheritance tax, will prefer the latter. It is significant, as an indication of the recent development, to note that the German law of 1924 reserves the entire proceeds of the inheritance tax to the federal government, and bids the states to be satisfied with other sources of revenue.

What now are these other sources of revenue upon which our states can rely? In the first place we have the whole domain of real and personal property taxation, upon which the federal government cannot as a practical matter encroach. In the second place, we have the new engine of taxation of which advantage is only beginning to be taken by our states; the field of income taxation, both personal and business. This is indeed not an exclusive field, for it is occupied by the federal government as well. But the possible limits of a state income tax system are set only by considerations of taxable capacity. Compared with these two sources of revenue, real estate and income, the inheritance taxes play only a small rôle in the states. In 1922 out of total revenues of one and one-quarter billions the state inheritance taxes yielded only sixty-five millions or about 5¼ per cent.

It may be conceded, however, that the loss of even these sixty-five millions would be seriously felt in some of our states. From this, however, simply follows the conclusion that whatever arrangement be made in the future, the fiscal interests of the states must be safeguarded. The present suggestion of a division of the yield, to be considered in a moment, will result in at least as much revenue to the states as accrues to them at present.

If, therefore, we combine these two considerations, on the one hand the relatively greater future needs of the federal government as compared with those of the states, and on the other hand the guarantee that the fiscal resources of states must not be impaired, it follows that the argument in favor of a federal inheritance tax is by no means a weak one. If we add to this fiscal argument the other argument that the continuance of the federal inheritance tax may be made to solve the problem of uniformity of taxation, it seems difficult to resist the conclusion in favor of a federal inheritance tax. This conclusion is strengthened by two other considerations. The one is the possibility afforded by a federal estate tax of reaching effectively the mass of tax-exempt bonds, both federal and local, which it seems so difficult to bring into the dragnet of our income taxes, and the existence of which constitutes such a blot on the American endeavor to secure equality of taxation. The other consideration is that even when we have solved the problem of interstate double taxation we shall continue to be confronted by the difficulties of international double taxation. With these a system of state inheritance taxes is wholly incompetent to deal. For the separate states, without any international standing or treaty-making power, will be powerless to make arrangements with foreign countries analogous to those which have been initiated abroad and which alone promise an escape from an evil which is growing apace with the spread of the world economy. So that from almost every point of view a federal inheritance tax seems not only defensible, but necessary.

It is true that the recent Australian Royal Commission on Taxation of 1921-22 recommended the reservation of the inheritance tax for the separate states; but the Commission was able to arrive at this conclusion only by suggesting that in return all income taxes should be reserved exclusively for the federal government or what they there call the Commonwealth. A subsequent conference between the Commonwealth and the state executives in 1923 made a new proposal, viz., that the inheritance taxes should stay as they are, but that the income tax should be divided, the states to limit themselves to the personal income tax, the Commonwealth to the corporate income tax (or as it is there called the company tax). Neither of these plans has been adopted, but it is significant that agreements were concluded in 1925 between the Commonwealth and each of the states (except Western Australia) that the entire income tax, state and federal, should be collected by the federal authority, with only a single return from the taxpayer.

Whatever we may think of this income-tax solution, which is not now before us for discussion, it is clear that the proposal of the Australian commission to leave the inheritance tax to the states and the income tax to the nation would not be acceptable to us. If our states had to choose between an income tax and an inheritance tax there is little doubt that ultimately, if not at present, they would prefer the former. But the experience of the United States, like that of every other federal government, shows that they cannot have both. The states, in other words, must make up their minds that in addition to the tax on real and personal property, which they now enjoy, they cannot continue to demand the exclusive use of either the income or the inheritance tax. The time of such segregation of sources has gone by, here as in every other federal country. Whether or not we have state inheritance taxes, the federal inheritance tax will continue to form an indispensable element in our federal tax system. Even if the present treasury policy succeeds in abolishing the federal tax, it requires but little perspicuity to predict its ultimate reënactment. For in the conflict between reactionary and liberal fiscal policy, there is little doubt as to what will finally win out in the American democracy.

If then we must have a federal inheritance tax, the second question is what kind of an inheritance tax? It is necessary here only to revert to our earlier explanation as to the two forms of the inheritance tax, the estate tax and the share tax. In England the death duties comprise both categories; with us, as in Australia, the federal government levies one kind and the state governments another kind. But if, as is here suggested, there should be primarily a single federal inheritance tax, it ought surely to combine both elements, for reasons not only of revenue but of equity. We raise at present from all our inheritance taxes, federal and state, about two hundred million dollars. With a uniform, improved, and adequately guarded system we could secure, at the same rates or even with somewhat lower rates, over double what we are now raising. In England, where the social income is only about one-third of that of the

United States, the proceeds of the inheritance tax are very much greater than in the United States, amounting in 1924 to about two hundred and seventy-five millions of dollars. Were our tax as successfully administered as in Great Britain and with similar rates, the revenue would be some seven or eight hundred millions. The trouble with our federal inheritance tax is not in the rates, as our esteemed Secretary of the Treasury thinks. The English rates are higher, and the French rates are much higher than with us; all of which does not prevent England and France from raising far larger and continually increasing revenues from this source. We have a defective law and a still more defective administration. With an improved law, with the enforcement of the gift tax, with the rendering impossible the evasion of the inheritance tax through our absurd incorporation of invividuals, and with a proper kind of administration, we should soon find that our revenues would be greatly augmented, even though the rates were diminished. With a revenue of several hundreds of millions, it would then be possible to hand over to the states a portion of the yield, whether it be twenty-five per cent. or seventy-five per cent., with the result not only that the federal government would get more than at present, but that the states would secure as much as they now receive or could in the future secure through independent action.

IV. *The Interests of the States*

The next question is this: If a part of the yield is to be apportioned to the states, how shall the division be carried out? It would be simple to say, as for instance until recently in the German empire, that there should be returned to each collecting district a fixed proportion of the whole. This solution would not be satisfactory for us, partly because of the divergence of economic interests alluded to above. The criterion of apportionment ought to be constructed in a manner comparable to the prosperity index in the Dawes report as to the taxable capacity of Germany. In that case it is a question of paying; in this, a question of receiving. But the principle is the same. There are several such possible criteria which in our judgment ought to be combined. One obviously is relative population; another is relative real-estate values. As these, however, would favor the creditor states, they should be supplemented by some such criteria as relative railroad trackage; telegraph and telephone wire mileage and instruments; agricultural mortgages; coal, oil and mineral deposits; water kilowatt power and the like.

A final advantage of such a plan would be the elimination of the great variations in the yield of the state taxes. In death taxes the narrower the base, the greater the oscillations in revenue. In New York, *e.g.*, the annual variations have reached 300%, making any accurate budgetary forecast most difficult.[1] A federal tax with its more stable annual returns would be a fiscal benefit to the states.

We come, finally, to the last point which is that of avoiding any impairment of state rights. The project, as outlined above, does not say to the states that they must not levy any inheritance taxes. It asserts that the federal government will stand ready to return to the states as much as, or more than, they are now getting for themselves, and that too with an avoidance of all the difficulties of double taxation under which their citizens now suffer. In all this there is no impairment of state rights. It could easily be made to satisfy the states from the fiscal point of view. But if a particular state should be discontented, it would still be at liberty to levy an additional inheritance tax of its own, as at present. It is unlikely, indeed, that it would do so, inasmuch as all of its citizens would already be subject to

[1] Typical figures are (millions omitted):

1910	$8,214	1916	$5,984	1920	$21,259
1913	12,724	1917	15,078	1922	15,385
1915	8,263	1918	11,433	1924	19,369

the high federal tax. If any state, however, desired to levy such a separate tax, it ought to be held in line by the simple condition that it could receive its allotted share of the federal tax only in case it observed, in the levy of its own tax, the above criterion designed to avoid double taxation. This also would involve no impairment of states' rights—it would simply extend to the inheritance tax the principle of affixing certain conditions similar to those that are now found in our system of federal grants or allotments for roads and for other purposes.

It might be claimed that the plan of apportionment here sketched is open to constitutional objections. As to this, it is to remembered that as far back as 1837 the federal government distributed its surplus revenue among the states, and that for some years it has been making annual grants to the states. If it be contended that this practice is not equivalent to apportioning among the states particular taxes collected by the federal government, the answer is that here also we have a precedent. During the Civil War the federal government collected a direct tax which was subsequently distributed among the states. If the government may repay one hundred per cent. of a tax, it obviously has the right to repay thirty-five or fifty per cent.

If doubts still remain on that score, they can be dispelled by utilizing the present twenty-five per cent credit. In other words, a portion of the tax can be credited to the states and even, if so desired, collected by, and paid to, state officials, while only the surplus would then be collected by federal officials. To this method it is difficult to see any possible constitutional objection.

Finally, if it be argued that the method of apportionment is apt to lead to extravagance, we have only to point out that the balance of advantages seems to be in favor of the practice, as witnessed by the rapid spread of the recent movement toward federal grants. Above all we must not forget that this arrangement is simply an extension of the method of apportionment of state revenues to localities which has long been practiced in state finance to the advantage of all concerned.

The present plan of allowing twenty-five per cent reduction of the federal estate tax for state taxes is ingenious, and marks a step forward in avoiding to a certain extent interference with state revenues. But it has two defects: twenty-five per cent. of the present federal estate tax affords too little relief to many states which now secure more than this from their own inheritance taxes. Furthermore, it does nothing to remedy the worst of existing evils, namely multiple taxation. If, nevertheless, this provision be retained it is suggested that the proportion be increased to fifty per cent. or even more; but only on condition that each state observe the criterion of apportionment designed to remove double taxation.

The project developed in this chapter would be more far-reaching than the existing plan, even if amended. It accomplishes four purposes: it gives the federal government a greater revenue than at present and renders possible a further reduction of the income tax; it gives the state governments at least as much revenue as at present; it lightens the burden on individual taxpayers because it spreads the load over a greater field, extending the tax to many who ought to bear their share but who now contrive to escape; and it removes once and for all the intolerable evil of simultaneous double taxation. From the point of view of adequacy, of equality, of uniformity, the proposed plan offers a distinct improvement over existing conditions.

We see then that it is possible for the federal government to help in accomplishing a much needed reform. A continuance of the present situation is unbearable. A way out of the difficulty, so far as double taxation among the states is concerned can indeed be found by interstate agreements—universal or regional. But even such a system will not obviate the possible rivalry of the future between the federal and the state governments. Is it not wiser to attempt to solve both problems at once, that is, to retain for the federal government a revenue which will in the future be increasingly indispensable to it, to afford to the state governments all the revenue which they can reasonably expect from this source, and to achieve at one blow the uniformity of taxation which is ardently desired by all? We need in the inheritance tax, as in many another domain of fiscal and economic life, the disappearance of the feeling of opposition between state and nation and the growth of a feeling of coöperation. Instead of thinking in terms of sovereign states and federal encroachments we must learn, in finance as in economics, to speak more and more in terms of a coöperative effort which will preserve all that is best in local and sectional vigor and yet at the same time bring our institutions into line with the fundamentally changed conditions of a national life. Uniformity of taxation as among all our citizens is one of the imperative needs resulting from this change of conditions: let us not lightly turn away from the possibility of its achievement by utilizing the joint endeavors of state and nation alike.

CHAPTER NINE

THE TAXATION OF NON-RESIDENTS IN THE NEW YORK INCOME TAX

[This originally appeared in the *Bulletin of the National Tax Association,* vol. v, 1919.]

The question of the taxation of non-residents has become especially urgent with the advent of the income tax. The problem was, indeed, obvious in principle from the very beginning of interstate taxation. But it so happened that as the economic relations between the states in this country assumed some importance, the administration of the general property tax left much to be desired, so that in practice the tax was not enforced in such a way as to create any considerable difficulties. When the inheritance tax was introduced, the enforcement was more rigorous, and we began to hear more of the difficulties of interstate complications. With the advent, however, of the income tax, we are confronted by the problem of double taxation in all its intensity. For under modern conditions, local and state lines are of only very slight consequence in the reception of incomes.

There is an additional reason, however, why the situation is still more complicated in states like New York. In many less advanced states of the union the great majority of incomes within the state are earned by residents of the state; that is to say, there are comparatively few non-residents who sojourn for a protracted period within the state. On the other hand, most of the residents of the state secure all or a very large part of their revenue from property situated or business conducted within the state. In New York, however, the situation is very different. In the first place, New York City, as the great metropolitan center, attracts people from all over the country. Not only do they swarm to New York for weeks or months at a time, but a large number of wealthy individuals, who still retain their legal residence in other states, erect princely mansions in New York and live there most of the year. On the other hand, New York City is the financial center of the country: we know that more than one-third of the individual income tax of the entire country is paid in New York. That means that the wealthy residents of New York own a large part of the property of the nation and that the incomes received in New York are to a considerable extent received from sources outside of the state. Finally, New York as the industrial center of the country is crowded with hundreds of thousands of members of the professional classes and of wage-earners who get their living in the city but who commute to the suburbs. Northern New Jersey and, to a less extent, southwestern Connecticut, are in reality suburbs of New York.

Thus from both points of view the question of double taxation, i. e., the taxation of non-residents on income received within the state and of residents on incomes received without the state, assumes in New York a significance which in practice far transcends that in many other parts of the country.

Although, as stated above, the question of double taxation has never been of great importance in the administration of the general property tax, the courts have gradually elaborated some general principles to govern the situation. In the case of real estate, it was comparatively easy to reach the conclusion that real estate ought to be taxed where it was located, irrespective of the residence of the owner. In the case of personal property the situation was more complicated. So far as intangible property is concerned, the rule of law that gradually came to be accepted was *mobilia personam sequuntur,* or "movables follow the person"; i. e., the controlling element is the legal residence of the owner. This decision was obviously due to the fact that we can scarcely speak of the situs of intangible property. When, however, the attempt was made to deal with tangible personalty, a real difficulty arose. Since tangible personalty has a definite location, the question arises why, despite the rule that movables follow the owner, the rule governing real estate should not also be applicable here. The consequence has been an uncertainty on the part of the courts and our legislators. In some states the rule of *situs* governs, in others the rule of *mobilia personam sequuntur* applies. The result would of course be intolerable if the tax were actually enforced; for in some cases the tangible personalty would then be taxed in neither the state of location nor the state of residence, while in other cases it might happen that it would be taxed in both states. Since a more recent decision of the Supreme Court (in the refrigerator case) a part of the difficulty has been removed in that no state can henceforth impose a tax on tangible property permanently located outside the state.

I. *Benefits versus Ability*

When we come to consider the theory underlying the American practice, we find that it was an outcome of the general economic and political doctrines of the day. The ordinarily accepted theory of the relation of the individual to the government, which had come down from the eighteenth century political philosophy, was that the chief object of the state was to protect the individual, and that he ought to pay for this protection by supporting the government. Accordingly, a man ought to be taxed where he permanently resides, for the reason that the government protects him in the state of his residence; and, on the other hand, the tangible property ought to pay where it is located, because it receives the protection of the government there.

In reality, although it was not recognized, two different

theories were implicit in this treatment of the matter. On the one hand was the theory that the government affords protection—the so-called protection theory. On the other hand was the theory that the individual receives a benefit from this protection—the so-called benefit theory. These theories are by no means necessarily identical. The protection theory states that the government ought to be reimbursed for the protection it affords, i. e., that the government ought to be paid for the expenses involved in affording protection. This is the cost-of-service theory; that taxation ought to be in accordance with the cost of the service.

On the other hand, the benefit theory holds that the individual ought to pay in accordance with the advantage or benefit that he receives. This is the value-of-service theory—that taxation should be in proportion to the value of the service. In the one case we regard the giver; in the other the recipient. Now it is to be noted that there is no necessary correlation between cost of service and value of service. The same service of the government to two different men may be valued very differently by them. The rich man may need for the protection of his person no more police than the poor man; the cost of service may be the same: and yet there may be a great disparity in the value of the service. According to the strict protection theory, the rich man would pay no more; according to the benefit theory, he would pay much more. Even if we consider the property, rather than the person of the individual, the protection theory and the benefit theory are not necessarily coterminous. It may, indeed, côst the government more to protect the large property than the small property; but the wealthy owner of the large property may decide not to depend upon the government and may choose to employ private watchmen, detectives and the like, so that he would not get as much benefit from the government protection as the owner of the small property who relies entirely on the police. In that case, while the cost of protection would be greater, the benefit received would not be greater. It is obvious, therefore, that the protection theory and the benefit theory are by no means identical.

The American courts, however, like the economists and publicists from whom they adopted the theory, made no such fine distinction. The only difference is that while the writers generally speak of the benefit theory of taxation, the courts have usually called it the protection theory.

As a matter of fact, however, this theory, although so deeply ingrained in the legal thinking, has been abandoned by economic and fiscal scientists. It has been retained in the courts to a certain extent and in popular and untutored thought by the mere force of tradition. The theory of protection really is untenable. It is as inapplicable to the person of the taxpayer as to his property; it is unsatisfactory from the point of view of both the cost of protection to the government and the benefit to the taxpayer.

The theory arose at a time when the chief expenditures of the government were devoted to military purposes and other forms of protection. In modern times, however, the state has assumed all kinds of new functions, among which that of protection counts for relatively little. In the city of New York, for instance, the only protection that the person of the taxpayer gets is from the police and perhaps in a wider sense from the courts; and even in the case of property there is to be added to these only the cost of the fire department. But all these combined do not by any means form the major part of the cost of government. Education, street cleaning, charities and corrections, recreational expenditures and the like, bulk continually larger in modern budgets. Government, nowadays, does far more than merely protect the individual; to measure the obligation resting upon the taxpayer by the cost of protection gives an entirely inadequate picture of the situation.

On the other hand, even if we abandon the cost-of-protection theory, and take refuge in the benefit theory, the situation is equally unsatisfactory. For, in the first place, the benefits accruing to the individual from governmental action are to a very large extent not susceptible of measurement. Who can measure the benefit received by a particular individual from the expenditures on the courts or the navy? How can we measure the benefits accruing to the property of an individual, as a merchant's stock in trade, from the millions spent by the city of New York on elementary schools? But even to the extent that we can measure the resultant benefits, the theory labors under the obvious weakness that in many cases the poor benefit more than the rich. The poor man sends his children to the public schools, the rich man to a private school; the rich man has his own night watchman and Pinkerton detectives, the poor man depends on the police; the rich man has his own garden or country house, the poor man enjoys the public parks; the rich man goes to his private hospital, the poor man in a large measure to the municipal hospitals; the rich man contributes to the charities, the poor man is a beneficiary of charities. Modern government ministers in increasing measure to the needs of the masses. If it were possible to measure benefits in dollars and cents, the benefit received from a not inconspicuous part of modern government outlays would be in inverse proportion to wealth. So that, if benefits were to be the test of taxation, the poor would frequently be called upon to pay more than the rich.

Without going into all these subtleties, however, the basic reason why the protection or benefit theory is not applicable is that it gives an erroneous explanation of the relation of the individual to the government. The modern democratic theory of taxation, which rests upon the more organic theory of the state, is that of faculty or ability to pay. As we have sought to express it elsewhere,[1] the modern theory of political science recognizes the fact that

[1] *Essays in Taxation*, 10th ed., 1925, pp. 337 *et seq.*

the public collective wants are as much a part of the nature of civilized man as are his individual private wants; and that the essence of taxation is a moral, as well as a legal, obligation. The government, indeed, must do something for the community in return for the support which it receives. But this reciprocal obligation on the part of the government is not toward the individual as such, but toward the individual as a member of the group. The special benefit is swallowed up in the common benefit. The special benefit to the individual is, in most cases, not even measurable; for the distinguishing characteristic of modern civilization is the spread throughout the community of these impalpable, non-material results of good government which make for the common welfare, and particularly for the higher life. In its ideal form, at all events, the state must be likened not to a joint-stock company, but to a family. The citizens are not stockholders but brethren, animated, if they are patriots, by the same ideals and by the same fine sense of coöperation in the common interest. Whatever the test of this moral obligation to contribute to the support of the whole may be, it is, in the state as little as in the family, assuredly not the measure of benefit received. Not only is the test impracticable, but if it were practicable it would be inadequate.

It must, of course, not be understood that this exhausts the explanation of the relations of the individual to the government. The government often does things for the individual where the principle of equivalents rather than the principle of ability comes into play, i. e., where the government does a particular thing for the individual and the individual receives a special benefit in return. The government in such a case functions, as it were, in a business capacity; it acts to a great extent as a private business man would act. It gives something to the individual which is of special value to him and it demands a payment in return for the particular service. But such payments, as has been fully explained elsewhere,[1] are called prices or fees or special assessments, and are not to be confused with taxes. Taxes —or direct taxes at least—should be levied in accordance with the principle of ability to pay: other charges of government may be assessed on the principle of benefits.

The contrast between the principle of ability and the principle of benefits is, however, less sharp than is often supposed. This is largely due to the fact that the interpretation commonly put upon the ability theory is the one formulated by John Stuart Mill who maintained that the ability of the individual to pay taxes is to be measured by the sacrifice imposed upon him in paying the taxes. In other words, the ability theory was identified with the sacrifice theory.

There has, however, been much confusion about this concept of sacrifice. In a wider sense, the sacrifice theory may indeed be defended, although the term employed would even then be inexpedient. In the narrower sense, however—that is, in the sense in which it was employed by Mill and in which it is commonly understood at present—the sacrifice theory, or the sacrifice concept of ability to pay, is incorrect, because inadequate. Let us make this clear.

We must remember that there are two sides to every man's economic activity—the production or acquisition of wealth and the consumption or disposition of wealth. The acquiring of the wealth normally costs some effort; the parting with the wealth also involves a pain. Now if by sacrifice we mean the costs involved, i. e., the costs of acquisition as well as disposition, then indeed the sacrifice theory is correct in the sense that from the point of view of economic psychology the test of ability to pay taxes is an amalgam of both of these costs or sacrifices.

The term sacrifice, however, as conceived by Mill and as commonly understood, refers only to the pains involved in parting with wealth. Sacrifice, thus interpreted, means

[1] *Essays in Taxation*, pp. 436-446.

a sacrifice of disposition, a sacrifice of consumption. The common defence of progressive taxation, for instance, is that the relative sacrifice of parting with the tax diminishes with the amount of one's wealth. When we speak of sacrifice, we think in such a case only of the interference with the enjoyment or consumption of wealth.[1]

This, manifestly, is a one-sided or inadequate view. For, just as there are differences involved in the disposition of wealth, so there are differences involved in the acquisition of wealth. These differences in the ease of acquisition may be termed acquisition costs or production costs as over against the disposition costs or consumption costs. If the term "sacrifice" is employed to designate the latter cost, the term "opportunity" might be used to designate the former. There are all manner of differences in opportunity which explain the relative ease of acquiring wealth. The most important of these differences, apart from those inherent in the very nature of things, depend, so far as the government or the social sanction is concerned, largely on the question of privilege. Society and state afford the individual all manner of privileges, most of them entirely legitimate, which help him to add to his wealth. It is, therefore, defensible to contrast privilege with sacrifice. The economic privileges conferred upon the individual in the acquisition of his wealth affect his ability to support the government no less than do the relative sacrifices imposed upon him in parting with his wealth. In other words, instead of there being one aspect or test of taxable ability, there are two: the privilege side as well as the sacrifice side, the acquisition side as well as the disposition side. A man's ability to pay taxes is to be measured not only by the relative burden imposed upon him in parting with his wealth, but also by the relative ease with which he has acquired his wealth.

[1] This point is more fully elaborated in Seligman, *Progressive Taxation in Theory and Practice*, 2nd ed., 1908.

Now, inasmuch as, and to the extent that, the privileges enjoyed by individuals result in actual benefits to them, the privilege theory may be in part at least interpreted in terms of the benefit theory. It is clear, then, however, that the real objection to the old protection or benefit theory is not so much that it is false as that it is exaggerated. It represents only a part of the truth, and only a small part. But the same thing may be said of the sacrifice theory. It also represents only a part, even though a larger part, of the truth.

In its proper formulation, then, the benefit theory is not opposed to the faculty theory, but really forms a part, although a minor part, of the ability theory. It is only to the extent that the benefits or privileges conferred upon the individual augment his ability to pay that they deserve any consideration at all. To erect the benefit theory into an all-embracing theory is incorrect; to say that benefits or privileges are one of the elements modifying the ability of the individual is justifiable. The benefit or protection theory is not an independent theory, standing side by side with the faculty or ability theory: it can be upheld only as one of the two constituent elements that compose the ability theory. It is because the ability theory has been incorrectly identified with the sacrifice theory that this confusion has resulted. Ability or faculty to pay is the fundamental explanation of all taxes; but ability to pay is composed of two elements, the privilege element and the sacrifice element. Benefits may be contrasted with sacrifices; the benefit theory cannot correctly be contrasted with the ability theory.

This confusion of thought has led many writers astray. Some of the leading continental writers on finance [1] hold, for instance, that the line can be drawn between the general state taxes, to be imposed upon the principle of ability, and local taxes which are imposed on the principle of benefit.

[1] Wagner, *Finanzwissenschaft*, part 2, 2d ed., 1890, pp. 138 *et seq.* Wagner is followed by many German writers.

This is clearly illogical, for it is obvious that the extent of benefits received has no connection in principle with the question as to whether we are dealing with local or state government. A piece of land, for instance, which is often chosen as an example, may indeed have its value enhanced by local causes; but it is equally possible that the value of the land may be enhanced by general state or national legislation, as, for instance, by a protective tariff on agricultural products. Similarly, some American writers[1] commit an error in trying to distinguish between certain taxes that are levied on the principle of protection and others that are assessed on the principle of ability. There is no such distinction. Taxes differ from other forms of public revenue in that none of them is levied on the principle of benefits, even though it may be entirely legitimate for some taxes to emphasize the element of privilege and for others to emphasize the element of sacrifice found in the principle of ability.

The American legal theory, however, so far as it has been applied to the general property tax, although incorrect, works out in practice much better than might have been supposed. This is a characteristic of Anglo-Saxon politics and jurisprudence, which have always been stronger in practice than in theory. For if the ability of an individual to pay taxes is measured by his property, there is no doubt that the obligation to pay taxes is due in part at least to the jurisdiction where the property is situated. The theory, however, as we know, not only breaks down in the case of intangible property, but also pays no attention to the other element in the conception of ability, *viz.*, the element of sacrifice. Above all, the American legal theory becomes defective when we desire to apply it to the income tax rather than to the property tax. It is necessary, therefore, to seek another approach to the problem.

[1] See the *Draft Report of the Committee of the National Tax Association on a Model System of State and Local Taxes*, 1919, pp. 19-30.

II. *Residents and Non-residents*

As a preliminary to working out the principles of double taxation or the taxation of non-residents, it is necessary to recall the familiar distinction between personal and impersonal taxes. A personal tax is a tax levied on the person as such; an impersonal tax is a tax levied on the thing rather than on the person. When the land tax is assessed, as in the state of New York, upon the plot of ground rather than upon the person who owns the land, it becomes an impersonal tax, or what the lawyers call a tax *in rem*. In other words, although of course someone must pay the tax, the law pays no attention to the personal situation of the owner; the tax is imposed upon the land, irrespective of how much the owner may have borrowed upon it. So in the same way, the tax may be levied upon capital or personal property, irrespective of who owns it; or the tax may be levied upon a business irrespective of who carries it on. As opposed to these impersonal taxes, we have the personal taxes; and as the wealth of the individual may be measured in terms either of property or of income, the personal taxes are either property taxes or income taxes. What we have to deal with here are specifically income taxes.

The income tax, however, may either be a general income tax, as in the United States, or it may consist of a series of special income taxes, i. e., taxes on the income from special sources. The French income tax, e. g., consists of both kinds; it is composed of a series of special or so called schedule taxes on the various categories of income supplemented by a tax on the entire income. These special income taxes may be of several kinds. In the first place, there may be a tax on the income either from the ownership of land or, where there is a distinction between ownership and cultivation, from the cultivation of land. In the next place, there may be a tax on the income from capital or what in this country is called personal property. This may take the form of a tax on the income either from tangible personalty or from intangible personalty, like securities. In the next place, we may have a tax on the income from professions or occupations, including taxes on wages as well as salaries. Finally, there may be a tax on the income from business.

These special income taxes are really akin to the impersonal taxes. It is true indeed that, as in all other income taxes, an allowance may be made for the personal situation of the taxpayer, so far as concerns the question of indebtedness or of exemptions or abatements. But to the extent that they are assessed on the source of the income, or on the income with respect to the source, they partake to a certain extent of the nature of impersonal taxes levied on the source. Consequently when it is possible to divide a general income tax into its constituent elements and to levy special income taxes, these are more properly to be considered as impersonal, rather than personal, taxes.

In considering the problem of the taxation of non-residents we must always bear in mind this distinction between general income and special income taxes, and between personal and impersonal taxes. If we are dealing with a general income tax, then if the individual earns his income in one jurisdiction and spends it in another the tax ought, from the standpoint of abstract justice, to be equally divided between the two jurisdictions. This solution proceeds on the assumption that the element of privilege is just as important as the element of sacrifice in the conception of ability. If, however, this is not accepted and if a greater importance is attached, as may well be the case, to sacrifice than to privilege, a proportionately larger share of the tax ought to go to the jurisdiction where the individual lives and spends his income than to the jurisdiction where he earns his income. In practice, however, neither the one nor the other solution is of great consequence; for the attempt to apportion the tax-paying ability of individuals in such a way would, in the absence of any effective national regulation, involve almost insuperable difficulties. Under actual conditions there are only three possible solutions of the problem.

In the first place, the income tax might be regarded as a combination of special income taxes and everybody, resident and non-resident alike, might be taxed only upon that part of his income received from sources within the state. The theory here would be that as each state would levy nothing but special income taxes, or taxes from the income of special sources, each individual would in the end pay a general income tax as a summation of the taxes imposed on the source of income within each state. Taxes on all the sources of income amount finally to a general tax on all income.

The obvious objection to this course, especially so far as residents are concerned, is that the other state or foreign country where part of the income is received may not impose an income tax, so that the individual would not be paying a fair share as compared with his neighbor whose income is received entirely within the state. There would in practice be no such combination of special income taxes as to constitute a general income tax. In addition to this general objection, however, there is another formidable difficulty. For even if the above objection were removed, so that the tax might be considered a general income tax, this solution, however acceptable in a debtor state like Wisconsin, would be open to the objection adverted to above, that in a financial center like New York the proportion of income received from its inhabitants from sources outside New York forms the overwhelming percentage of the whole. A creditor state like New York would accordingly find such a solution fiscally inadmissible. The revenue which it would receive from the taxpayers would be insignificant when compared with the expenditures which it would be called upon to incur because of their presence within its borders. The solution, in short, would be theoretically unsound because of the over-emphasis put upon the opportunity or privilege side of faculty as compared with the sacrifice side. We must, in a general income tax, bear in mind not alone income earned but income spent—not only the production side, but the consumption side, of ability to pay. The Wisconsin principle is as defective in principle as it would in New York be hopeless in practice. If the time should ever come when capital, industry and population would be equally distributed throughout the union and when every state would impose an income tax of its own, then, and only then, would the above solution be relatively satisfactory as among the separate states, although still open to criticism in its international aspects. But in default of these two vital conditions, the principle is unacceptable at present in a state like New York, so far as the individual income tax is concerned. The matter is, of course, quite different with a corporate income tax, where this principle is not only legitimate but actually applied in New York. For, as we shall see below, not only is the conception of faculty or ability to pay to be interpreted differently in the case of corporations as compared with individuals, but corporations are taxed in virtually all states, upon either their income or the sources of the income.

In the second place, residents might be taxed on their entire income and non-residents might go scot-free. This would proceed on the theory that each state levies a general income tax, so that no individual will escape his due share. The difficulty with this solution is equally great. For, in the first place, there is no assurance that the other state will impose an analogous income tax, in which case residents will be subject to a disadvantage. Why, for instance, if New Jersey imposes no general income tax, should its residents who carry on their business in New York in competition with New Yorkers be exempt from taxation in New York on that business or on the income derived from the business? Why should the New Yorker who is pursuing his occupation side by side with the Jerseyite be put at this manifest disadvantage? In the second place, this solution of the problem would involve the important practical consequence that any New Yorker who desired to escape his taxes could easily do so by transferring his legal residence to his summer home in New Jersey. It is well known that the chief reason why the general property tax has broken down so completely in New York City is the facility afforded to wealthy New Yorkers to claim their legal residence in the environs. The one great advantage of the income tax over the property tax is that it tends to decrease this movement. Such a result, however, would be entirely defeated if non-residents were exempted on their income earned within the state of New York. No solution of the problem which fails to put a stop to this deplorable practice of local expatriation can be acceptable. The exemption of non-residents from income taxation would fail to cure the existing inequality of the general property tax and would create a new and still more indefensible inequality.

We are led, therefore, to the remaining solution as the only possible one, namely, to subject residents to a general income tax on their entire income, from whatever source derived and to subject non-residents to the special income taxes; that is, to arrange that non-residents should be liable only on such income from special sources as is received or earned within the state.

This solution, satisfactory as far as it goes, is open to the criticism that if two states impose a similar tax and follow the same principle they may create cases of unjust double taxation by superimposing in practice special income taxes upon a general income tax. For if individual A earns his money and spends it in one state, he would be taxed only once on his entire income; while B, with the same income, who earns his money in one state and has his legal residence in another, will be taxed twice, once by the state where the income is earned and again by his state of residence.

A simple escape from this difficulty can, however, be

found in a provision whereby the state where the income is earned permits the non-resident to make a proportionate deduction of such tax on the income earned within the state from the tax, if any, which may be levied by the state of residence. This was the solution suggested by the present writer and adopted in the New York law.[1] The working-out of the system in practice would then be as follows.

If New Jersey, for instance, imposed no income tax at all, the Jerseyite would be subject to taxation in New York on his income earned within the state. To this special income tax there can surely be no objection. For if the tax be regarded as a general income tax New York is assuredly justified in seeking to reach the privilege side of the Jerseyite's taxable ability; if New Jersey elects not to attempt to reach the sacrifice side of his taxable ability, that is its own concern. But if the tax be regarded, as is more properly the case, as a special income tax on the non-resident, the defence of the solution is even stronger. Not only is the method defensible, but for New York to refrain from action would involve an inequality. If two contiguous pieces of land are owned respectively by a New Yorker or a Jerseyite; if two competing business houses are occupied respectively by a New Yorker or a Jerseyite; if two dentists, one a New Yorker and the other a Jerseyite, carry on their professions on opposite sides of the same New York street, is there any reason why, in the absence of any income tax by the state of New Jersey, the Jerseyite should be preferred to the New Yorker? Why should the sources of income within the state be taxable to some and not to others? Far from imposing

[1] Section 363: "Whenever a taxpayer other than a resident of the state has become liable to income tax of the state or country where he resides, upon his net income for the taxable year, derived from sources within this state and subject to taxation under this article, the controller shall credit the amount of income tax payable by him under this article with such proportion of the tax so payable by him to the state or country where he resides as his income subject to taxation under this article bears to his entire income upon which the tax so payable to such other state or country was imposed; providing that such credit shall be allowed only if the laws of said state or country grant such similar credit to residents of this state subject to income tax under such laws."

any additional burden upon the Jerseyite or interfering in any way with interstate commerce the taxation of the Jerseyite would bring about substantial equality in treatment with that of the New Yorker. To do less than this would give him an unjustifiable preference.

As a matter of fact, however, such a preference is actually given to him in one respect in the New York law. While the resident is taxed on his entire income including that from intangible personalty, the non-resident is exempt from income tax on his intangibles, unless these are employed in his business. This preference to the non-resident is explicable on the ground that otherwise the market for New York securities and the preëminence of New York as a financial center might be jeopardized. Favor to a non-resident is preferable to the decay of New York. Equality of taxation may be made to bow to general economic expediency, just as Great Britain in her recent *post-bellum* loan exempts foreigners from income tax on the bonds. The point remains, however, that in this respect non-residents are actually favored. But because they are favored in one point, there is no reason why they should be favored in other points, where there is no compelling economic consideration. Great Britain exempts foreign bondholders, but does not exempt landholders or foreign business men or foreign capitalists from income tax. Why should New York do so?

On the other hand, New York does something which Great Britain and other countries do not attempt to do. New York is careful to prevent unjust duplicate taxation. If New Jersey should levy an income tax, New York allows the Jerseyite to deduct from the New York tax a proportionate part of the tax levied by New Jersey—subject, indeed, to the condition of reciprocity, i. e., that New Jersey will agree to treat New Yorkers in the same way. The consequence of this would be that if New Jersey imposed an income tax at the same rate as that of New York, the Jerseyite would in final result pay little or nothing in New York. Inasmuch, however, as he would pay an equivalent tax in New Jersey, this would operate to accomplish two important results. In the first place, it would preclude any financial advantage to the Jerseyite, and, far more important, secondly, it would prevent the great evil alluded to above, i. e., the inducement on the part of wealthy New Yorkers to claim a legal residence in New Jersey. The law, therefore, will operate not only to prevent the fictitious emigration of New Yorkers but also to subject bona-fide Jerseyites to the same burdens as those borne by their New York competitors. It does not impose any additional burden on them and it does not create any discrimination against citizens of another state.

This solution of the problem, therefore, constitutes a forward step in the treatment of non-residents. In subjecting non-residents to taxation on the income derived from sources within the state, the law does not differ from either the federal law or any other important income tax law. In every country foreigners are taxed upon their income from sources within the country, with the minor exception of foreign-held bonds in certain cases. The chief difference between the New York law and that of most countries is that in the latter cases no such equitable provision is made for a proportionate and reciprocal deduction of the tax where the home country imposes a tax on the same income. The New York law hence marks a distinct advance in the treatment of this problem. Residents and non-residents alike are subjected to taxes on income earned within the state; residents are subjected in addition to a tax on income from all other sources; and non-residents are freed from double taxation by a reciprocal deduction which operates similarly to free residents of New York from double taxation by a sister state. The net result is equality all around.

There is only one minor point in which residents and non-residents are not treated alike in the New York law.

In the case of resident taxpayers the law allows an exemption of from one to two thousand dollars together with two hundred dollars for each dependent person. It would seem that the absence of any such exemption in the case of non-residents constituted a real discrimination. As a matter of fact, however, something may be said for such a difference in treatment.

The theory underlying the law is, as we have seen, that the state of residence may also impose an income tax. If New Jersey or Connecticut were to impose an income tax it could avoid possible injustice to its residents on the part of New York by permitting an exemption similar to that granted by New York to its residents; through the reciprocal provisions of the law just mentioned all the difficulties would then at once be adjusted. If New Jersey preferred not to grant such an exemption, the discrimination would be chargeable not to New York but to New Jersey. The only possible case of inequality chargeable to New York might arise where New Jersey, for instance, does not impose any income tax at all, and where the income of the Jerseyite is wholly or almost wholly earned within New York. Such a situation, not contemplated by the framers of the law—who looked forward to the speedy adoption of income tax laws by the neighboring states—can, however, be easily remedied. The non-resident might be permitted to file a declaration of his entire income within and without the state of New York and might be granted such proportion of the statutory exemption as corresponds to his income within the state. A still simpler solution of the problem would be to grant to non-residents whose income from wages, salaries, or professional earnings in New York were under a modest figure, say five or ten thousand dollars, the same exemption as that accorded to residents. But this provision should be enforced only as long as New Jersey does not levy an additional income tax of its own.

It appears, therefore, that in the main the New York law

meets all the legitimate demands of interstate comity. It does not subject non-residents to any additional burden; and it paves the way for the adoption of a system whereby all individuals would be treated on an equality according to a fairly correct interpretation of the principle of taxable ability to pay taxes. To do anything more than the law now states, with the possible exception of the minor and temporary amendment suggested in the last paragraph, would be to accord an unfair advantage to non-residents and to create an artificial inducement to an illicit emigration of residents.

It is also not to be overlooked that in the treatment of individuals the New York law is more favorable to non-residents than is the case in the existing corporate income tax or the so-called Emerson law applicable to corporations. It is a principle long since adopted by the American states and upheld by the American courts that non-resident or foreign corporations should be subject to taxation as well as domestic corporations. In the case of New York, indeed, as is true of the most advanced states, resident corporations are taxed not upon their entire income but only upon so much of the income as is earned within the state. This distinction between natural and artificial persons or between individuals and corporations is, as mentioned above, entirely justifiable, owing to the fact that in the case of corporations the element of sacrifice in the concept of ability is of less importance than that of privilege. When compared with individuals the corporation as such does not consume its earnings: it distributes them to the stockholders who are the final consumers. It is reasonable, therefore, that corporations should be taxed only upon that part of their income earned within the state. The significant point, however, to be emphasized here is that while foreign corporations are also taxable upon their income earned within the state, there is no reciprocal provision in the case of corporations as in that of individuals which permits the corporations to deduct any part of the tax payable in New York. In the case of foreign corporations there is no possibility that the state of New York would fail to receive any revenue at all; whereas in the case of non-resident individuals, as we have seen, there is every likelihood that the state of New York would receive no tax, whenever the state of residence imposed a similar tax. Individuals therefore are treated by the new income tax law more favorably than are corporations. Since the method of dealing with corporations has been upheld by the courts there is no reason to suppose that the more favorable treatment accorded to individuals will be disallowed.

The only other difference in treatment between residents and non-residents in the New York law is that in the case of non-residents the employers are obligated to withhold the tax from the salaries of their employees. If the principle of the law itself is sound, however,—namely, that of the equal treatment of residents and non-residents—there can be no valid objection to this administrative provision. For from the administrative point of view it would be practically impossible, or certainly most difficult, otherwise to ensure the payment of the tax from non-residents who are engaged in salaried occupations in New York. The intent of the law is to reach all those who are taxable under its provisions. In the case of residents the taxpayers can be reached through the ordinary processes of law; in the case of non-residents, a personal tax cannot be assessed with any assurance of equal enforcement in any other way than in the manner indicated. The difference in administrative treatment between residents and non-residents is thus simply a method designed to secure a real equality of taxation. It imposes no discriminatory burden upon non-residents, but on the contrary endeavors to prevent a discrimination against the resident, who would otherwise be subjected to a more severe burden. The intent of the law here again is equal treatment: the ostensible inequality resolves itself into a higher equality.

It is clear from the above review that the taxation of non-residents is only a part of the great problem of double taxation. No final solution of this problem is possible in a federal union like the United States without a uniform rule which can either be imposed from above or adopted from below. This uniform rule can be imposed either by the national legislature, as is the case in Switzerland, Germany, and some other federal unions or, what is far more probable in the United States, by a series of rulings of the Supreme Court binding upon the separate states as in the case of the federal judicial regulation of the national bank tax. It is clear, however, from what has preceded that we are not yet ready, and probably shall not be for some time, for such a federal regulation in detail. The economic differences between various states and various sections of the country and the great problem of the debtor *vs.* the creditor state may make such a solution, which is abstractly equitable, bear with great hardship on certain states and sections. New York, as we have seen, is in a very different position from many of the western and southern states, and a rule which would be acceptable elsewhere might be entirely inadmissible in New York. Until the time comes when there is a much greater equality of economic conditions in the United States, a far more satisfactory solution of the problem will be found in that accepted by the state of New York. Provisional though that solution be, it is nevertheless one in harmony with considerations of economic expediency and the dictates of economic justice.[1]

[[1] The law was upheld in *Travis* vs. *Yale & Towne Manufacturing Co.*, 252 U. S. 60 on all the counts mentioned above with one exception. The court disapproved of the non-allowance of the $1,000-2,000 exemption to non-residents, especially as New Jersey had not yet imposed an income tax. In all essential points, however, the Supreme Court has sanctioned the system as elaborated in this chapter. The general problem is further treated in the *Report on Double Taxation* rendered to the League of Nations in 1923 by the so-called "experts," Professor Bruins of Holland, Senator Einaudi of Italy, Sir Josiah Stamp of Great Britain, and the present writer; and in the subsequent *Report* of 1925 by the practical experts.]

CHAPTER TEN

FISCAL RECONSTRUCTION

[This chapter, originally written before the end of the war, first appeared as a contribution to the volume entitled *American Problems of Reconstruction: a National Symposium.* Edited by E. M. Friedman, 1918.]

In the domain of public finance, even more than in any of the other topics at present in the public eye, the subject of reconstruction presents almost insuperable difficulties at this time. It is uncertain as to how long the contest will last and what will be the future drain upon our resources. No one can foretell how large will be the ultimate public debt, nor to what extent the necessity of meeting the outlays of the war will affect our future productive capacity. The destruction of capital and the depletion in the numbers or the strength of the labor force which we shall suffer are both unknown factors.

Since the extent and the nature of the necessary reconstruction are alike uncertain, the methods of procedure must themselves lack precision. But whatever be the final result, there are at least three difficulties which will confront us after the close of the war and which will need a statesmanlike discussion and solution, irrespective of the length of the war and of the gravity of the situation. In any event, we shall have a huge debt; we shall have to find the means of defraying the vastly increased expenditure of the post-bellum period; and we shall have to consider, as never before, the problems of economy and efficiency in public finance. In other words, the three great problems of fiscal reconstruction will be those of public debt, of public revenues and of the budget.

I. *The Debt*

Were this a discussion of war finance, rather than of reconstruction, the subject of the public debt would loom even larger than is actually the case. For it would then be necessary to discuss the problems connected with the creation of a public debt, such as the desirable proportion of loans to taxes,[1] the length of the loans, the character of the bond issues, the conditions of emission, and the provisions for amortization. In short, almost the whole theory of public credit would need elucidation.

As we are dealing with the problem of reconstruction, however, we must take all these things for granted. We must assume the existence of a huge debt bequeathed to us by the war. There will then remain two basic problems, that of the conversion of the debt and that of the payment of the debt.

With the first problem it is impossible to deal at the present time. In the case of a long-continued war the rates of interest at which successive war loans can be floated naturally rise. They will rise not only because of the progressive weakening of the government credit, but also because of the increase in the general rate of interest which inevitably accompanies the destruction of capital during a war. The process has already begun in the United States. Our three liberty loans have been issued at the continually rising rates of 3½, 4, and 4¼ per cent. What the future has in store for us no one knows. All that can be said is that if the war should leave us with a huge debt, one of the first duties of reconstruction will be so to readjust the debt as to take advantage of the restoration of credit and the fall in the interest rate. The larger the debt and the higher the rate of interest paid by the government, the greater will be the need of a skillful utilization of the sound principles of conversion.

[1] This problem is treated in the chapter "Loans versus Taxes in War Finance" in Seligman, *Essays in Taxation*, 10th ed., 1925.

The other problem—that of the payment of the debt—is on a different footing. For here we have the question, not only as to whether the debt should be paid at all, but how rapidly it should be extinguished. Peculiar as it may seem to the average American, the problem of a perpetual debt has by no means been finally solved. Some forms of indebtedness, to which even Americans have become accustomed, do not call for eventual repayment at all. In corporation finance, as in our railroads and other public utilities, there is neither need for, nor especial advantage in, paying off the mortgage indebtedness. The capital of our railroads is none the less capital because it is cast in part in the form of bonds. No demands of sound corporate finance require the total substitution of stocks for bonds. The same is in large measure true of public indebtedness for productive and self-supporting enterprises. There is no reason why Australia or Prussia should pay off the public debt which represents the investment in its railroads; there is no reason why New York should pay off the Croton water bonds or the dock bonds or the subway bonds, the interest on which is more than met by the respective earnings of operation. A perpetual debt in all such cases is a mere bookkeeping device. It constitutes no burden of any kind upon the community.

In the case of debts contracted for war purposes the practice, if not the theory, in the chief European countries has been the same. Great Britain has made only a slight effort to extinguish the debt contracted during the Napoleonic wars; the war debt of France accumulated during the nineteenth century has likewise not been substantially diminished. The chief arguments in favor of a perpetual debt, even of this kind, have been two in number. It is argued, in the first place, that with the progressive increase in the wealth and productive capacity of modern nations a fixed debt constitutes a continually diminishing burden upon the community. In the second place, the argument is advanced that, at all events in so far as we have to deal with a domestic debt, there is virtually no burden upon the community as a whole. What actually takes place, so it is said, is a payment from the right hand to the left hand, a transfer of income from the taxpayer to the bondholder. If the debt is accompanied by an appropriate revenue scheme, these mutual debits and credits will be satisfactorily adjusted from the point of view of public policy. Nothing will then be lost by the decision to maintain a perpetual debt. On the contrary, it is urged, the attempt to pay off the capital of a huge debt may involve dangers to the productive capacity of the nation which will outweigh any possible benefits.

The American theory has been the reverse, largely for reasons dependent upon the disparate economic conditions of the United States. In the first place, the tempo of economic growth has been much more rapid in a new community like ours. The growth of our wealth and social income has been so prodigious that the country has experienced no appreciable discomfort in getting rid of a continually diminishing burden. So productive and so easily tapped have been the ordinary sources of revenue that from the war of 1812 to the period after the Civil War the extinction of the debt took place almost automatically. Our fiscal troubles during the nineteenth century have almost always been connected with utilizing a surplus rather than with providing for a deficit. Our embarrassment has been not how to pay the war debts, but what to do with our excess revenues.

The second consideration which differentiated American from European debts was that while in England and France the debts were almost exclusively domestic debts, our debts were in large part foreign debts. Instead of diverting the revenue from the taxpayers to the bondholders within the country, we were under the necessity of sending a portion of our annual production abroad in order to satisfy foreign creditors. Under such conditions there could be no doubt of the existence of a burden on the community; and with the realization of this burden there came a determination to get rid of it.

After the conclusion of this war, however, the disparity between American and European conditions will be far less than has previously been the case. In the first place, now that all our free land is virtually gone, the conditions of economic growth will not be so different in the United States from those to be found in Europe. Now that we have left the period of economic puberty behind us and have to confront the necessity of a public expenditure suited to a fully developed economic community, we shall not find the waters gush forth so plentifully from the sources of public revenue. We have reached the period of fiscal maturity, with all its complications and its embarrassments. In the second place, the relative position of Europe and America is now completely altered. For while our public debt must needs be well-nigh exclusively domestic, we shall have been lending such large sums to the Allies that, in these cases at least, no mean part of the debt will be owing from abroad. The conditions of the nineteenth century will, in short, have been reversed.

Does this mean, then, that the European countries will accept the theory of debt repayment and that we shall adopt the principle of a perpetual debt? Whatever may be the conclusion arrived at by the European countries, there is little doubt that we shall none the less oppose the theory of a perpetual debt and shall seek to extinguish ours as soon as possible. There are two reasons why fiscal reconstruction after the war will demand a rapid payment of our war debt.

In the first place, we must recognize the fact that in a community like ours new demands will continually be made upon the government for expenditures of a social character. With the growth of real democracy the community will begin to spend constantly larger sums relative to the growth of wealth. We are only in the first stages of really socialized democratic expenditure. When even Great Britain is already devoting tens of millions of pounds to a single item like social insurance, we can easily look forward to the time when the American governments will be spending their hundreds of millions of dollars for communal purposes of a more or less immaterial character, the very import of which is only faintly grasped at present. In proportion as this feeling spreads there will be a growing reluctance to devoting so large a part of the social income permanently to the service of the debt. We see even now the difficulties created in New York City by the narrow margin left in the debt limit and by the growing inability of the city to increase its revenues to the point where a constantly greater surplus above the interest on the debt is available for needed purposes. The coming social democracy in the United States will insist upon removing what at all events seems to be an incubus and will cheerfully undergo the greater sacrifices needed for a time for the payment of the debt in order to wipe the slate clean and to allow the future to deal with its own expanding problems.

The second reason why there is need for a payment of the debt is to be found in the fact that there will in all probability be no such equitable adjustment between the taxpayer and the bondholder as is assumed in the theory of the burdenlessness of a public debt. In a consideration of the adjustment between poor or rich bondholders and taxpayers there are four possibilities:

First, there may be a wide distribution of the debt in the sense that most of the bonds are held by people of little means, while the system of taxation may be so arranged as to burden primarily the wealthy.

Second, there may be the same wide distribution of the debt, but the taxes may fall chiefly on the consumption of the poor rather than on the wealth of the rich.

Third, the bonds may be held predominantly by the wealthy classes, and yet the burden of taxation may rest on the poor.

Finally, both the bondholders and the taxpayers may be found to an overwhelming extent among the wealthier classes.

Whatever may have been the situation in the past, it is evident from what is happening at present throughout the world that recent industrial development combined with modern democracy conspires to make the fourth alternative probable. The immense increase of wealth in recent times renders it almost inevitable that the great mass of the colossal war loans should be subscribed by those classes which really have at their disposal a surplus of either capital or credit. On the other hand, the tendency toward democratic justice in taxation forcedly leads to the placing of the burdens where they can most easily be borne. The necessary result will be that both bondholders and taxpayers will be found primarily in the well-to-do classes of the community.

It would be a mistake, however, to conclude from this that there will be a substantial identity of interests between bondholders and taxpayers. On the contrary, there is going on at present a decided differentiation of taxation between two clearly marked subdivisions of the wealthy class. This distinction may be expressed as one between enterprise and property. It is the same distinction that is sought to be emphasized in the British classification into earned and unearned income. Modern taxes are being more and more clearly differentiated between taxes on individual wealth and taxes on business. While it is indeed true that the wealthy individual may have a business and that business prosperity may lead to an accumulation of wealth, it is none the less a fact that in a rapidly growing and shifting community like ours the burdens upon enterprise as such are coming to be sharply differentiated from those on property or on the income of property. With the need, seen everywhere today, of supplementing taxes on individual income or property by taxes on business or enterprise, a new division is created and a new argument for the rapid payment of a war debt emerges. For while the bondholders will necessarily be found in the propertied classes, the business man will more and more object to the burden of raising a substantial part of the revenue required to defray the interest of a perpetual debt. He will use all his influence toward having the debt paid off rapidly out of the revenue of the class in which the bondholders are to be found.

The disparity of interests, therefore, that may be expected after the close of the war is not so much one between wealth and poverty as between property and enterprise. The greater the accumulations of wealth in modern times as compared with earlier decades, the stronger become the arguments for debt payment.

Our conclusion, therefore, is that in a country like the United States a perpetual debt is inadvisable. The old argument has indeed been replaced by new ones of a different character, but of none the less compelling a nature. One of the first problems of reconstruction will be the rapid payment of the war debt.

At the outbreak of the war the present writer, who had this contingency in mind, advocated the emission of relatively short time (ten-year) bonds.[1] This suggestion was not followed in the first and second liberty loans, the length of which was fixed at a considerably longer period. In the third liberty loan, however, the Government has seen fit to adopt the suggestion, and the bonds are to run for only ten years. It is to be hoped that this example will be followed in future issues, even if the other suggestion of throwing the issue into the form of serial rather than sinking-fund bonds fails of acceptance. In any event, however, we are putting ourselves into a position which will be favorable to a comparatively rapid extinction of the debt. That is the first task to which we shall have to address ourselves after the war.

[1] *How to Finance the War*, Columbia University War Papers, no. 9.

II. *The Tax System*

In order to make this rapid repayment of the debt possible it will be necessary to provide the wherewithal. The situation, however, is complicated by the fact that even without this necessity the public expenditures will be on a vastly augmented scale. In the first place, there will be the increase of expenditures directly bequeathed by the war. Foremost among these will be the provisions of the insurance law, replacing the hitherto existing system of pension legislation. The longer the war lasts and the greater the number of casualties, whether fatal or otherwise, the more colossal will be the outlay for compensation calculated on a liberal scale. In the second place may be put the expenditures indirectly due to the war. Although the exact nature and amount of these outlays will depend to a considerable extent on the conditions of peace, it is entirely likely that the military and naval expenditures of the United States will in the future be on a scale of far greater magnitude than before. Finally, in the third place, it is scarcely open to question that the democratic movement which will almost surely result from the war will engender a change also in the attitude of the legislator toward the vastly increased expenditure which will be demanded for the common needs. In the domains of transportation, of education, of public health, of social insurance, of science and art the demands for augmented outlays will become rapidly more insistent.

Both of these streams—that of vastly increased normal expenditures and that of provision for the rapid payment of the war debt—will converge into a mighty torrent of rising expenditures. Here, as in Europe, one of the fundamental problems of reconstruction will be the provision for this colossal increase of Government outlay.

In many of the European countries publicists and statesmen are despairing as to the possibility of making both ends meet through the resource of taxation, ordinary or extraordinary. Almost simultaneously the idea has arisen in Germany as in England, in Austria as in France and Italy, of utilizing the powers of government in new and untried ways. These suggestions have taken two forms—government monopoly and government control of industry. In the first class we find schemes for the government assumption of the railways in those countries where private ownership still existed before the war, with the demand that the railways be run, as in Prussia, on the principle of profits, so that hundreds of millions may be derived in each country from this source alone. Widespread, in the next place, is the demand for the governmental assumption of coal mines. Next in order is found the demand for government monopoly of the manufacture or sale of whiskey, of beer, and of tobacco. To these are added the demands for government monopolies in a variety of other commodities, like sugar, salt, gunpowder, petroleum and matches. In some countries we even find the growing demand for government monopolies of other raw materials and necessaries of life.

Where this prodigious step in the socialization of certain forms of industry seems to be attended with peculiar local difficulties, the substitute suggestion is offered that the government should exercise a far more rigid control, partly for fiscal purposes, over industry in general. It is well known, for instance, that in Germany, at present, many of the important industries are rapidly being converted into trusts or combinations. Not only does the government refuse to look with suspicion upon these combinations, but it actually compels every producer, whether he wills it or not, to enter such a combination. A great part of German industry is being compulsorily trustified. The reason for this is indeed only partly fiscal. It is due primarily to the fact that German economists and statesmen realize that industry in the future is to be on a large scale and that the well-meaning efforts of those who, as in the United States, have attempted to apply the political ideals of individual liberty to the industrial field are mistaken. It is true, indeed, that there is a great future for democracy in industry as well as for democracy in politics; but it must be a democracy not of small-scale but of large-scale production. The chief difference between what is going on in the United States and what is developing in Germany is that the movement with us is progressing in spite of the law and of an uninformed public sentiment, while in Germany and other European countries it is developing in harmony with the law and a new public policy. Abroad, however, the corollary of compulsory industrial combination is strict supervision by the government, just as with us railway combinations and traffic associations developed with increasing government control. What has already been decided in some of the European States is that the government shall exercise a rigid control over these combinations in the interest not only of the consumer but of the general producing public as well. What has not yet been settled, but what is being actively discussed, is the amount of revenue which the government shall demand as the first charge on the industry.

Both of these methods—that of governmental monopoly and that of government participation in industry—are within the range of possibilities in the United States. But in view of our past history and of the peculiar characteristics of American life it is unlikely that we shall be compelled to resort to either. Not until all our other resources have been taxed and not unless the war should continue to the point where the country should be completely exhausted and the need of collective action become as imperious as during the war itself—only in these unlikely contingencies is it probable that we shall have to adopt these expedients. Leaving a consideration of these matters, therefore, to a future which we may all hope will be successfully averted, let us turn our attention to the more modest task of considering the demands of fiscal reconstruction through a change, comprehensive though it may be, in the methods of taxation.

To the attentive student of the history of taxation the development of fiscal systems during the last generation is full of important lessons. Not only has there been a great change in the fundamental attitude toward taxation on the part of all modern democracies, but the methods employed in giving expression to this newer attitude have themselves been affected by the marked alterations in the economic structure of society.

If we were to attempt a broad generalization as to this fundamental change of attitude we would say that taxation is no longer regarded as a burden to be exacted from an unwilling victim but as a contribution cheerfully rendered by those who are alive to the sense of collective responsibility implicit in the very conception of democracy. The only limitation on this idea is the insistent demand for equality and uniformity of treatment, giving to those terms the broadest interpretation that has resulted from modern enlightenment. In principle this means the definitive adoption of the conception of ability or faculty—a conception to which lip service was rendered in part in former times but which has received a newer and a richer content during the last generation. More and more we are beginning to realize that there are two aspects of the doctrine of ability to pay or faculty in taxation. The one which was emphasized by the earlier writers almost exclusively is that of sacrifice—the idea, namely, that the test of real ability to pay resides in the sacrifice imposed upon the taxpayer. More recently, however, we have become familiar with the second aspect of the principle, namely, that of privilege. This is the idea that the taxpayer's ability to pay is to be measured also by the privileges which he enjoys. We accept nowadays the obvious fact that wealth must be produced in order to be consumed, and we realize that while the conception of sacrifice applies more particularly to the consumption of wealth, the conception of privilege applies to its production. The consequences of this will be seen below.[1]

[1] See above, pp. 187-190.

Hand in hand with this distinction there has come more recently an appreciation of the further distinction between taxes on persons and taxes on things, or, as we prefer to term it, the distinction between personal and impersonal taxation. Of course this has reference only to the immediate and not the ultimate phenomena. For, in the end, the money has to be subtracted from the pockets of the individual who has the final control of the thing in question. But the distinction is none the less a significant one. Whereas democracy has, on the one hand, manifested a decided tendency toward the adoption of personal taxation, the imperious needs of modern government are disclosing the necessity of a fresh resort to impersonal taxation, although in new forms and with a new content. The fiscal reconstruction after the war will inevitably be effected along these two lines. Let us analyze them.

The characteristic marks of the change in our conception of personal taxation are the replacement of property by income as the most satisfactory test of faculty and the alteration in our conception of expenditure as the measure of sacrifice.

In former times wealth was measured in terms of capital rather than of income—as a fund rather than a flow. In primitive society, where everybody was supposed to work, where there was little complexity or differentiation in production, where there were no very rich and no very poor the conception of a fund of wealth was as natural as it was legitimate. In the United States, as elsewhere, the democratic content given to this conception of ability to pay was the general property tax. But modern economic life has brought about a change. The homogeneous mass of property has been split up into its constituent parts; earnings are not necessarily transmuted into capital but may be spent; the modern institutions of speculation and credit often stand in the way of a correlation between actual income and capitalized income; the character of modern enterprise and the opportunity afforded to business ingenuity create a disparity between invested capital and business profits. In short, the whole modern tendency is to emphasize the importance of wealth as a flow rather than as a fund. As a consequence we find everywhere the replacement of property taxation by the taxation of profits or income. Where the tax is imposed upon the individual as such—that is, where we have to deal with personal taxation, modern economic development is leading to the substitution of the income tax in lieu of the older general property tax. Where the individual is still taxed on his general property, the tax is becoming either an exceptional measure, as in war finance, or a subordinate and ancillary addition to the income tax.

With the adoption of income as the test of faculty, however, there have come two further developments. The one is the adoption of the principle of graduation or progressive taxation; the other is the acceptance of differentiation or the distinction between different kinds of income. The first principle, that of graduated taxation, was until recently introduced only timidly.[1] In England it came only about a decade ago. But in the United States, where we have the greatest democracy in political theory side by side with the greatest distinctions of wealth in economic fact, the war has seen the insertion of the wedge of graduation until at present, in 1918, the recipient of the maximum income is under certain conditions subject to a tax of 77 per cent., namely, the sum of 65 per cent. normal tax and 12 per cent. surtax. While these precise rates may not be retained after the war, it is not at all unlikely that public opinion will demand, for a time at least, the continuance of a steep scale of progression. Our hand having been put to the plough, it is unlikely that we shall desist. Sharply graduated income taxes must form a part of the policy of fiscal reconstruction until a more normal budgetary situation has again been reached.

[1] *Cf.* Seligman, *Progressive Taxation in Theory and Practice*, 2 ed., 1908.

The other phase of the problem, however, has not yet been attacked in this country. Whereas Italy accepted the principle several decades ago and England adopted it in 1909 by separating earned from unearned incomes, we have still to introduce the much needed reform. The higher equality in taxation can never be attained until we differentiate between the various kinds of income according to the criteria not only of the sacrifice imposed in parting with the income but of the privilege enjoyed in creating the income. While progressive taxation is, at least in part, the result of the conception of sacrifice—the relative sacrifice in paying a tax diminishing with the growth of the income or the property—the other aspect of faculty, that of privilege enjoyed in creating the income, leads to the demand for distinguishing between earned, partly earned, and unearned incomes. Differential taxation, like graduated taxation, is a corollary of the modern theory of ability to pay. We have adopted the latter; we must before long accept the former.[1]

The second change in our modern conception was stated above to be the altered attitude toward expenditure. In former times taxes were in large measure imposed upon the necessaries and conveniences of life, thus burdening primarily the expenditure of the poor. Modern democracy has set its face resolutely against such widespread taxes on commodities, on communication and on transactions. In this we find the secret of the growing antipathy to the so-called, but misnamed, indirect taxes. But the retention of certain imposts on particular commodities, even in modern democracies, shows the need of a distinction. In the United States, as in Great Britain, the chief so-called indirect taxes are levied upon articles like whiskey and tobacco, which properly represent either luxurious or baneful consumption. What has not yet been done and what is, nevertheless, a logical corollary of the principle of ability to pay is to extend this system of expenditure taxation to more and more

[1] [This has now been adopted, in principle at least, by the law of 1924.]

luxuries and to apply here as elsewhere the principles of graduation and differentiation. When expenditure taxes are restricted to those on truly luxurious and harmful consumption, expenditure will be restored to its rightful place as a proper norm of faculty in a democratic scheme. One of the problems of fiscal reconstruction will be to work out a realization of this principle.[1]

While the income tax and to a lesser degree the expenditure tax will form the principal elements of personal taxation, the future probably has in store for us a reformulation of the old system of impersonal taxation, or taxes on things —a reformulation of which the beginning can already be seen. If we regard the taxable thing, rather than the taxable person, we find that there are three chief categories, namely, land, capital apart from land, and business. Each of these is likely to play an important part in fiscal reconstruction.

Land everywhere forms the basis of our State and local taxation. In only a few places in the United States, however, is the land tax treated as a tax *in rem* instead of a tax *in personam.* But even in the greater part of the United States where land is taxed to the individual as a part of his general property the tendency is clearly perceptible to differentiate land from the rest of the property both in the rate of assessment and in the actual process of collection. In some states this process has gone through its normal evolution and the tax is assessed on the land *in rem,* irrespective of the owner. While the single-tax movement has but little chance of success because of its exaggerations, the kernel of truth in the idea is to be found in the conception of privilege as applied to land and in the fact that there is a difference, not indeed in kind as the single-taxers assume, but in degree, between land and other forms of property. For while the progress of the community helps to enhance the

[1] [The eighteenth amendment has destroyed alcoholic beverages as a source of revenue; but the development of the automobile is rapidly bringing gasoline to the front as a fiscal substitute.]

value now of this thing and now of that, the value of land is apt to be more uniformly and consistently augmented by the growth of population and wealth. This difference in degree renders legitimate the demand, not for a single tax but for a special and additional tax on land, which will take account of the socially enhanced increment of value. In proportion as public opinion comes to realize the importance of privilege side by side with sacrifice as a test of faculty in taxation, a special land-value tax—may come to be considered a necessary part of the fiscal reconstruction after the war.

The second form of impersonal taxation is a tax on capital, irrespective of the owner of the capital. This may assume several forms—a tax on capital in general or on special kinds of capital. The chief example of the former is to be seen in the inheritance tax. It is true that where the inheritance tax is imposed upon the shares, it can be considered a personal tax on the accidental income of the recipient. But where, as is now the case in our national government and to an overwhelming extent in Great Britain, the tax is imposed upon the estate as a whole, it may more properly be regarded as an impersonal tax on property. It is, in part at least, a tax on the thing, fitly supplementing in a democratic community the personal tax on the income of the individual.

Here also, before the war, only faint beginnings had been made in the United States. But at present, under the stress of war, we have a tax which rises in certain cases to 50 or 55 per cent., the maximum being 25 per cent. for the federal tax and 25 to 30 per cent. in some of the state taxes.[1] While such a combined rate may be exceedingly rare, the very existence of such a steep graduation shows the possibilities of the system in post-bellum finance. Whether they should be levied by the nation or by the states is perhaps

[1] [By 1925 the rates had increased, the possible maximum being 75 per cent., 40 per cent. federal and 35 per cent. state.]

open to question;[1] but that highly graduated inheritance taxes have come to stay and that they will form an important element in our program of fiscal reconstruction is scarcely open to doubt.

In contrast to this general tax on capital, we find taxes on special kinds of capital. If we distinguish between consumption capital and production capital it may be said that the tax on consumption capital may be fitly represented by the taxes on luxurious or harmful consumption discussed above. So far as production capital is concerned, the history alike of the United States and of Europe teaches a significant lesson. There are only two fiscally important forms of production capital—capital represented by the intangible forms of wealth known as securities, and capital invested in business enterprise; for capital invested in land is taken care of by the land tax.

Of these two forms experience has everywhere shown that the better method of taxing securities consists not in attempting the difficult task of assessing the securities as a part of property but in reaching their yield as a part of the income of the individual subject to the personal income tax. Whatever may be the future of the so-called low-rate intangibles tax in some of our states, it is improbable that a special tax on this form of capital will loom large in any policy of reconstruction.

The situation is different when we deal with business capital. Here, however, the conception has been broadened so as to comprise the business itself, irrespective of the capital invested in the business. Thus the capital tax merges into the business tax. The business tax, like the land tax, is a tax on the thing rather than on the person. Just as the land tax is coming to be a tax on the land instead of the landowner, so the business tax is coming to be a tax on the business instead of the business man.

The business tax has gone through an interesting develop-

[1] [For a discussion of this problem see *supra*, chapter eight.]

ment. In the continental countries of Europe, when the old personal taxes of the Middle Ages were abolished by the French Revolution, they were replaced by a system of impersonal taxes, or taxes on things, of which the business tax was one. In the course of the last generation or two, however, there was a decided trend back to personal taxation in the newer form of the income tax, and the business tax was accordingly allowed to lapse. More recently, as the inadequacy of a system of pure personal taxation again disclosed itself, we find a return to the taxation of business, but this time not as a substitute for but as a supplement to the personal tax.

In the United States the development was slightly different. With us business enterprise soon took the form of corporate activity, so that America became the earliest home of corporate taxation. Our corporation taxes developed, therefore, side by side with the property taxes on individuals. While it is true that business enterprise here takes the predominant form of corporate activity, the most recent addition to our tax system—the excess-profits tax—has quickly become a general business tax, including corporate as well as non-corporate business. This business tax, like the similar war taxes in other countries, before long constituted the most important feature of our tax system. And although it was calculated primarily for the duration of the war, the possibility of its retention, in some shape or other, as a permanent element in our revenue system is by no means excluded.[1] Now that the great fiscal possibilities of the system are becoming evident, the desirability of a continuance of some form of business taxation, preferably, however, through an extension of the corporate income tax, is in fact becoming increasingly clear. In considering this problem only two points need to be emphasized at present. One is that any modern and equitable business tax must

[1] [For a criticism of the excess-profits tax as it developed during the war see Seligman, *Essays in Taxation*, 10th ed., 1925, p. 700 *et seq.*]

deal with the results rather than the processes of business. The other is that the tax must be so arranged as to interfere to the least possible degree with social production.

It is evident, then, that in the program of fiscal reconstruction at least five important taxes will call for careful consideration—the income tax and the tax on luxurious consumption representing the personal taxes; the land tax and the business tax representing the impersonal taxes and the inheritance tax with its combination of personal and impersonal characteristics. If these taxes are developed with a due regard to the principles of sacrifice and of privilege and with a due appreciation of the modern demands preferred by a social democracy of the truest type, we may confidently look forward to a system of public revenues which will be entirely adequate to the demands of the reconstruction period.

III. *The Adjustment of Revenue and Expenditure*

There still remain two problems which, however, can only be briefly touched upon. The one is the general relation of federal, state and local finance in the post bellum period. The war has rudely dispelled many cherished notions. The doctrines of state sovereignty and of local government have given way to the imperious needs of a centralization undreamt of in our past history. The fiscal needs of the future will be distributed in a far different fashion between federal and state or local authorities. The old-time clear distinction between the sources of federal and of state revenue is vanishing. The former sharp line of separation between federal and state expenditures is being rapidly blurred. What has hitherto been no problem at all bids fair to become one of the chief problems of fiscal reconstruction—namely, the selection of the true principle to guide us in the elaboration of a system which will respond to the intermingled needs of federal, state and local governments. To discuss this principle here would take us too far astray; it must suffice to emphasize the importance of turning the thoughts of the statesman and the expert to this new range of problems.

Even more important than this, however, is the need of budgetary reform. The growing pressure of our taxes and the increasing recognition of the lack of efficiency and economy in American fiscal arrangements have led within the last decade to the beginnings of a consideration of budgetary reform. The immensely greater pressure of the impending burden, however, and the need of rigid economy will coöperate to put this topic in the forefront of every program of reconstruction. The problem is all the more difficult because of our political embarrassments—not merely those of political fact but those of political theory. The thoughtful citizen is only awakening to a recognition of the fact that our entire theory of government rests upon an error. We are the only civilized community which has erected a mistaken theory into the fundamental basis of our political structure. The theory of the separation of powers was a generalization which Montesquieu evolved from an erroneous interpretation of the British constitution as it then existed. Although that theory was never accepted by the British writers and was soon refuted in practice by the development of the British constitution, it found a lodgment in American minds and was before long introduced into American practice. In no part of the British Empire, not in Great Britain or Canada or Australia or Africa, is this principle of the complete separation of powers accepted. On the contrary, the executive is everywhere else simply an organ or a representative of the legislature. What is often called the parliamentary form of government, found almost everywhere else in modern democracies, is contrasted with the presidential form of government, characteristic of America. This unfortunate sharp separation between the executive and the legislative in the United States is the chief reason why we lag so far behind every other country in the adoption of a modern budget. Our shortcomings are due not simply to inefficient administration but to fundamental errors in political organization. The sooner this fact is recognized the easier will be the process of reconstruction after the war. Fiscal reconstruction will demand, as a necessary prerequisite, political reconstruction. Far from having solved our basic constitutional problems, as we used to think, we are only at the very beginning of constitutional reform.

But while an entirely modern system is well-nigh hopeless of accomplishment in its entirety without fundamental constitutional changes, much can yet be done, even under our present political system, in improving upon the budgetary anarchy which is found in federal and state governments alike. With the detailed principles of such a budgetary reform this is not the place to deal. We shall be content to have pointed out its paramount necessity.

It is evident, therefore, that the problems of fiscal reconstruction are by no means among the minor problems that will confront us. Social prosperity depends at bottom upon economic considerations. Government, as the war has now so convincingly shown, is becoming an increasing factor in shaping the scope and limits of these economic considerations. Government can carry on its work, however, only if it is provided with adequate means. Thus we are brought face to face with the fiscal problems which must be solved if we are to have social progress. Fiscal reconstruction is the cornerstone of the social edifice of the future.

CHAPTER ELEVEN

THE REFORM OF MUNICIPAL TAXATION

[For several years before the war the fiscal embarrassments of not a few American cities were multiplying, and increasing difficulty was experienced in securing adequate revenues. In New York City in especial, the situation was complicated by a movement in favor of freeing buildings from the real estate tax. In April, 1914, Mayor Mitchell appointed an advisory body of twenty-five citizens as a Committee on Taxation to study the two problems of the untaxing of buildings and of the securing of additional revenues. Mr. Alfred E. Marling was made chairman of the committee and the present writer chairman of the executive committee. After many hearings and the publication of several interim reports there appeared in 1916 the *Final Report of the Committee on Taxation of the City of New York,* in three volumes. Inasmuch as the majority reports on the various projects were drafted by the present writer, we venture to include them in this collection, and we add a memorandum which, although concurred in by a number of the committee, failed to secure the assent of the majority.]

I. *The Untaxing of Buildings*

Your Committee believe that it would conduce to a clearer understanding of the problem if the arguments on both sides were presented in summary. If we characterize those who advocate the plan of untaxing of buildings as the affirmative, and those who are opposed to the untaxing of buildings as the negative, it may be convenient to discuss the arguments under four heads:

1. The alleged advantages of the scheme as advanced by the affirmative;
2. A rebuttal of these arguments by the negative;
3. The alleged disadvantages of the scheme, as propounded by the negative;
4. A rebuttal of these arguments by the affirmative.

1. THE ALLEGED ADVANTAGES OF THE SCHEME AS ADVANCED BY THE AFFIRMATIVE

The advocates of the scheme for the untaxing of buildings who appeared before the Committee may be divided into three classes: (1). The out-and-out single taxers who espouse the views of Henry George, and who consider private property in land to be an anachronism; (2). The social reformers who allege that taxation must be used primarily for social purposes, and who think that great social benefits would accrue from the change; (3). Those who, while not single taxers, believe that, largely for fiscal reasons alone, there is some warrant for considering the propriety of the untaxing of buildings. Of the arguments herewith submitted, some would appeal to one of these three classes, and some to another. The arguments themselves have been urged with insistence before your Committee. They may be summed up under seven heads:

(1). Land is something entirely different from the products of labor. Land is a gift of nature; ordinary commodities are the product of human energy. Land values are entirely the creation of the community; all other values are labor values. Since land value is a social product or a community product, land rents should go to the community, or, at all events, all taxes should be derived, in the first place, from land. Houses, being products of labor, should, therefore, be exempted from taxation. This exemption of houses from taxation will lead to an increased production of buildings, and this increased production of buildings will tend to increase wages and to diminish unemployment.

(2). Land is essentially a monopoly, since the supply of land available for building cannot be increased. Buildings, like all other products of labor, are subject to the influence of competition, and their value, therefore, will be limited to the cost of production. Since land is a monopoly, its price, like that of all monopolies, ought to be controlled by the government; and the best method of such control is through the agency of taxation. Buildings, being subject to the ordinary competitive law, do not need this control. Therefore, buildings should be exempted from taxation, while land alone should bear the burden.

The existing monopoly of land, both of acreage and of land value, in New York City, make the proposed change especially just and appropriate. There are, in New York, one hundred families who were the owners of record of land, assessed in 1915 for $473,808,075, approximately one-ninth of the total assessed value of land in the city. The assessed value of their improvements was only $157,515,235, or less than a third as much, while the value of the building of a small home owner is usually about three times as much as the value of his site.

It is estimated that eight hundred families are the owners of record of land assessed for about eight hundred millions, between one-fifth and one-sixth of the total assessed value of land; and that less than three thousand families own, directly or through real estate corporations which they control, approximately two-fifths of the assessed value of land in the city. Assuming even eight persons to a family, twenty-four thousand people, out of a population of five million three hundred thousand, own about two-fifths of the total assessed value of land in the city.

Most of these families acquired their land years ago for a small part of the present selling price. Almost every wealthy family in the city owning a mansion would pay more taxes under the proposed change. The Astor family alone are the owners of record of land assessed for nearly as much as the total land owned by nearly all of the smaller home owners of the city. Several families or corporations own from one hundred to several thousand lots in the outlying boroughs, which they are holding for high prices.

(3). Land speculation is one of the great evils of modern city life. People who buy land in order to keep it out of use until some future time when its value should be considerably enhanced are the real enemies of society. Their profits are exorbitant. They take for themselves what really belongs to the public, with the result of giving to our American cities that straggling appearance which is the despair of the reformer. Land speculation results in large tracts of land held out of use, and is one of the chief causes of high rents, and one of the chief reasons for the need of exorbitant sums for supplying rapid transit facilities. Moreover, in the City of New York, the normal annual increase of land values is very great. During the past decade, for instance, land values have increased by over a thousand million dollars, while business in general is very poor. It is only fair that the chief beneficiaries of our economic system should be compelled to suffer the burden.

Increases in the selling price of land are a waste in the cost of production, irrespective of whether one land speculator loses what another gains, or whether it is a net clear acquisition of any one land speculator. The average annual increase in the selling price of land in New York has been for the last decade about $125,000,000. The total increase for the decade has been about $1,250,000,000. Calculating interest at five per cent., and net ground rent also at five per cent., this means an annual charge of $125,000,000 on a decade's increase in land values, to be paid by manufacturers, business men in general, tenants and home owners. This constitutes a dead-weight fixed charge upon the workers of the city, of no use to any one except land speculators.

The gradual transfer of taxes from buildings to land values, during a period of ten years, would prevent most of the speculative increase in the selling price of land, and would save the community this fixed but wasteful charge, which tends to increase the cost of living and interest rates, and to keep land out of use longer, thus restricting employment.

Speculation in land differs from speculation on the stock market. Speculation in land lays a burden in perpetuity upon the city; speculation on the stock exchange is a game in which only gamblers lose or gain. Those who complain of their heavy burdens on real estate ignore the fact that, while in 1880 real estate paid 87 per cent. of the taxes for the city, in 1913 real estate paid only 75 per cent.

(4). The untaxing of buildings will lead to the lowering of rents. More houses will be built, and the competition of these houses will bring down rents, not only in the outskirts, where the new houses are built, but in the city's slums and centers. These lower rents will apply not only to the tenants of residential apartments but to the tenants of commercial structures. In either case, there will be an economic saving, due to the lower rent. In the case of tenements, the lower rents will mean an increased surplus to be divided for general purposes, which will tend to increase wages and to lessen unemployment. In the case of lower rents for business purposes, it will make New York City more attractive to industrial ventures, and will, to the extent of lessening of taxes, increase the funds available for the payment of wages or the investment of capital, and thus contribute to general prosperity.

(5). The untaxing of buildings will tend to lessen congestion in the City of New York, either by the lowering of rents or by providing larger rooms and better accommodations at the same rental. The untaxing of buildings will tend to replace the dark and noisome rookeries by improved, light and airy dwellings; it will help to stamp out tuberculosis; it will better the physique and the morals of the whole population.

(6). The untaxing of buildings will lessen the tendency that is now seen in New York to the erection of tenement houses and flats. It will make it more profitable, and therefore more attractive, to intending owners of small homes in the suburbs to build their own homes, and will thus help to prevent the repetition in the outskirts of the city of the slum conditions in the center.

The change would save the smaller home owner of the city about $50 a year taxes on the average, and would only retard the rate of increase in the selling price of his land.

(7). Finally, apart from any of the above considerations, buildings ought to be exempted from taxation because the financial benefits of city expenditure accrue exclusively to the land owner. The building of a school house increases the value of the adjoining lands. The construction of a new subway creates or augments land values. Everything that is spent by the city ultimately accrues to the advantage of the land owner, and if there are any advantages at all that come from city expenditures to other members of the community, they have to pay for these advantages in the increased rent that they give to the owners of the real estate. For these reasons buildings should be exempted from taxation.

2. REBUTTAL OF THESE ARGUMENTS BY THE NEGATIVE

On every one of these points opposing arguments are advanced, and either the benefits are alleged to be chimerical or the arguments are declared to be inconclusive. Let us take them up in order:

(1). As a general philosophy of economics and social life, it is denied that land is so entirely different from other kinds of wealth. It is true that land is a gift of nature; but it is also true that a great part of the so-called products of labor are also gifts of nature. The wood that goes into a table, the wool that goes into a suit, and the pearl that goes into a necklace, are all gifts of nature. Furthermore, it is denied that we can, at all consistently, distinguish between land values as community-made values, and other values as man-made values. What gives value to everything is demand. Without demand no labor product would have any value whatever. If people spend their time in making things for which there is no demand, those things will have no value. The demand is as important and insistent in the case of labor values as it is in the case of land values. Again, in reply to the contention that values depend upon the relation between demand and supply, it is an error to state that the supply of land cannot be increased while the supply of other things can be increased. To all intents and purposes the supply of land can be increased. Assuming that there is sufficient demand, land will be taken from the outskirts, and turned into building sites. Finally, and above all, value in modern life comes not so much from the application of labor as from all sorts of relations and privileges. These speculative relations and actual privileges enter so importantly into all forms of modern income that it would be illegitimate to draw so hard and fast a line between land and other things.

(2). Land monopoly exists only in the imagination of the affirmative. As a matter of fact, land in the City of New York is not held out of use for any appreciable length of time. The vacant parcels in the Borough of Manhattan, for instance, apart from those used for coal or wood yards, and so forth, are so insignificant as to be entirely inappreciable. As a matter of fact, any attempt to hold land out of use would, under existing conditions of taxation in New York, be a losing venture. It is not denied that in some other cities vacant land is not assessed at all, or assessed at only a fraction of its value; and where the system of special assessments is not in vogue, this might become a serious problem. Even then, the proper solution of the difficulty is by levying a special tax on vacant land. In the City of New York, however, such conditions are practically non-existent, as land is brought into use just as soon as it will pay the land owner to put up a building thereon. To speak of land monopoly is a great mistake. Moreover, it must be remembered that in the City of New York land, as a rule, changes hands frequently. In the City of Chicago it was shown by a recent investigation that each parcel of land changed hands on an average every twenty-seven years. There is no reason to believe that the average is far different in New York City. It is true that there are some large holdings of land by individuals, but the fortunes of even these large landowners are insignificant today as compared with the fortunes of our capitalists, financiers and captains of industry. While no careful statistical investigation has been made, it is fairly demonstrable that there are about 200,000 individual landowners in New York City. On the general assumption that the head of the family represents his wife and three children, and on the further assumption that the great majority of landowners are married men, there would be one million people directly or indirectly owning land. Moreover, it was brought out in the testimony that by far the greater part of New York City lands is mortgaged, and that the quantity of real estate owned free and clear is exceedingly small. Since, therefore, the equity is slight, the owners of the mortgages are, to all intents and purposes, part owners of the land. Real estate mortgages in the City of New York are held to an overwhelming extent by savings banks, life insurance companies, and similar institutions, so that the real owners of the greater part of New York real estate are the depositors in savings banks and the policy-holders of the insurance companies. To speak of land monopoly in such a case is illegitimate.

(3). Speculation in land is not the bugaboo that has been made of it. Speculation in land is not essentially different from speculation on the stock or the produce exchange. It is not denied that abuses exist in the one case as in the other; but, as every careful thinker knows, speculation is an essential element in all modern business enterprises. Without speculation, there would be far greater fluctuations in the prices of ordinary commodities. The speculative expert is the one who takes the risk for the community. The speculator in land is, therefore, just as legitimate and as necessary as the speculator in anything else. Moreover, two great misapprehensions should be removed. The first is the idea that land speculators, as a class, or land owners as a class, whether they speculate or not, make any more money than any other members of the community. We are often presented with the picture of the man who invests a certain sum in land and then travels and leaves the land alone for years or for decades, in order finally to reap the immense increment in its value, a value which, we are told, is produced by the community. As a matter of fact, if the same man, instead of putting his $10,000 into a piece of vacant land, had put it into the bank and allowed it to increase at compound interest, he would find that, at the end of a term of years, he would be better off than if he had invested the same amount of money in a piece of vacant land subject to increasing taxation and to all kinds of special assessments. The large profits of landowners and land dealers are fanciful. As a class, they do not earn any more than any other class in the community. During the past few years, in New York City, at least, they have earned far less than the other classes of the community. Speculative profits in land in New York City, as a social danger, are a myth.

The other misapprehension comes from a failure to understand the real function of the owner of real estate. In the City of New York, as in most American cities, the same man who owns land owns the building. Investments in real estate, therefore, constitute one of the productive industries of the United States and, in many respects, the most important productive industry. In lieu of being a menace to, or a drag on, the community, the landowner—the land speculator, in the better sense of the term—is really one of the indispensable classes in the community. We must be careful to distinguish between the use and the abuse of a system. The stock exchange may have its abuses, but no sensible man would desire to do away with the stock exchange.

In answer to the contention that land values have increased during the past decade disproportionately to everything else, two points are made. In the first place, a large part of the so-called increase of land values is due to the arbitrary raising of assessed valuation which was resorted to during the years 1910-1911, in order to make possible a broader basis for addition to the city debt, required primarily by the new expenditure for subway construction and by other permanent improvements.

In the second place, it must be remembered that in not a few sections of the city the nominal increase in the value of land which has been normally improved is due to improvements on the adjoining land, such as the Woolworth and other skyscrapers. In reality, the owner of the adjoining property which is already covered by the normal improvement, instead of enjoying a benefit from this ostensible increase in valuation suffers a detriment; and this detriment will continue, at all events, up to the time when the actual value of the land increases to such a point, making allowance for a proper amortization of the buildings, as to make it profitable to destroy the existing improvement. Finally, it must be remembered that a not inconsiderable part of the ostensible increase in land values has been offset by the accumulated taxes and by the payment of special assessments of all kinds that may have been levied upon the lands. It not infrequently happens that the burden suffered by special assessments is in itself made the basis for an increased valuation, and, therefore, an increased payment of taxes to the city.

Finally, the claim that in 1880 real estate paid 87 per cent. of the taxes for the city, while in 1913 real estate paid only 75 per cent., is specious. What has happened, as a matter of fact, is that a number of taxes have been added to the general property tax, thus reducing the proportion paid not only by real estate but by all property in general under the general property tax. As a matter of fact, in 1913, real estate paid a much larger percentage of the general property tax than it did in 1880, and entirely apart from percentages the actual burden of real estate has increased enormously. Not only have the tax rates themselves increased very greatly, but assessed valuations have been raised from 60 per cent. or 70 per cent. to almost 100 per cent., so that there can be no question about the very much greater burden upon real estate at present as compared with that of a generation ago.

(4). In answer to the contention that rents will be lowered as the result of the untaxing of buildings, it is pointed out that while it is true that the incidence of a tax on buildings is different from the incidence of a tax on land, it does not follow that in actual life rents would really be lowered. Entirely apart from the argument to which attention will be directed below, showing that there would be countervailing forces tending to more than overbalance the influence of the remission of taxes, it is argued that in actual life we must consider the influence of friction. In many portions of New York City, for instance, it has been pointed out that the rate of taxation has been going up for the past five or ten years, but that there has been in those quarters no increase of rent. If an increase of taxation has so slight an influence on the rent, why should a remission of taxation have any greater influence? Far more important than any change in the rate of taxation are the other economic factors involved, such as general conditions of industry, rapid transit, etc. Even if it be conceded that, in the long run, lower taxes on houses might lead to lower rents, the results would be slow in showing themselves, and the changes would be far less than are imagined. Again, it must be remembered that there are countervailing influences at work in preventing a decrease of rents. One of the most important facts here is that house owners in

New York City count upon a future normal appreciation of land values to make good the inevitable deterioration in the value of the building; in other words, the expected growth in land values takes the place of a deterioration fund or amortization fund for the house. If, now, by a change in the methods of taxation, this virtual amortization fund disappears, it will be necessary to put into operation an actual amortization fund. This, however, will *pro tanto* increase the carrying charges of the building and will tend to augment rather than to reduce the cost. So far as this point is concerned, therefore, the tendency of rents would be to increase rather than to decrease.

Moreover, the benefits, so far as the question of wages and employment are concerned, are entirely exaggerated. Wages and rents move along together. It is absurd to claim that since all wealth is divided into rent, wages and interest, if more goes to the payment of rent less will be available for wages and interest. This may be true of a hypothetical static condition; that is, where there is a given sum to be divided; but it is not true of actual life, which is a dynamic condition and which continually changes. If rents rise because of greater population and greater prosperity, it is just as likely that wages will rise at the same time, because of the greater prosperity and the greater demand for the products of industry. The only correlation between rents and wages that is at all sure is that if rents go up, wages must go up also. The scale of wages and professional earnings is far higher in the City of New York than in the small neighboring towns, and the difference is very largely measured by the difference in house rents. If, therefore, rents were to fall in New York as the result of the untaxing of buildings, it is probable that wages would also fall. The untaxing of buildings would, therefore, not benefit wages.

Again, there is no truth in the contention that the untaxing of buildings will lead to greater employment. It may be true, it is conceded, that the immediate result of the untaxing of buildings might lead to an overbuilding of the city; but as soon as the first impetus had spent itself after a year or two, and a new equilibrium had been reached, there would be only the normal increase in building due to the normal increase in population, which would come with or without the change in building operations. There would, therefore, be no continuous tendency to more employment.

Moreover, there is a fallacy in the argument that the savings of the merchant and manufacturer in his store or factory, assuming that rents would fall, would lead to more employment. The surplus, it is true, would now go into the hands of the merchant or manufacturer instead of into the hands of the landowner; but in the one case, as in the other, the surplus would either be spent unproductively in riotous living, which would give little or no employment to labor, or it would be turned into the bank and then invested in some productive enterprise. For the purposes of the community, it is immaterial whether this capital is productively employed through the medium of the land owner, or through the medium of the merchant or manufacturer. In every case it is an addition to social capital.

Thus, it is a gross economic fallacy to argue that the untaxing of buildings would be of any benefit to the laborer in the way of greater employment. It is the old fallacy of Henry George, which has not been accepted by any modern economist of repute.

(5). With reference to the argument as to congestion, it is replied that the affirmative regards only one kind of congestion, the congestion of population per room. The other kind of congestion is the congestion of population per acre. Whatever good results might ensue from diminishing congestion of the first kind would be more than outweighed by the congestion of the second kind. It is indubitable, for instance, that the untaxing of buildings will lead to a more intensive use of the land, simply because it will pay better to economize in the use of the land. The results will be, without any doubt, that all vacant land, so far as there is any, will tend to be covered with buildings, and that there will also be a tendency to replace all low two- or three-story structures by skyscrapers in the business districts, and by lofty tenements in the slums. In so far as this will lead to the destruction of some of the poor and outworn tenements, it may be conceded that this is a good thing. But the benefits of this are far more than overbalanced by the conversion of whole sections of comparatively low buildings into sections of high and densely populated structures. The congestion per acre would be enormously increased and all the dangers to life and safety which would be removed in one way would be reintroduced in another.

The affirmative argues that all this might be prevented by proper laws limiting the height of buildings and by proper zoning systems. The attempt, however, to carry out this scheme, if made at all, ought to be made after, and not before, these laws are passed. To permit the untaxing of buildings now, and to hope that the other laws will come subsequently is a very naive argument. We must consider the proposition on its merits. If it is true that the untaxing of buildings will of itself increase congestion of the second kind, the argument of the affirmative is *pro tanto* weakened.

(6). The alleged advantage to the small householder is largely illusory. Almost all improvements in New York City are made through mortgage loans. The decrease in the capital value of land, due to the increased rate of taxation on land, will so impair the security for loans that either the rate of interest will rise or a smaller percentage of the capital will be loaned at the same rate of interest, since it is customary in this city to increase the rate of interest on loans with the proportion of the loan to the real value of the property. In either case, there will be an increased expense to the intending home-builder, which will tend to offset whatever advantage might accrue to him from the decrease in taxes.

In the second place, the point is made that just as in the country at large it is the expected increment in land values which was chiefly responsible for the settlement of the West by individual farmers, who sold out and moved on whenever the value of their farms reached a certain figure, so it is the anticipated increase in the value of the land that forms the greatest inducement to intending home-builders. When a man builds a house of his own and borrows most of the capital necessary, he hopes that, while in the course of time the value of the house will depreciate, the value of the land will appreciate to a much greater extent, so that when land values have gone up to a certain point, he can then sell out and, by reason of his profits on the land transaction, pay off his mortgage and come out clear. Even if, as a matter of fact, many small home owners do not sell out under these conditions, it remains none the less true that the knowledge that the capital value of their investment has risen prompts them to bear with greater ease and equanimity the annual burden of the mortgage debt. If, now, we take away from the intending house-builder this expectation of being able ultimately to finance his building operations without difficulty, we manifestly decrease the inducement to build.

Combining these two points, the increased interest rate and the removal of the anticipated increase in land value, we have a very decided obstacle to building small homes. This obstacle will more than outweigh the advantage both of the remission of taxes and of the decrease in the cost of the land. The net result of all these factors will be a decrease, and not an increase, in the inducement to build small homes.

(7). Finally, the argument that the benefits of city expenditure accrue exclusively to the landowner is completely false. Most of the city expenditures redound to the benefit of the community as a whole. The expenditures for fire protection redound to the benefit of people who own houses and to people who live in structures; the benefit of the police is to protect every property owner, whether his property consists in land or in personal property, from theft, and to protect every individual, whether he owns any property or not, from violation; the benefit of the courts is to dispense even justice between individuals, whether or not they are landowners; the benefit of the school system is to give advantages primarily to the children of the poor; the benefit of the city departments of Charities and Corrections goes to the weak and the suffering; the benefit of the city hospitals accrues to every one, whether or not he owns land; the benefit of the subways goes to all those who use the subways, and especially in the case of the large mass of wage-earners increases opportunities for work. In short, even from the narrow point of view of monetary compensation, it may be said that the expenditures of a great metropolis like New York result in increased opportunities for gain. Laborers, merchants and manufacturers would not flock to New York unless they earned more money here than they would elsewhere.

It is not denied, of course, that with increasing prosperity there comes an increase of land values. But it is denied that the landowners are the only beneficiaries. It is true, indeed, that the value of property does not normally increase as land values do; but it should not be forgotten that the opportunities for increased income grow in about the same proportion as the increase in land values The larger the city, the higher the wages; the larger the city, the greater the profits of the merchants and manufacturers, and the greater the income of the salaried and professional classes. It is contended by the affirmative that even though some benefits accrue to the public at large, these benefits are swallowed up in the higher rentals paid to the land owners. To this there is a double answer: First, it is not true that the benefits to the community are swallowed up in higher rents. Rents indeed are higher, but unless there was a growing surplus or margin over and above these higher rents, there would be no inducement for merchants, manufacturers, professional classes, or even laborers to congregate in New York. The very fact of the gradual increase of population shows that there is a margin or surplus over and above the increase of rents.

Secondly, even assuming that the foregoing is not true, there is no reason why the burdens of taxation should be put exclusively on the landowners; for then, even according to the arguments of the affirmative themselves, the community at large, such as merchants, manufacturers, professional classes and laborers would receive a benefit from city expenditures, but would pay nothing at all, even in the rentals, since buildings would be untaxed. That is to say, the community at large would have a double exemption; they would pay no direct taxes of any kind to the city, nor would they pay any taxes indirectly to the landowners, since it is conceded by the affirmative that a tax on land values would not be shifted to the tenant. The net result, then, would be that all the expenses of the city would be borne by the landowners alone, although a large part of the benefits would accrue to other classes as well.

We have now considered the arguments advanced by the affirmative, and the rebuttal of these arguments by the negative. We now proceed to consider the alleged positive disadvantages of the scheme advanced by the negative, and shall then discuss the rebuttal of these arguments advanced by the affirmative.

3. DISADVANTAGES OF THE SCHEME AS SET FORTH BY THE NEGATIVE

(1). The first point made by the negative is the so-called confiscation-of-property argument. It is pointed out that under our laws, as they have existed, people have been encouraged to invest in land as well as in other things. What possible reason is there for the government now to step in and, by utilizing the engine of taxation, to take away from present owners a part of their property? Here is a man who has worked hard for years, gotten together the sum of, say, ten thousand dollars, and invested it in a piece of real estate, where the improvements, as frequently happens, are worth far less than the land. He works hard, perhaps, in managing his piece of property and in keeping the building in good condition and in looking after the continually changing tenants. Here is another man who has inherited ten thousand dollars from his father, or has made ten thousand dollars by a lucky plunge in Wall Street, and who buys corporate stock, or deposits his cash in a bank, and runs off to Europe to have a good time. The landowner finds, as a result of the untaxing of buildings, that the value of his property falls to eight thousand dollars. He loses not only a fifth of his capital invested, but must pay more money out every year in taxes. The successful stock speculator enjoys in perpetuity the full amount of his property and, perhaps, pays no taxes at all. This is a travesty of justice. It is an unendurable utilization of government powers, and results in practical confiscation. Several of the witnesses who appeared before the Committee and who were owners of vacant land have testified how anxious they were to improve their property, and how impossible it was for them to secure the loans needed for this purpose under the circumstances. They have called our attention to the fact that the change contemplated would simply wipe them out. Owners of more modest houses in the Borough of Manhattan, on both the east and west sides, have claimed that, as a result of the untaxing of buildings, they would be unable to keep their heads above water, and that they would have to sell out at a great loss.

It has been contended that a large part of the two hundred thousand owners of real estate, representing about a million of the population in New York City, are in a condition where the value of the land considerably exceeds the value of the structures. In all such cases, and they are far more numerous than is supposed by those who think simply of the Astor Estate, the result would be disastrous. This objection would be only slightly weakened by the proposition to decrease the rate on buildings gradually for a term of years. This would be like pulling a man's teeth out one by one instead of pulling them all out together. The net result in the end would be equally unfortunate.

The exemption of buildings is defensible only on the theory that property in land is unjust, and that all land ought to be confiscated by the government. Only an infinitesimal number of people in the City of New York, less than one-hundredth of one per cent., hold any such opinion. How absurd, then, to make such a change in the fundamental principles of the city tax policy in order to satisfy the misguided demands of a minute fraction of the population.

(2). The immediate result of the adoption of the scheme would be a great real-estate panic. It would lead to the instant stoppage of the loan of mortgage funds by the great investing companies, and would produce such an apprehension that there would be a calling in at once of all existing loans. This would mean a wiping out of all existing equities, and would lead, under actual conditions in New York, to an unheard-of disaster. All panics are psychological in character, and are often the result of unreasoning fear. Whether or not the actual contemplated injury to property would ensue is immaterial. The apprehension or the fear of such injury, either at once or in the future, would be enough to bring about the panic. This apprehended injury, moreover, would not be confined to the idea of any immediately added burdens, but would consist to a large extent of the apprehension that the present project was simply an entering wedge for a much more complete scheme of confiscation of land values for the benefit of the community.

(3). Entirely apart from the question of confiscation of property, the scheme would lead to an undue and unjust burden on all property owners where land values were greater than building values. Under existing conditions in New York, immense sums of money are invested by people of small means in modest shares of real estate parcels. It is unjust to add to the existing burdens on real estate. Real estate, as a business, is in a most depressed condition in New York. To increase the burdens at this time would be suicidal policy.

(4). The untaxing of buildings would tend to increase the city expenses, as it would increase the congestion per acre. Immense sums would have to be expended for breathing spaces and city parks; streets would have to be widened to permit the increased traffic; fire hazards would be augmented, and in every way the difficulties in the cost of municipal administration would be increased.

(5). The general financial condition of the city would also be rendered more difficult. It is an acknowledged maxim of taxation never to narrow the base in the face of an anticipated increase in the amount to be levied. Under actual fiscal conditions in New York, there is great need of increased revenue, yet the proposition is to reduce the base in the face of this needed increase. The Constitution provides that the amount to be raised by taxation, exclusive of debt service, shall not exceed two per cent. on the value of the property. The contention of the affirmative that the assessed value of the property will remain the same, notwithstanding that, as is proposed, the rate on buildings should be reduced to one per cent. of the rate on land, is erroneous. As a legal proposition, it is clear that if the tax rate on buildings is reduced so as to be only one-hundredth of the rate on land, the courts will undoubtedly hold that, for the purposes of this constitutional provision, either the assessed or the selling value of the buildings should be estimated as only one-hundredth part of their real value.

(6). A similar argument is advanced with reference to the city debt, which, by the Constitution, is limited to ten per cent. of the assessed valuation of real estate. Here, however, the argument is even stronger than in the preceding cases. If, as is conceded, the higher tax rate on land will lead to a diminution in the value of the land, the margin for future debt will be wiped out, and there may even be an impairment in the city credit owing to a lessening of the underlying security for the present debt. To make such needless experiments with the city finances is reprehensible in the extreme.

4. REBUTTAL OF THESE ARGUMENTS BY THE AFFIRMATIVE

(1). The affirmative contends that there is nothing in the confiscation argument. The cry of confiscation has been raised whenever any improvement in the condition of the working classes is suggested, from tenement house laws to the abolition of child labor. The more extreme advocates of the scheme go so far as to say that all land owners are thieves, and that they ought to be well content to get off with only a slight loss; for, in reality, the community ought to take back all of their ill-gotten gains. The process must be considered not as confiscation but as a resumption by the community of what has been taken by extortion.

The less extreme advocates of the scheme do not characterize land ownership as robbery, but contend, nevertheless, that there is really no confiscation. They concede that the value of the land may be diminished, but they say that there is no divine right guaranteeing the owner forever in his property. They call attention to the fact that a sudden change in the tariff or in the system of internal revenue taxes may, under certain circumstances, bring about a loss to the owner of certain kinds of goods or property, and we do not recognize this as an essential injustice.

Still another class of advocates of the scheme concede that there will be a loss and deplore this loss in the case of what they confess to be innocent holders; but, say they, in any great change we must always weigh the good against the evil. If, as they claim, the adoption of the scheme would lead to very great social benefits, the property loss to owners of land, while regrettable, must not be deemed sufficiently important to interfere with the greater good to be accomplished.

Finally, still another class of the advocates of the scheme think that there will be no loss at all to property owners, because, in their opinion, land values will really increase rather than decrease, owing to the greater demand for land which will come from the increase in building and from the additional incentive to the gross population.

The assertion that there is no general interest in the subject is belied by the fact that over 40,000 voters in the City of New York have asked for a referendum on the question.

(2). With reference to the alleged panic, this is a mere figment of the imagination. The affirmative rely especially on the opinion of the head of a large loaning company, and upon a certain other gentleman connected with a savings and loan association. They quote the testimony of these two gentlemen, to which they attach more importance than to all the other real estate experts who testified. Their argument, in short, is that as more houses would be built, it would be to the interest of the lenders, through pressure of competition, to supply funds for the same, while money, now sunk in speculative increases in the selling price of land, will be available for buildings.

(3). The argument as to the injustice of increased expense to the owner is sought to be rebutted by the affirmative by the statement that an increase of expense is only the fair return for what will sooner or later be an increase of revenue.

(4). The argument that the expenses of the city will be increased is denied. It is conceded that more money may have to be spent for parks, etc., but it is claimed that there will be a saving in expense by a more compact city, which will, among other things, diminish the need of very expensive subways, etc.

(5). The argument as to the constitutional dangers in taxation is sought to be met in a double way. In the first place, we ought not to be prevented from accepting the change because of constitutional doubts. If the change is a good one, the Constitution can easily be altered. In the second place, the legal argument is incorrect, and no matter what the rate of taxation is, as long as the assessed values are not changed, the fiscal conditions are not altered.

(6). As to the debt, several points are made in rebuttal. In the first place, it is held that it is a good thing to put obstacles to the creation of further debt. It is claimed that the huge debt that has already been piled up is utterly unnecessary, and even if necessary it has been contracted for the sole benefit of the landowners; therefore, it is held that either we should stop short in adding to the debt, or that we should make the land owners pay for it. In the second place, others who take a slightly different view of the debt and the city credit, contend that we must not be deterred by the constitutional provision, but that contemporaneously with the change proposed, we must seek to secure an amendment to the Constitution.

It is contended by others, finally, that no change in the Constitution is needed, and that notwithstanding the diminution of the value of the land, the enormous increase in land values to be expected from a growth of the population would give the city all the leeway that is needed, and that, therefore, no impairment of the credit is to be expected.

5. CONCLUSIONS OF THE COMMITTEE

Your Committee have carefully weighed all of the above arguments and counter arguments. Three conclusions have been forced upon us: (1) The complexity of the situation is apparent. As regards each particular point, the arguments both for and against have been very vigorously presented and in not a few cases the issue of fact or probability seems to be in more or less doubt. (2) Many of the arguments on each side are inconclusive and are destroyed by opposing arguments on the same side. (3) Many of the arguments, as to both the advantages and the disadvantages of the scheme, have obviously been exaggerated by each side. As in almost every controverted question, where much bitterness has been engendered, it is important to estimate both the benefits and the dangers that are advanced.

Another point that ought to be disposed of at once is the appeal by both sides to the experience of Canadian or American towns that have tentatively made the experiment. On this phase of the subject, the Committee concur with the conclusions of its expert, Dr. R. M. Haig, who has made a thorough study of these experiments.[1] Dr. Haig sums up the Canadian experience as follows:

"It has been customary to think of Western Canada as a region where single tax measures have been uniformly and conspicuously successful. Such is not the case. In some places the measures have been conspicuously unsuccessful from practically every point of view. * * * In some places the plan has worked well; in other places it has

[1] Cf. R. M. Haig, *The Exemption of Improvements from Taxation in Canada and the United States. A Report prepared for the Committee on Taxation for the City of New York*, 1915.

worked poorly. In particular cities it has given satisfaction at one time, and dissatisfaction at another."

Dr. Haig tells us again that even in those cases "where the system was successfully introduced, land values were increasing enormously," but that with the stoppage of the boom the situation changed entirely. He tells us again that "the Canadian experiments have been confined to young cities," and that "the Canadian experience offers no evidence as to what the effect may be where land values are increasing unevenly, or where the margin between loans and securities is narrow." He says, furthermore, that the system is, even "under favorable circumstances, neither a plague nor a panacea." While he concedes that "certain definite and desirable social ends can be gained through its adoption," and that they "may be gained, under certain conditions, without an appreciable burden upon property owners," he also writes: "These conditions were present when the transition was made in the cities of Western Canada. They were not present when the change was made in the Alberta towns. These conditions do not obtain to-day in New York City." Again, as regards the American experiment, Dr. Haig's conclusion is, after careful investigation, "that there is little basis for drawing conclusions either in favor of or in opposition to the plan of exempting buildings from taxation." Finally, as to the situation in Pittsburgh and in Scranton, Pennsylvania, owing to the fact that the gradual exemption of buildings was only a very incidental feature in the great reform of abolishing the old classification scheme, Dr. Haig calls attention to "the hopelessness of expecting clear-cut immediate results under these circumstances."

In considering the evidence that has been submitted to the Committee, both in writing and at the public hearings, the Committee have been impressed by the following facts: The witnesses may be divided into five classes, viz., the single taxers, the real-estate dealers and the loaning interests, the representatives of the laboring classes, the owners of small parcels of real estate, and the scholars and publicists.

The single taxers, as was to be expected, were all in favor of the scheme as a matter of general principle. The real estate dealers and the experts in the loaning interest were all, with a single exception, opposed to the scheme because of the anticipated dangers; and there was one other prominent expert who, although not inimical to the proposition as a matter of theory, declared himself opposed to the scheme as a practical proposition at present. The representatives of the labor interests were in favor of the scheme because of their belief that it would lead to lower rents and more employment. The more modest owners of property were divided; that is, those who were owners in the suburbs, where land values are still less than building values, were in favor of the scheme. Those in other parts of the city, and especially in the borough of Manhattan, where land values are greater than building values, were opposed to the scheme. Finally, while the scholars and publicists, who might be supposed to take an impartial attitude, were divided in their judgment, the preponderance of opinion was opposed to the scheme, either as a matter of general principle or as a matter of immediate application.

As a final result of a careful weighing of all the evidence in the case your Committee have come to the following conclusions:

We believe, in the first place, that both the advantages and dangers of the scheme have been exaggerated by each side. We believe that there still remain, as a matter of principle, certain advantages as well as certain disadvantages. We think it entirely possible that there may be a temporary decrease of rents. We believe, however, that the extent of this decrease has been grossly overestimated. Moreover, we think that even if there should be a tendency to a permanent decrease of rents, it is not at all improbable that the result of decreased rents will be in the direction of lower wages. We also believe that there will not be any substantial final difference in the demand for labor.

On the other hand, we cannot but be sensible of the disadvantages of the project, both as a general proposition and in its practical application to the City of New York. We think that it has been clearly proved that the tendency of the project would be toward a more intensive use of land and that, therefore, it would be out of the question to adopt it without first enacting laws to regulate the height of buildings and to provide for a proper zoning system. Without such preliminary measures the project would not be defensible, even as a general proposition. In the second place, while we think that the financial dangers have been somewhat exaggerated, we believe that it would also be prudent to provide for a change in the constitutional provisions affecting the tax rate and the debt limit before we could even think of recommending the scheme in general.

Apart from these general doubts as to the advisability of the project, there are particular circumstances in the City of New York which afford ground for serious hesitation. New York is the greatest metropolis of the New World, and is probably destined soon to be the greatest metropolis of the entire world. Business operations of the greatest delicacy and the greatest magnitude are common. The complexity of property interests is enormous and the conditions of land-holding differ from borough to borough and almost from street to street within the same borough. In our opinion, the probable result of the contemplated change would be to benefit some property owners and to injure other property owners. After careful investigation, our expert, Dr. Haig, has pointed out that, while the anticipated benefits to the home owners in the outlying boroughs might be very slow of realization, there is no doubt as to the effect of the change on the magnitude of taxes payable by the owners of the single-family dwellings in Manhattan, and that it would lead to a depressing influence upon land values.[1] It has, moreover, been proved to our satisfaction that, in the Borough of Manhattan, at least, the burden would be relatively heavier upon the owners of the less expensive parcels of real estate, and that in a not inconsiderable number of cases the actual diminution of value to the owners of property would be considerable.

This is, in our mind, the chief consideration that impels us to doubt the wisdom of the contemplated change. Even if the anticipated benefits of the scheme were to be immediate and unquestioned, it would still be doubtful, in our opinion, whether these benefits on the one hand would not be outweighed by the added burdens on the other. But where, as is undoubtedly the case here, the benefits of the scheme have been much exaggerated and would be slow in coming; where, in other words, the extent of the benefits is questionable, and the fact that the added burdens to certain classes is unquestionable, the conclusion in our minds is irresistible. It would, in our opinion, be neither fair nor wise to cause the owners of real estate, and especially the owners of the more modest parcels of real estate, to suffer diminution in the amount of their invested capital because of vague and uncertain benefits to other classes that might ultimately be expected. As in every practical problem of statesmanship, the losses and the gains must be weighed against each other. In the opinion of this Committee, the losses to the community as a whole, under existing economic conditions in New York City, would outweigh any probable gains. We have, therefore, come to the conclusion that it would be unwise in the City of New York to exempt buildings from taxation.

[1] Robert Murray Haig, *Some Probable Effects of the Exemption of Improvements in the City of New York*, 1915.

II. *Projects for Increase of Revenues*

1. THE INCOME TAX

When your Committee originally considered the advisability of an income tax, they were confronted by the fact that as the problem was a purely local one we could not discover any administrative machinery which would make a direct municipal income tax feasible. Under existing conditions, we thought, and still think, it impracticable to localize income for the purposes of a municipal income tax.

An entirely different complexion has, however, been given to the problem by the creation of the Joint Legislative Committee of the State, and by the possibility of instituting an income tax under general state law.

Your Committee have always been of the opinion that, in principle, the direct income tax is one of the fairest of all taxes. They believe, furthermore, that a bill can be drawn which, if passed, will make the income tax entirely workable under general state law, and they agree that such a tax, carefully devised, would go far toward solving the fiscal problem of New York City as well as that of New York State. While your Committee do not deem it proper, in view of the anticipated report by the Joint Legislative Committee, to present any definite bill, and while they reserve the right to criticize or even to oppose any special provisions of the project which may be submitted by the Joint Legislative Committee, your Committee believe that the following general principles ought to be observed in an income tax applicable to the conditions of New York:

First. All incomes ought to be taxed, whether they accrue to residents of New York or whether, if they are within the State of New York, they accrue to non-residents. The adoption of this principle, which, in the opinion of your

Committee is legally entirely possible, would completely differentiate the income tax from the personal tax.

Second. Only so much of the income tax should be taxable within New York as fairly belongs to New York in the face of interstate relations. A just system of allocating income both within and without the State, and within and without the localities of the State, ought to be devised.

Third. The exemption from income tax ought to be reduced below the level of that existing in the present federal tax. The exemption, however, ought not to be so low as to trench on the income of the wage earner who is compelled to spend virtually his entire income.

Fourth. The rate of income tax ought to be proportional and not graduated, as the larger incomes are already reached at a higher rate by the federal tax. A very low rate, as will be seen below, will be adequate to yield a substantial revenue.

Fifth. The administration should, as far as possible, be in the hands of central authorities so as to ensure both expertness and impartiality.

Sixth. The returns ought to be made, as far as possible, duplicates of the returns for the Federal income tax, with such minor additions as may seem necessary.

Seventh. Use should be made, as far as possible, of the principle of information at source, in preference to the system of collection at source.

Eighth. Complete secrecy should be required of all the officials and employees with regard to any details disclosed in any income returns.

Ninth. The personal property tax should be abolished, or if that be found to be impracticable, the amount paid as a personal property tax should be deducted from the amount payable as income tax.

With the observance of these principles, your Committee believe that an income tax would be desirable.

Two possible methods of safeguarding the fiscal interests of the City of New York might be adopted. In the first place a 2% income tax might be levied by the state, of which 50% or 75% might go to the localities. We believe that an income tax on the lines sketched above, even if all public-service corporations were exempted from income tax and continued to be taxed as at present, would yield at the rate of 1% from $20,000,000 to $25,000,000. Allowing for the deduction of the personal property tax a 2% income tax would yield not far from $40,000,000. If 50% went to the localities, the share of the City of New York would be somewhere around $15,000,000, and if we were to add to this the remission from the direct state tax there would accrue to the City of New York about $30,000,000. If, instead of giving to the localities 50%, the share of the localities were to be increased to 75%, the advantage to New York City would naturally be greater.

On the other hand, if, for some reason, it seemed unwise or impracticable for the state to levy a direct income tax, your Committee would recommend that by state law there should be given the privilege to the City of New York to substitute for the direct state tax on property, an income tax to be levied according to general rules laid down in the state law, and with such additions to the rate of income tax for municipal purposes as might be recommended by the municipal authorities. To this extent, we are in favor of the plan of local option even in taxation, for it would be an option carefully guarded.[1]

[1] [The above suggestion of the Committee for a state income tax with a share going to the localities was finally carried out in 1919. For a more extended discussion of the arguments *cf.* chapter xx in Seligman, *Essays in*

2. THE CLASSIFIED PERSONAL PROPERTY TAX

The second project mentioned by the Joint Legislative Committee is the classified personal property tax, or the low-rate tax on intangible personalty, to be followed later by a low-rate tax on tangible personalty. Your Committee see no reason to depart from the conclusions at which they arrived several months ago, and which were embodied in a special report made to the Mayor. Without repeating all the considerations which have been previously urged, your Committee content themselves by summing up the objections to a low-rate tax on personalty, as follows:

1. It will require for its successful operation a listing system, which has always been repugnant to the citizens of New York. The listing system as applied in other states to the property tax, has always resulted ultimately, with the publicity that has by law everywhere attended it, in an increase of perjury rather than of revenue.

The schedules required to be filled out for the existing federal income tax cannot be considered as a counter argument. Secret returns of income are in their practical operation very different from the public listing of personal property, including assets of all kinds and thus necessarily disclosing business secrets.

2. The low rate on personal property would only slightly diminish the temptation to evasion. A rate of four or five mills represents a 10% income tax on 4% or 5% bonds, and an additional income tax of 10% is not likely to remove temptations to evasion, especially in a state like New York where, under the law, residence for the purpose of taxation can be so easily changed.

3. Even a low rate of taxation on personal property would jeopardize the interests of New York City. If levied upon securities it will be an intolerable burden upon all

Taxation, 10th ed., 1925. The further suggestion as to an additional rate for municipal purposes was seriously considered by the New York state legislature in 1925, and will probably lead to favorable action in the near future.]

of these interests that deal in securities and whose profits are in very slight relation to the amount of securities they may hold for sale.

In the case of merchandise, a low-rate tax will be a tax on assets and on stock in trade which will bear with peculiar hardship upon merchants, as in the large wholesale centers stock in trade has no net direct relation to profits.

4. A low-rate tax on personalty is confronted by the problem of debts. If no allowance is made for indebtedness, the tax is clearly unjust. If allowance is made for indebtedness, inducement is given to the creation of fictitious debts, which will again result in inequality.

5. No system of taxation, whether low rate or high rate, can be profitably levied upon property as such, with the exception of a local tax on real estate. The whole tendency of modern times is to estimate tax-paying ability in general in terms of profit or income, not in terms of property.

6. A low-rate tax will entirely fail to reach those who are in possession of large incomes from salaries or professional exertions.

7. A low-rate tax will not begin to yield the revenue that is required. In the few states where the low-rate tax has been employed, the increase in revenue has been only moderate and far from what would be needed in New York. In some of these states, like Iowa, there has even been an actual and considerable diminution of the revenue.

We believe, therefore, that in the existing situation of New York, a classified personal property tax would be a step backward and not a step forward. It would scarcely, if at all, help us in the fiscal emergency and it is based upon an erroneous principle of public finance.

3. THE ABILITY OR PRESUMPTIVE INCOME TAX

If the direct income tax is found to be impossible, your Committee would repeat its recommendation of last winter, viz., that the State permit the City of New York, as well as the other cities if they so desire, to reach incomes indirectly rather than directly by the so-called ability or presumptive income tax. Several members of your committee would even go so far as to prefer, under actual conditions in New York, the ability tax to the income tax.

What is here called the ability tax is a tax on the abilities of those who benefit from the opportunities afforded by the City of New York. Conceding that the fairest test of ability to pay is income, the proposition here is to reach the income indirectly and by outward signs or criteria, utilizing certain definite facts of expenditure as affording some indication of relative income. The ability tax as a presumptive income tax would, therefore, be composed of three parts, viz.: the habitation tax, the occupation tax, and the salaries tax, with provisions by which only one of these taxes would be payable by any particular person.

A. *THE HABITATION TAX*

The habitation tax is a tax upon individuals occupying habitations—that is, houses or apartments for residential purposes. The tax proceeds upon the theory that what a man spends for rent is a rough indication of his ability to contribute to the public burdens. Inasmuch, however, as the ratio of house rent and income decreases as the amount of rent increases—that is, inasmuch as people with smaller incomes must spend a relatively larger share of their income for rentals, it is obvious that in order to secure approximate justice the tax must be rather sharply graduated, so that the tax will increase not only in proportion to the rental, but more than in such proportion.

The schedule of the tax ought to be so arranged that every individual will pay a sum that is about equivalent to one per cent. of his income, as indicated by his house rent. According to the consideration just mentioned, the real income of the taxpayers may be considered to increase at a greater rate than do the rentals which they pay. If, for instance, we assume that for the more modest rentals a man spends about a fifth of his income for his house rent, we would have to multiply the yearly rental by five in order to get his presumptive income. In the case of the higher rentals the multiplier would have to be more than five, running up to six, seven, eight, nine, ten, and even more, as in the latter case of rather expensive rentals it is to be assumed that a man's income would be at least ten times and more the amount of rent that he pays. The tax, therefore, will have to be based upon a progressively graduated scale, so that the higher the house rent the progressively higher would be the amount of tax.

In order, however, to prevent miscarriages of justice and to obviate the criticism that the presumptive income may be far from being the real income, and that two men living in precisely similar houses may yet have very different real incomes, it should be provided that if any one finds that the tax which he is called upon to pay amounts to more than one per cent. of his actual income, he shall have the right to declare and to prove his actual income and to have his tax reduced to one per cent. of his income. This would happen in only a comparatively few cases, but would effectually dispose of the criticism. This provision is not found in the draft bill herewith appended, but should be, and could easily be, added thereto.

It is further provided that if a man lives in his own house, the rental value shall be calculated at seven per cent. of the assessed value of the property. Provision is also made for people who live in hotels or apartments, and the tax should be applicable to those who have occupied apartments continuously for at least three or four months.

Several criticisms, which, however, are not valid, might be urged against the habitation tax. In the first place, it might be alleged that the tax is a tax on the poor man. In reality, however, the opposite is the case. Under the project of your Committee, all rentals below $50 a month, that is, $600 a year, are entirely exempt from taxation. This corresponds to a total expenditure of from $2,500 to $3,000. Every one, therefore, with a presumptive income under this amount will pay no tax at all. Moreover, the amount of tax on slightly higher rentals is exceedingly moderate, because of the fact that, according to our recommendation, $2,000 should be exempted in every case from the presumptive income in order to reach the taxable income. On the very high rentals, however, this exemption is of no importance, and the tax will be very much greater. From the scale, which is worked out in detail in the bill appended hereto, we make the following extracts to show the operation of the law:

Rental	Multiplier	Presumptive Income	Taxable Income	Tax
$600- $700	5	$3,500-2,000	$1,500	5
700- 800	5	4,000-2,000	2,000	10
1,000- 1,100	5	5,500-2,000	3,500	30
2,000- 2,100	5.1	10,710-2,000	8,710	87
2,900- 3,000	5.5	16,500-2,000	14,500	145
4,000- 4,100	6	24,600-2,000	22,600	226
10,000- 10,200	8	81,600-2,000	79,600	796
25,000- 26,000	17	442,000-2,000	440,000	4,400
90,000-100,000	17	1,700,000-2,000	1,688,000	16,880

From the above table, therefore, it will be seen that the habitation tax entirely exempts all these with incomes under $2,500 or $3,000; that it imposes an insignificant burden on those with an income between $3,000 and $6,000 or $7,000 a year, and that it considerably increases the burden as the income augments. The habitation tax is thus not a tax upon the poor man and not an appreciable burden upon those in moderate circumstances.

In the second place, it might be alleged that the habitation tax falls upon the real estate owner for the reason that a prospective tenant of, let us say, a $650 apartment, would insist upon having his rent reduced to $600 in order to escape the tax. This argument, however, is to a great extent fallacious.

As a matter of fact, the $650 tenant will never secure the owner's consent to a reduction of $50 in rent in order to enable the tenant to save $5 in taxes. The same would be even more true of higher rentals, because, according to the scale proposed, a reduction of every $100 in rental would involve the saving of only $5 in each case. So that even at the very worst it would only be at the margin of each class of tenants that there would be any pressure at all to demand a reduction of rent. But even this is open to considerable doubt. The only way in which a landlord could be induced to grant a reduction of rent would be through the fear of having his apartments vacated. If, however, the tenants of a particular grade of apartments would actually be induced to move to a lower-priced apartment because of the tax, the place vacated by them would be filled by the influx of tenants from the next higher grade of apartments who would, under the hypothesis, in like manner be induced to seek lower-priced apartments. The fact that there are relatively less higher-priced apartments would only slightly retard this tendency. Therefore, what might possibly be lost in one way would in large measure be gained in the other; and the only apartments which might suffer a possible reduction of rental because of a threatened disappearance of their tenants would be the highest-priced apartments in the city. These, however, are occupied by the wealthiest classes, and the amount of taxes to which they would be subjected would be such a small proportion of their entire income as, in all probability, to lead to no such transfer at all.

Thus it will be seen that the argument that the habitation tax falls on the real estate owner is largely fallacious. If it is shifted at all to the real estate owner, only a small part will fall upon him and the rest will still be paid by the tenant, while only the owners of the most expensive apartments could suffer. But even these, as we have seen above, will probably not suffer at all, or to any perceptible degree.

Above all, however, it must be remembered that even if it is true that the habitation tax would fall to a very slight extent on the real estate owner, it is a question of choice between the habitation tax and an increased rate on real estate. If the additional revenue must be raised by a direct tax, which is practically a tax on real estate, the real estate owner will have to pay all of it. If the necessary revenue is derived from a habitation tax, the real estate owner will at the very worst pay only a small part of it, and, in all probability, as we have seen, he will pay none of it. As between the habitation tax, therefore, and the real estate tax, the habitation tax is in the interest of the real estate owner.

The habitation tax is, therefore, not a tax on the poor man, nor is it a tax on the real estate owner. It is a tax on the presumptive income of everybody who resides in New York City. Its chief value, as compared with our present system of taxation, is that it reaches the man who is not in business in New York City and also that it reaches the rich man who now escapes taxes entirely by living here and claiming a residence outside of New York. The habitation tax does not depend upon legal residence. It must be paid by all with incomes of approximately $2,500 to $3,000 who rent apartments or who live even for a limited time in New York City.

The habitation tax, however, will not affect those who earn their living in New York City but who do not live here. These classes also possess an ability which ought to be reached, and in the City of New York they form an exceptionally numerous class. These it is proposed to reach by the business residence tax to be considered on the next page under the name of an occupation tax.

B. *THE OCCUPATION TAX*

This is a tax on the premises occupied for business or for securing a livelihood. It reaches the non-resident and the resident alike. Your Committee, after considering the various methods employed in different parts of the world, have come to the conclusion that the occupation tax should be levied on the basis of the annual rental value of the business premises. In some of the Canadian and European cities where this tax is in force, an attempt has been made to graduate the occupation tax according to the character of the business, on the assumption that different businesses will require varying degrees of floor space for their purposes. After a study of the world's experience, your Committee have come to the conclusion that the greater degree of theoretic fairness which would follow from such a system of classification would be more than outweighed by the complexity of the scheme and by the inability after all to secure exact justice. Your Committee, therefore, believe that we should follow the example of the most important cities, and should impose a flat tax on business rentals. We accordingly suggest a tax of 7% of the annual rental value of all business premises, and we propose, in order to lighten the burden on the small man, a deduction of $20 tax in every case, with a complete exemption of all business rentals up to $50 a month.

The occupation tax, it will be seen, is, therefore, not a tax upon the small business man. Business premises are liable to be taxed only when the rent exceeds $50 monthly, or $600 a year, and as the tax is levied at the rate of 7% only on the rental exceeding that sum, with the further provision that $20 is deducted in every case, the amount of the tax would be insignificant on even the more moderately successful business man. With business rentals of $1,000 a year, for instance, the tax will be only $50. Where a man occupies his own building for business purposes, or for purposes of a livelihood, the rental value is estimated, as in the case of the habitation tax, at 7% of the assessed valuation. Moreover, if a person is subject to both the habitation tax and the occupation tax, he may deduct the one from the other. Finally, it may be pointed out, that in the occupation tax, as in the habitation tax, if any one should be held to pay a tax on his personal property, he would be entitled to deduct the amount of the personal property tax from the occupation tax or the habitation tax as may be.

It may be conceded that the occupation tax is not an ideal tax, but it must be remembered that it is far better, even so far as the business man is concerned, than a tax on personal property or a tax on his stock in trade. At the present time, the business man contributes virtually nothing to the expenses of the city. An attempt to tax him on his stock in trade without deduction for debts, which would be a result of levying a tax on his tangible property, would be both more onerous and less equitable than the occupation tax.

Neither the occupation tax nor the habitation tax would, however, reach the salaried classes who secure large incomes in New York City, and who neither live in New York nor themselves pay any rent for business purposes. All these, for instance, who receive large salaries from corporations would be exempt from taxation. Your Committee feel that this would be unjust and they, therefore, recommend an addition to the habitation tax and the occupation tax of

C. *THE SALARIES TAX*

This is a tax on all salaries paid or received in the City of New York except salaries paid by the federal government. The exemption should be, in all cases, about $2,000, and the tax should be graded from the rate of one per cent. up to the figure of five per cent. on the excess of all salaries over $30,000. Provision is made in our bill for the reporting of salaries by employers and for the withholding by them of the tax at the source.

As before, where the taxpayer, subject to the salaries tax, is subject to either the habitation tax or the occupation tax, he may deduct the one from the other; and, in the same way, he may also deduct any tax that he happens to pay on his personal property.

Here, again, several possible misconceptions ought to be removed. In the first place, it would not be true to state that the salaries tax is a tax on the small man. Since all salaries up to $2,000 are exempt, and since the rate is only one per cent. on the excess over that amount, the recipient of even a $3,000 salary would pay only $10 a year as his entire tax to the city. On the other hand, higher salaries, like that of the more successful professional man and of the well-paid corporation official are taxed at considerably greater figures. The salaries tax is, therefore, in reality a tax upon large incomes derived from personal exertion. It is a tax upon the wealthier classes, not upon the poor man.

In the second place, it would be equally fallacious to state that salaries are taxed while other incomes are not taxed. Business incomes are supposed to be reached by the occupation tax; other incomes, in general, by the habitation tax. Nobody has to pay more than one of these three taxes. The purpose of the salaries tax is not to single out for taxation people with salaries; but, on the contrary, to prevent people with large salaries from entirely escaping taxation—especially the recipients of large salaries in this city who live outside of New York City. The salaries tax, instead of being an unequal tax on a special class, is an endeavor to secure equality of taxation by reaching those who would otherwise escape.

If we consider the ability or presumptive income tax in general as to all of these three parts, it will be realized that it has two great advantages. In the first place, it will be exceedingly easy, as well as inexpensive, to administer. Moreover, it can be readily executed by the city officials without any necessity of depending upon the state administration. As regards its practicability, its certainty, and its inexpensiveness, it satisfies three of the cardinal rules of taxation.

In the second place, the revenue will be large. Your Committee estimate, on the basis of figures furnished to them by the internal revenue department at Washington, that in the City of New York alone, at the rate suggested, the revenue would be from $20,000,000 to $25,000,000.

In the face of these great advantages, the only possible objection to the scheme is that it is not absolutely equal. We concede this at once, but urge its other advantages. Theoretically, our personal property tax is in many respects unobjectionable, but in actual operation it is open to the gravest criticism. We must remember that a fairly rough approximation to justice which is administratively simple and workable is far better than a more ideal scheme which does not work out in practice. Under our present system vast classes of the population escape and a very small proportion of the population bears the burden. Under the project herewith submitted, many classes will be reached who now are not reached, and while ideal justice will not be attained, a step forward will have been taken. As in every question of tax reform, we must consider the proposition not from the point of view of ideal justice, but from that of substantial progress. It is easy to criticize any project for reform, but it is far more difficult to submit a constructive proposal. We ask that the entire project be regarded from the point of view not of the ideal, but of the practicable.

4. THE INCREMENT TAX ON LAND VALUES

In the early part of this report your Committee have called attention to the fact that from forty to fifty millions of dollars would before long be needed in the shape of additional revenue. We have pointed out that a very substantial part of this increase can be derived from either a direct income tax or a presumptive-income or ability tax. There still remains, however, a material sum that must in all probability be raised. This leads your Committee to take up again the question of taxation of land. Some members of your Committee are in favor of this, quite irrespective of the other recommendations.

While it is true, as your Committee have already pointed out, that of all possible times this is the most inopportune to increase the burden on land, because of the great depression of real estate, and while both in view of the particular conditions of New York and of the general principles involved, your Committee have previously stated that they do not believe in the exemption of buildings from taxation or in the imposition of any heavier burden upon existing land values, it remains none the less true that we should regard with open minds the general question of the advisability of raising in the future an additional revenue from land values.

On this point, we agree with the majority of modern economists that land values afford an especially promising and suitable basis for local taxation. We do not indeed believe that land values should form the exclusive basis of taxation. We hold, however, that under certain conditions, to be described in a moment, a larger revenue may in the future be derived from this source than is the case at present. Land values in a growing city tend to increase, notwithstanding periods of temporary regression. Landowners, moreover, as a general class, are in a position to amortize a burden of taxation, and if care be taken not to decrease the capital value of the investment in land in the hands of present owners, since future purchasers may be depended upon to buy themselves free of any increasing tax burden that has accrued in the interval, it is possible to secure additional revenues from land without injustice.

How can this be accomplished? In the first part of the report, your Committee have indicated their reasons as to why they disapprove of the exemption of buildings from taxation. It will be remembered that the chief objection was stated to be that land, especially in the present depressed condition, is already bearing more than its due share of taxation; and that, in the opinion of your Committee, it would be inequitable to frame any scheme of taxation which would reduce the capital value of land in the hands of existing owners. Your Committee, however, have considered whether some scheme of land taxation would not be possible without exposing it to the objection mentioned above.

In the opinion of your Committee, it is still possible to accomplish the desired result by imposing a tax on the future increase or increment of land values. Your Committee recommend that there be levied a flat one per cent. on all future increases of land values, making the basis from which the future increment is to be estimated the value, with the exception noted below, at the time when the law is enacted. Owing, however, to the present depression in real estate, the basis from which the increase is to be calculated should be not the year 1916, but any year between 1910 and 1914 which marks the highest assessed valuation, provided the property has not been sold in the meantime. If, for instance, a plot of land in the year 1912 was assessed for $10,000 and in the year 1916 at only $8,000, then if its value in 1917 or thereafter should rise, it would not be subject to the increment tax until the value would again rise to over $10,000. Moreover, in assessing the increment tax, allowance should be made for any sums paid for special assessments which would increase the value of the land.

In considering the application of the increment tax, attention should be called to a distinction which is of considerable practical importance. There is no doubt in our minds that if the increment tax be accepted it should be immediately adopted in the case of all vacant land, as well as in the case of underimproved land. Where, however, there are existing normal improvements on particular plots of land, it is susceptible of proof that unless great care be observed considerable injustice may result. As a matter of strict equity, no increment on land values ought to be figured until the value of an existing normal improvement, properly amortized, merges into the value of the land. There are, for instance, many examples in the City of New York where, at a given time, entirely proper improvements, as, for instance, six-story tenements or apartments, were put upon the land. So rapid, however, is the change in conditions in New York City that after the lapse of ten or fifteen years land values in particular sections may increase so much as to make it profitable to cover an adjoining vacant or underimproved lot with a twelve-story structure or even a skyscraper. This will, of course, relatively depreciate the value of the six-story structure which was an entirely normal improvement and which is as yet by no means worked out or obsolescent. The owner of the six-story structure finds that the value of his land is under normal circumstances increased considerably; but the total value of his property is now less than before, because the structure is worth practically nothing and his total income is very much less than before, because his six-story structure will be more and more deserted for the better accommodations in the neighborhood. Although the selling value of his structure has virtually disappeared, the assessed valuation on the tax books has decreased little, if at all. He is, therefore, paying actually more taxes and is getting less revenue than before; that is, he is hit at both ends and has really suffered a detriment. If, now, in addition he has to pay an increment tax because of the increased value of the land, he will suffer a third time.

There is, perhaps, no city in the world where there are such rapid shifts as in New York. It is not unusual for the same plot of land to be successively covered by three or four different kinds of structures within a generation. The situation is far more common than is ordinarily thought. Your Committee, therefore, believe that a perfectly equitable increment tax could be applied in such cases only where the value of an originally normal improvement, when properly amortized, merges into, or is overtaken by, the value of the land. It is only from that point on that the increment in land values should be considered taxable. It would be relatively simple, moreover, for the tax authorities to provide a proper amortization rate for each kind of building as they now provide for the factors of assessment.

It need scarcely be pointed out, however, that if a proper zoning system, with reasonable limitations upon the height of buildings, were adopted in the City of New York, the above considerations would not apply. For, in that case, it is not likely that a twelve-story apartment or skyscraper would be erected immediately adjoining a six-story structure until the whole character of the neighborhood had so completely changed as to render existing improvements sub-normal, thus bringing about an alteration in the character of the zone itself. If, accordingly, the above rather complicated considerations are to be avoided, it is in the highest degree desirable that the introduction of a land increment tax should be attended by the adoption of a zoning system.

In considering the increment tax, it must be borne in mind that the two objections that might be advanced against it are really destitute of foundation. It might be said, in the first place, that the land increment tax is an entering wedge of the single tax. This is an error. The single tax contemplates the taxation in part or in whole of existing land values, thus diminishing or destroying the capital value of land. Entirely different, in our opinion, is the increment tax, which affects only future increases of land value, and which is founded on, and recognizes to the full, the existing capital value of land. Increment value taxes, which deal only with the future, should not be confused with taxes on existing land values.

In the second place, it might be objected that the increment tax imposed additional burdens upon real estate as a whole. This, again is, in our opinion, erroneous. The increment tax in reality levies a tax where taxation ought to rest, namely, upon those best able to pay. Is it not true that when a landowner secures an appreciable increase in the value of his land, either through the action of the government or through the general growth of the community, he is really making a profit, a part of which might equitably go to the government?

Apart from this general consideration, it may be pointed out that the increment tax must be considered as primarily a burden on the particular owners who are especially benefited. The completion of the vast scheme of rapid transit, costing about $350,000,000, and for which the taxpayers have, in large measure, to pay, will substantially increase land values in some sections of the city and, perhaps, in all the boroughs. The imposition of an increment tax diminishes the burden on the landowners who may suffer a decrement or whose property remains stationary; for, if there were no increment tax, the ordinary tax rate on real estate would be raised throughout the city. The burden which in this way is removed from the landowners who do not benefit is thus borne by those landowners who are best able to pay, namely, those whose land enjoys an increase in value. The increment tax really amounts to a supplementary income tax or ability tax.

The revenue to be derived from this increment tax would, indeed, not be great at first, but it would substantially increase, from year to year. In proportion as there will probably come within the next few years a restoration of prosperity in the real estate situation, and even on the assumption that the average increase of land values during the next five or ten years will be only $75,000,000 or $100,000,000 a year, the land increment tax will, within a very few years, yield a considerable revenue to the city, and not the least claim to our consideration is the fact that it forms a revenue which will be derived without interfering in any degree with the existing property rights of land owners in the City of New York.

5. THE SUPER-TAX ON LAND VALUES [1]

Although, as a member of the majority of the Committee, I have expressed my conviction that both according to the general principles and in view of the particular situation in New York, the exemption of buildings from taxation is inadvisable, it nevertheless remains true, in my opinion, that we should regard with open minds the advisability of placing in the future an increasing burden upon land values.

While I hold the arguments of the single taxers to be erroneous, I agree with the majority of the modern economists in the belief that land values afford an especially promising and suitable basis for local taxation. I do not believe that land values should form the exclusive basis of taxation, but I do think that, under certain conditions, a larger revenue may be derived from that source than is the case at present. The majority of the Committee are clearly of this opinion, as is evidenced by the fact that they

[1] [The report of the Committee proper closes with the preceding paragraph. This section was signed by the present writer and received the support of several members of the Committee.]

have recommended an increment tax on land values. While I have been glad to sign that recommendation as a member of the Committee, I feel that very much the same argument may be utilized in favor of a carefully devised super-tax on land values. I do not, of course, believe that both an increment tax and a super-tax on land values should be levied at the same time; but I desire to set forth the reasons why, in my opinion, a super-tax on land values may, if necessary, be utilized in lieu of an increment tax on land values.

As has been pointed out in the majority report on the untaxing of buildings, I do not agree with many of the stock arguments advanced by the single taxers. I do not think that land is so entirely different from other forms of property as to justify the single tax. I do not believe that an increment tax on land values is needed to force land into use, since under present conditions of taxation in New York City it does not pay to hold land out of use. I do not believe that taxes should be levied on land in order to free products of industry, because this assumes that taxes are generally, or must otherwise be, levied upon such property; whereas, as was stated in the majority report, the whole trend of modern taxation is to take income and not property as the basis of taxation; and there are many incomes in modern times which are derived not from property, but from all kinds of privileges and relations of an economic kind. I do not believe that land values should be taxed for the reason that property in land is unjustifiable. I do not believe that land values should be taxed in any exclusive sense in order to lessen the number of those who get incomes without earning them; for, in my opinion, not alone is land only one of the sources of such unearned incomes, but the revenue from land is sometimes earned in the same sense as the revenue from anything else which is based upon care, attention and good business judgment.

Despite these facts I think that a good case may nevertheless be made out for a greater taxation of land values. Land values, in a growing city, are apt to increase, notwithstanding periods of temporary regression. Land owners, while they do not form the only class of people that benefit from city expenditures and while they are not the sole class of the community that possess an ability to contribute to the communal burdens, are nevertheless in a better position than almost any other class to amortize any increasing burden of taxation.

Furthermore, while land, indeed, does not constitute a monopoly (for the supply of urban land may undoubtedly be augmented by drawing upon outlying districts) land none the less differs, not indeed from all other kinds of wealth, but from many other kinds of wealth, in that the increased supply can be secured only at an increased cost; that is, while the tendency of most manufactured products is to fall in price with the development of science, the price of land like that of most raw products tends to increase in price. The growth of demand, therefore, acts differently in the case of land and natural products from what it does in the case of most manufactured products. It is not a clear distinction between land, on the one hand, and labor products on the other; but it is a distinction between those forms of wealth which respond to an increased demand at the same or a decreasing cost, and those which respond to this demand at an increasing cost. Land differs from other things, in short, not absolutely in kind, but simply in the degree to which increase in demand affects change in price. Moreover, the land value tax is perhaps of all taxes the simplest to assess and the easiest to collect. The land value tax, again, is perhaps, of all taxes, the one to which a community can most readily adjust itself. The land value tax, finally, is one, which if carefully devised and administered, will tend to cause the least interference with economic and social conditions. In short, while land does not

differ in essence from all other forms of wealth, it does differ in degree from some other forms of wealth, and it is precisely this difference in degree which justifies, in my opinion, a somewhat higher tax upon land.

The principles, which, in my judgment, should obtain in applying the doctrine of a super-tax on land values are as follows:

(1). A portion of the increased revenues that are needed should come from other sources. In the opinion of a majority of this Committee this portion of additional revenues, as we have seen, should come from a tax on the general income of the inhabitants, through either a direct income tax or a presumptive income tax. The remainder may well come from an additional tax on land values either in the shape of an increment tax or in the shape of a super-tax.

(2). Care must be taken not to interfere with existing land values. The chief objection as we have seen, to the untaxing of buildings, is that it may decrease the selling value of the property of entirely innocent holders. Such a glaring infraction of property rights could be justified only by considerations of overwhelming necessity, and such considerations are entirely lacking in this case. It is, therefore, highly desirable that in the assessment of any super-tax on land values a provision be introduced that the additional tax when capitalized should never exceed any intervening increase in land values; for only in this way can the above injustice be prevented.

It will be asked what is the difference between a super-tax and an increment tax. The difference is obvious. It is true that the tax will not be assessed in either case unless there has been an increase in land values; but in the case of an increment tax, the tax is proportionate to the increment, while in the case of the super-tax the tax stands in a definite relation not to the increase in land value but to the capitalized value of the land. The super-tax, in other words, is a more comprehensive tax than the increment tax.

The difference can be illustrated by an arithmetical example. Let us assume, for instance, that a given plot of land has increased in value in a definite period from $10,000 to $12,000. An increment tax of say one per cent. on the $2,000 increase would amount to $20. These $20 capitalized at five per cent. amount to $400, thus making the selling value of the land $11,600 after the tax was imposed. On the other hand, let us assume that a super-tax of as much as three mills on the dollar is needed. A three-mills tax on $12,000 would amount to $36. Thirty-six dollars capitalized at the rate of five per cent. equals $720. The consequence is that the property will advance in price from $10,000 to $11,280 and that the tax will stand, because the capitalized tax, or $720, is less than the increase of land values, or $1,280. If, however, the increase in land values had been less than the capitalization of the super-tax, the super-tax would have to be diminished in proportion.

The practical difference between the increment tax and the super-tax is that the super-tax would tend to take a larger share of the increment, and that it might be simpler to levy a low super-tax than a high increment tax.

The advantages of a super-tax as against the untaxing of buildings are, therefore, as follows:

(1). There would be no injustice done to the present owners of land.

(2). There would be no reduction in the assessed valuations of real estate, thus eliminating all possibility of embarrassment in either the debt situation or the tax situation.

(3). There would be only a slight slackening in the increase of land values which may be normally expected in a growing city.

(4). If the super-tax is definitely fixed in advance, it would be so amortized as to create practically no embarrassment to future holders of land.

(5). To the extent that the super-tax is levied, it would tend to prevent that part of the increase of rent which is due to a tax on buildings. It would be a mistake, indeed, as was pointed out in the majority report on the untaxing of buildings, to think that a change in rent is to be measured by the change in the rate of the tax on buildings; for there are many other factors, as we have seen, which affect the relative cost of buildings. While, however, due allowance must be made for these other factors, it is none the less probable that a failure to increase the rate on buildings will tend, on the whole, to prevent any corresponding increase in rents.

I think, then, that the future of municipal revenues, not alone in the United States but throughout the world, has in store for us a reliance on the one hand on a share in increased income taxes, in order to tap the abilities of those who profit by the opportunities of our large cities; and on the other hand, on an increase of revenue from land values in order to reach the abilities of those who derive additional and increased benefits from the special privileges afforded by our growing cities.

I believe, in short, that a super-tax on land values, carefully restricted and equitably enforced, will form a precious source of increased revenue to the cities of the future; that it will tend, on the whole, to secure advantageous social results; and that it will not be attended by injurious consequences either to innocent property owners or to the community at large.

CHAPTER TWELVE

THE FRENCH COLONIAL FISCAL SYSTEM

[This was originally printed in the *Publications of the American Economic Association,* Third Series, vol. i, 1900.]

I. *History and Present Extent of the Colonies*

The history of the French colonies begins in the fifteenth and sixteenth centuries when sailors of the crown took possession of lands in the new world and on the African coast. Under Richelieu and Colbert came the period of greatest expansion. In the seventeenth century France owned vast possessions in Canada, in Louisiana, in the Antilles and in Hindustan. With the peace of Utrecht in 1713 the dismemberment of the colonial empire began; until by the treaty of Paris in 1814 France had been stripped of most of her possessions with the exception of several of the Antilles and of minor settlements in Africa and Asia. Very shortly thereafter, however, a new period of progress set in, starting with the gaining of a foothold in Algiers in 1830, and slowly progressing in other parts of Africa during the next half century. But with the beginning of the eighties a new and more vigorous policy was adopted. More than two-thirds of the colonial empire existing at the end of the nineteenth century was added to France in the preceding fifteen or twenty years. The chief acquisitions of these recent decades are: Tunis, large tracts in Central Africa, the island of Madagascar and the countries in the neighborhood of Cochin-China and Tonkin.

At the close of the nineteenth century the French dependencies comprised the following:

I. America: (1) French Guiana; (2) Martinique, Guadaloupe and dependencies in the Antilles; (3) Saint Pierre et Miquelon near Newfoundland.

II. North Africa: (1) Algiers; (2) Tunis.

III. West Africa: (1) Senegal; (2) French Soudan; (3) French Guinea; (4) Ivory Coast; (5) Dahomey and Bight of Benin; (6) French Congo.

IV. East Africa: (1) Obock and Somali Coast; (2) The Comoro Islands and Mayotte; (3) Reunion; (4) Madagascar.

V. Asia: (1) French India (Pondichéry, Chandernagor, Yanaon, Mahé, Karikal, etc.); (2) Indo-China; (*a.* Cochin-China, *b.* Cambodia, *c.* Annam, *d.* Tonkin).

VI. Oceanica: (1) New Caledonia and New Hebrides; (2) French Oceanica (*a.* Tahiti and Moorea, *b.* Marquesas Islands, *c.* Society Islands, *d.* minor islands).

Outside of Algiers, Tunis and Indo-China, which occupy a place by themselves, the French dependencies may be divided into two groups: the first, or the colonies proper, including those which have a general legislative council (*conseil général*); and the second, often called the possessions in contrast to the colonies, with a more rudimentary administrative organization.

The first class comprises the following: Martinique, Guadaloupe and Reunion (1882)[1]; Guinea, Senegal and French India (1878); St. Pierre et Miquelon (1885); New Caledonia (1885); Tahiti, and the rest of French Oceanica (1885); and Mayotte and Comoro (1896).

The second group includes French Congo (1887); French Soudan (1893); French Guiana (1893); Ivory Coast (1896); Dahomey (1894); Somali Coast (1896); and Madagascar (1896).

As to the others, Algiers is treated as a part of France. It is divided into three departments, sends representatives to the French parliament and is subject in its different in-

[1] The date is that of the present administrative organization.

terests to the various ministers at Paris. Tunis, as a protectorate, falls within the province of the Minister of Foreign Affairs, as does also Madagascar. All the other colonies and dependencies are under the control of the minister of Colonies. Indo-China was formed in 1887; but in 1888 it was decided that for fiscal purposes Cochin-China, Cambodia and the protectorate of Annam-Tonkin should be kept separate. In Indo-China many of the expenses which in the other colonies are borne by the home government are defrayed by the colony itself. Not only this, but a large part of the revenues of this colony go to the home government in the shape of a "contingent," to be discussed below.

II. *Development of the Fiscal Policy*

Before the Revolution the French colonies were managed, very much as those of other nations, in accordance with the ideas of the Mercantile system. The colonies were supposed to exist for the sake of the mother country alone, and in their commercial and fiscal relations with the home government the interests of the colonists were made entirely subordinate to those of the mother country. In the nineteenth century, however, there have been several changes of policy. Beginning in 1825 we have the period of so-called autonomy, in which a large measure of self-government was granted to the colonies in fiscal as well as other matters. In 1841 there was initiated the second period, that of so-called assimilation, in which a far more rigorous dependence upon the home government in fiscal matters was insisted on. This lasted, however, only a short time; for 1854 witnessed the inception of the third period which has continued, with one important exception, to the present time,—the period of modified autonomy, in which a somewhat greater degree of independence was given to the colonies. The exception referred to is due to a change in the year 1892, by which the privilege of imposing independent tariffs was again taken from the colonies. Apart from this, most of the colonies are still regulated by the law of 1854, modified in some respects by the law of 1866, which forms the basis of the French fiscal colonial system. As has already been stated, however, Algiers occupies a position by itself and Indo-China possesses a fiscal system which differs in some details from those of the other colonies. Unless there is an express statement to the contrary, therefore, the general references in the following discussion apply to all the colonies with the exception of Algiers and Indo-China.

In general the fiscal relation of the colonies to the home government is one of partial autonomy. As a consequence of this lack of complete autonomy, there has been developed a curious and somewhat confusing arrangement. The expenses and receipts of the colonies are divided into two budgets, the one constituting a part of the budget of the home government, the other forming a separate colonial budget.

The home government is responsible for a number of expenses, the most important of which are those for the army and navy; for the salaries of the civil, judicial and religious officers; for the penal institutions; and for the so-called common expenses, which include the salary of the colonial minister and his office, as well as of the colonial inspectors. These expenses may be classed under two main heads: the expenses of sovereignty, and the subventions accorded to the separate colonies to aid them in defraying their local expenses. In 1898 the expenses for which the home government thus made itself responsible amounted to over 91 million francs. In addition to this large sum France also makes considerable grants in the shape of shipping subsidies (and to a minor extent, cable subsidies) to the lines having relations with the colonies. These grants, which amounted in 1898 to 23½ million francs, are also included in the budget of the colonies which forms a part of the home budget. Thus the total expenses chargeable to the colonies, but paid by the home government, amounted in 1898 to over 116 million francs. The details of these expenses are given in Table A on pages 291 and 292.

Against these expenses which appear in the French budget proper ought to be put the receipts from the colonies which go to swell the income of the mother country and appear in its budget. These receipts are of four kinds: first, the so-called "contingents" imposed on the colonies; second, the India rent; third, the deductions from salaries for civil pensions; fourth, the sale of state property and the proceeds of prison labor. The "contingents" comprise a number of small contributions, supposed to be paid by the various colonies. The purposes for which the contingents are paid are fixed by the law of 1866 which, it is to be noted, applies only to the three so-called ancient colonies, Guadaloupe, Martinique and Reunion; but the principles of the law of 1866 have been extended to the other colonies by subsequent legislation, especially in the eighties. Although the contingents are in general insignificant, the reverse is true of Cochin-China. In the budget of 1898 the total contingents amounted to 5,839,000 francs, of which Cochin-China alone was responsible for 4,510,000 francs. The remainder was distributed in small amounts among the other colonies. The above figures comprise not only the colonial contingents, so-called, as defined by the law of 1866, and its successors, but also the additional colonial "contributions" as fixed by the arrangement of 1893. In theory the "contingents" are supposed to be a payment on the part of the colonies in return for the expenses of sovereignty defrayed by the mother country and chargeable to the general French budget. On the other hand the so-called "contributions" are supposed to be payments toward the general expenses of the home government, whether these expenses have been incurred for colonial purposes or not. As a matter of fact, however, most of these contributions go toward defraying the expenses of certain institutions in Paris which have been created for colonial purposes. The contributions themselves are insignificant, amounting to less than half a million francs, as against the contingents of more than five million francs. Thus the sums raised in the colonies by both contingents and contributions are in fact spent for purposes which redound to the interests of the colonies themselves. Much dissatisfaction, however, is expressed with the system; Cochin-China in especial seems to be severely treated, for not only do more than four-fifths of the contingents come from that colony, but it has to defray out of its own resources most of the expenses which in the other colonies are chargeable to the subventions granted by the home government.

The other items in the receipts mentioned above may be dismissed with a few words. The India rent is a sum of 668,000 francs which has been paid since 1818 by England in return for the abandonment by the French of the salt monopoly in India. The deduction from the salaries of the colonial administrators for pension purposes explains itself. The miscellaneous receipts from the sale of property and the proceeds of prison labor amounted in 1898 to about a million francs. Table C (page 293) gives the complete list of receipts as contained in the French budget of 1898; Table B, on the same page, gives the "contributions" in detail. If we deduct the receipts from the expenditures, it would appear that the colonies cost France in 1898 over one hundred and eight million francs. This, however, does not include the sums due to the increased expenditure of the home administration, which are properly chargeable to the existence of the colonies. To differentiate these, however, would be impracticable.

In addition to this list of expenses and revenues contained in the French budget proper we have now to note the separate colonial budgets themselves.

III. *The Colonial Budgets*

It may be said in general that the colonies in fixing their own budgets have a large measure of autonomy, modified, however, in some important particulars. On the side of expenses, for instance, there are certain so-called obligatory expenses, for which each colony is compelled to provide in its own budget. On the revenue side the colonies have a free hand, except that since 1892 they have lost the right of fixing the rate of the tariff duties. This power is now reserved to the home government. The colonial budget itself is discussed and fixed by the General Council in all the colonies where that institution exists. It must then be submitted to the Colonial Governor who represents the home government. The powers of the governor, however, are carefully defined by the law of 1866. If the budget balances and if all the obligatory expenses have been provided for, the governor cannot modify the budget in any way; his consent is therefore in such cases a simple formality. If, however, there is a deficit, or if no adequate appropriation has been made for the obligatory expenses, the governor may intervene. The same holds true of the so-called supplementary credits, where intervention by the governor is also permissible.

Coming now to a consideration of both sides of the budget, we may say a word first as to the expenditures.

The most marked characteristic of colonial expenditures is their division into obligatory and optional expenditures. This division was clearly brought out by the law of 1866, which fixed the obligatory expenses for the three old colonies of Martinique, Guadaloupe and Reunion. The law declared the obligatory expenditures to be eleven in number: the payment of the debt; the maintenance of the government buildings and of the assistants connected with the governor's residence; the maintenance of the buildings for judicial and religious purposes; the rent and maintenance of the governor's private residence; the building and clerks of the governor's secretary; a part of the maintenance and salaries for public instruction, police, insane and poor children; the housing of the policemen; the return of immigrants; the cost of the publication of finance accounts; the contingent imposed on the colony; and, finally, certain unforeseen expenses. The laws of 1882 and 1885 extended this list to most of the other colonies. As we have already intimated, however, the obligatory expenses in the case of Cochin-China are considerably more numerous. All the colonies are compelled to provide for these obligatory expenditures in their budgets; and where they amount to large sums, as in Cochin-China, the discontent is very marked.

In contradistinction to the obligatory expenditures are the optional and extraordinary expenditures which may be fixed at pleasure by each colony separately.

The colonial revenues are derived from four sources: taxation proper; tariff duties (which in France are put in a class by themselves); income from colonial property; and subventions from the home government.

The system of taxation is supposed to be based largely on that of the mother country. Indeed, the colonial tax systems resemble those of the mother country primarily in the fact that by far the greater part of the revenue comes from indirect taxation. But so far as direct taxes are concerned the colonies differ in many respects not only from the mother country, but also from each other. This is due of course to the influence of local conditions and of the varying degrees of economic and social development. Table D (page 294) gives a survey of the sources of revenue in each colony. From this table it will be seen that what is common to almost all the colonies is the poll tax, the business tax, the export and import duties, the tax on spirituous liquors and the stamp tax.

The direct taxes of the mother country, as is well known, are of four kinds. They comprise the land tax, the "personal and movables" tax (being a combination of a poll tax with a tax on rentals), the door and window tax, and the business tax. Of these four taxes, that on doors and windows is entirely lacking in the colonies; the "personal and movables" tax has generally shrunk to a poll tax; while the land tax and the business taxes are assessed on very different principles from those observed at home. The land tax is found, with a few exceptions, in most of the colonies, but in several it applies only to land on which houses are built, thus becoming virtually a house tax. On the other hand, even where the land tax proper exists, it is not levied as in France, on the annual revenue, but, as in all primitive land taxes, it is assessed on the area or gross produce. In some cases it even takes the shape of a definite rate on different classes of land. In Tunis and Algiers, moreover, the original Arab land taxes are still in force, and in Algiers no real estate tax at all is levied on Frenchmen. In but one case, that of Reunion, is the tax assessed on property value, and even there it is applied only to houses, the rate being $^{35}/_{100}$ of one per cent. In the Antilles sugar lands are exempt from the land tax which is there replaced by an export duty on sugar. A similar principle applies to salt lands in New Caledonia, India and Cochin-China.

Of more fiscal importance than the land tax is the poll tax which, as is well known, has disappeared in almost all modern countries except the United States and Switzerland. The poll tax is not found in the Antilles, in the newer African possessions, or in Guinea. In most of these it has been replaced by a tax on rentals. But in the older African, and more especially the newer Asiatic, possessions the poll tax still forms an important part of the revenue.

The business tax is modelled quite largely upon the French "patentes" which at home is composed of a so-called *droit fixe* and a *droit proportionnel*. In the colonies, however, it is generally either the one or the other. Practically it is a kind of business license. It is found in almost all of the colonies, although it is of significance chiefly in the so-called old colonies.

In addition to these direct taxes we find in almost all of the colonies the so-called tax for the verification of weights and measures, which is in reality nothing but a fee, and which has been rendered necessary by the extension of the decimal system to the colonies. While the poll, land and business taxes are common to many of the colonies, we also find a few isolated taxes, which are levied in only a single colony, or at most in two or three colonies. Such are the carriage tax in Reunion and India; the boat tax in Cochin-China, Annam and Tonkin; the tax on mine rents in Guinea and especially in New Caledonia; and finally, for local purposes, a kind of income tax from intangible personalty in Martinique and Guadaloupe.

In treating of the direct taxes, a word must be said finally about Algiers. Although Algiers, as has already been stated, is treated to a certain extent as a part of France itself, in dealing with fiscal as well as with general administrative principles a line is drawn between the French citizens proper and the bulk of the native Arab population. In the case of the native population with its entirely different social and economic basis, the revenue system, is, as might be expected, completely different. The so-called Arabian taxes to which the native population is still subject are four in number: the *Hockor,* the *Achour,* the *Zekkat* and the *Lezma.* The *Hockor* is a tax on the lands still held in common, for in Algiers, as in all primitive countries, private property in land is an institution of slow growth. The *Achour* is a tax on the gross produce based mainly on the number of ploughs. It is still largely paid in kind. The *Zekkat* is a tax on the cattle owned by the nomadic population; while the *Lezma* is in some cases a tax on palm trees and in others a graduated poll tax. In Tunis also the native taxes are still levied.

Of greater fiscal significance than the direct taxes are the indirect taxes. Here, as in France, the stamp duties play a great rôle. They are found everywhere except in St. Pierre, and include a large variety of transactions. A still larger revenue is afforded by the tax on spirituous liquors, which is levied in almost every colony. Tobacco is not a state monopoly as in France, but is subject to an excise duty in a number of the colonies. In addition to these imposts we find isolated taxes on oil, on fats, on matches and on playing cards. Indirect taxes on commodities that do not exist in France are the following: on salt fish in Guadaloupe, on native gold in Guinea, on India rubber in Senegal, on rice in Cochin-China, on petroleum in St. Pierre, on dynamite in Senegal. Opium forms a colonial monopoly in Cochin-China and in Oceanica, and is taxed in Guinea and New Caledonia. Salt is everywhere exempt from taxation except in French India where it forms a colonial monopoly.

Scarcely less important than the taxes on liquors and tobacco are the tariff duties. These are levied on both exports and imports and, as has been stated above, are now fixed by the home government, not by the colonies themselves. The export duties are ordinarily confined to a few important articles. Thus in Martinique we find export duties on sugar and molasses, in Reunion on the so-called colonial goods (sugar, spices, etc.), in Cochin-China on rice, in Oceanica on mother-of-pearl. The import duties are in general those of the French tariff itself with a few concessions in the interests of the colonies. In several cases particular commodities are absolutely prohibited in order to protect colonial products. This is true of sugar in Martinique and Indo-China, of rum and molasses in Reunion and of opium in Indo-China and Mayotte.

Although the home government is invested with the duty of fixing the tariff for all the colonies, the colonial councils have the right of pointing out to the home government the modifications which are desirable for each special colony.

A few such changes have been made, chiefly in the direction of lower duties or complete exemption; but the deviations from the general French tariff are insignificant. There are only two colonies without tariff duties, namely, Obock and the towns of French India.

In addition to the general tariff duties, tonnage, navigation and harbor dues are to be found in almost every colony.

The purely local and municipal expenses are defrayed to a large extent by the *octroi de mer*. This is a tax on all kinds of commodities, especially articles of food coming in by water. It takes the place of the local octroi in the mother country. The *octroi de mer*, however, cannot be fixed independently by the colonies; they have indeed the right of formulating the tentative plan, but their decision must obtain the approval of the Council of State in Paris not only as to the tax itself, but also in respect to the methods of administration.

Of the remaining revenues, in addition to those derived from taxation and tariff duties, the third class includes the income from colonial property and enterprises. The most important element in this is the revenue from the postal and telegraph system, which is everywhere a government monopoly. The fourth and final category of colonial revenues is composed of the conventions or subsidies from the home government which have been considered above.

IV. *Conclusion*

From this summary it will be seen that the French government wavers between two lines of policy. On the one hand the movement toward local autonomy has granted to the colonies substantial rights of fixing their own sources of revenue and expenditure in accordance with the dictates of local expediency. On the other hand the movement toward centralization or so-called assimilation has taken away from the colonies the privilege of levying their own tariffs and has imposed upon many of the dependencies a system of taxation more suitable to the interests of the mother country than to those of the colonies themselves; has declared certain of the colonial expenditures obligatory; and finally has complicated the relations between the colonies and the home government by a series of subventions on the one hand and of contingents and contributions on the other. The most recent and enlightened colonial administrators themselves plead not only for a simplification of the relations between the colonies and the home government, but also for a larger share of independence and initiative on the part of the colonies themselves.

TABLE A

EXPENDITURES OF FRANCE FOR THE COLONIES IN 1898

I. *Expenses of Sovereignty and Subventions*

1. DÉPENSES COMMUNES

	FRANCS
Traitement du ministre et personnel de l'administration centrale	695,000
Matériel de l'administration centrale........................	137,000
Frais d'impression, publication de documents et abonnements..	108,000
Frais de dépêches télégraphiques........................	102,000
Service central des marchés........................	120,000
Service administratif des colonies dans les ports de commerce de la métropole........................	162,500
Inspection des colonies........................	311,000
Secours et subventions........................	44,500
Subventions à diverses compagnies pour les câbles sousmarins	707,500

2. DÉPENSES CIVILES

Personnel des services civils........................	489,561
Personnel de la justice........................	1,470,000
Personnel des cultes........................	602,000
Service des travaux publics........................	53,000
Matériel des services civils........................	17,100
Frais de voyage par terre et par mer et dépenses accessoires	325,000
Exposition permanente des colonies et renseignements commerciaux. Service géographique........................	43,400
Participation à l'Exposition universelle de 1900........................	2,000
Missions dans les colonies........................	210,000
Bourses coloniales........................	28,000
Études coloniales	10,000
Émigration des travailleurs aux colonies........................	75,000
Quatrième des quatorze annuités à payer à des exploitations agricoles pour la mise en valeur d'établissements français...	360,000
Subvention au budget local du Congo français........................	2,353,000
Subvention au budget local de Madagascar........................	1,800,000
Subvention au service local de certaines colonies........................	765,307
Subvention au budget annexe du chemin de fer et du port de la Réunion	2,508,500
Subvention au budget annexe du chemin de fer du Soudan français	768,000
Chemin de fer de Dakar à St.-Louis........................	1,270,000

3. DÉPENSES MILITAIRES

	Francs
Troupes aux colonies et comité technique	5,799,372
Gendarmerie coloniale	1,630,000
Commissariat colonial	871,500
Inscription maritime	60,000
Comptables coloniaux	346,000
Service de santé (personelle)	1,092,000
Service de santé (matériel)	1,474,000
Vivres et fourrages	3,310,000
Frais de voyage par terre et par mer et dépenses accessoires	1,400,000
Matériel de casernement, de campement et de couchage	274,000
Matériel des services militaires	1,444,000
Défense des colonies	1,200,000
Frais d'occupation du Soudan français	6,180,000
Route de Konakry au Niger	100,000
Dépenses des services militaires et maritimes en Annam et au Tonkin	23,250,000
Dépenses militaires à Madagascar	18,276,000

4. SERVICE PÉNITENTIAIRE

Administration pénitentiaire (personelle)	2,649,500
Administration pénitentiaire (hôpitaux, vivres, habillement et couchage)	4,129,900
Administration pénitentiaire (frais de transport)	1,170,000
Administration pénitentiaire (matériel)	1,439,900
Dépenses des exercices périmés non frappés de déchéance	Mémoire
Dépenses des exercices clos	Mémoire
Rappels de dépenses payables sur revues antérieures à 1898	Mémoire
Total	91,633,530

II. *Shipping and Cable Subsidies*

Subvention au service maritime de New-York et des Antilles, primes de vitesse	11,258,000
Subvention au service maritime de l'Indo-Chine et du Japon	6,083,688
Subvention au service maritime de l'Australie et de la Nouvelle-Calédonie	3,108,936
Subvention au service maritime de la côte orientale d'Afrique	1,925,640
Subvention au service maritime de la côte occidentale d'Afrique	500,000
Subvention à la compagnie concessionaire du câble reliant à St.-Louis du Sénégal les possessions de Rio-Nuñez, Grand Bassam, Porto-Novo et le Gabon	300,000
Subvention à la compagnie concessionaire du câble reliant la France à l'Amérique et aux Antilles	400,000
Total	23,576,264

TABLE B

THE COLONIAL CONTRIBUTION IN 1898

	FRANCS
Cochin-Chine	4,442
Annam-Tonkin	109,000
Martinique	65,032
Guadeloupe	71,060
Réunion	67,076
Guyane	32,435
Sénégal	16,805
Soudan	3,000
Guinée	3,600
Côte d'Ivoire	3,600
Dahomey	3,600
Congo	4,530
Madagascar	9,570
St.-Pierre et Miquelon	7,992
Mayotte	2,410
Comores	2,410
Taïti	11,821
Nouvelle Calédonie	33,619
Inde	25,780
Côte de Somalis	300
Cambodge	2,000
Total	469,472

TABLE C

COLONIAL RECEIPTS

(Forming a part of the French Budget in 1898.)

	FRANCS
Contingents et contributions	5,838,972
Rente de l'Inde	668,800
Retenues pour pensions civiles	859,400
Recettes diverses	966,400
Total	8,333,572

TABLE D

COLONIAL REVENUES IN 1898.[1]

	In Thousands of Francs																							
	Land Tax.	House Tax.	Poll Tax.	Business Tax.	Carriage Tax.	Dog Tax.	Boat Tax.	Total Direct Taxes.	Export Duties.	Import Duties.	Tonnage and Navigation Duties.	Liquor Tax.	Tobacco Tax.	Opium Tax.	Rice Tax.	Oil Tax.	Match Tax.	Taxes on Other Commodities.	Licenses.	Stamp Taxes.	Octroi de Mer.	Total Indirect Taxes.	Post and Telegraph.	Total.
Martinique	734	30	...	395	...	...	...	...	555	810	144	1,370	...	...	...	...	...	...	...	880	214	...	118	5,354
Guadeloupe	...	259	...	230	...	...	...	...	555	550	63	2,232	...	...	...	...	...	621	6	409	110	...	100	5,552
Guiana	...	36	...	60	...	...	...	...	354	276	48	260	48	30	...	...	...	297	...	280	...	...	30	1,894
St. Pierre et Miquelon	...	...	...	21	...	...	...	...	...	230	60	...	...	...	...	...	...	...	...	...	...	...	18	435
Senegal	...	50	15	180	...	...	...	...	140	2,040	48	800	...	...	...	...	...	...	...	119	...	...	183	3,958
Guinea	...	...	...	...	...	...	...	...	320	...	12	200	...	...	...	...	...	...	...	6	...	...	4	547
Congo	...	...	...	...	...	...	...	68	...	225	...	...	...	...	...	...	...	...	...	...	...	879	...	2,680
Reunion	...	75	220	243	34	...	...	...	294	18	40	1,950	120	...	...	...	...	...	...	638	60	...	125	5,243
Mayotte	62	...	60	22	...	...	...	...	...	21	9	18	...	...	...	...	...	...	...	22	...	...	...	257
Nossi-Bé	16	...	20	40	...	1	...	...	...	...	14	12	...	3	...	...	...	...	...	4	...	...	...	207
Madagascar	...	...	...	...	...	...	...	...	...	...	...	...	...	...	...	...	...	...	...	...	...	...	...	9,437
French India	...	...	...	...	...	...	...	358	...	...	39	...	...	...	...	...	...	...	...	142	...	...	10	1,835
Cochin-China (piastres)	830	...	688	169	...	...	76	...	1,660	1,484	...	30	...	3,196	636	...	...	...	...	90	...	...	85	10,200
Cambodia (piastres)	120	14	634	...	1	...	...	...	...	...	...	127	...	...	...	...	...	...	...	...	...	...	7	1,413
Annam-Tonkin (piastres)	6	2,412[2]	...	10	...	...	11	...	373	810	177	362	60	...	...	31	29	...	...	95	...	...	92	6,400
Oceanica	...	...	147	81	...	22	...	...	...	260	...	53	...	50	...	...	...	28	...	100	...	...	31	1,256
New Caledonia (1893)	105	...	...	140	...	...	...	...	...	...	...	510	212	...	...	...	...	...	...	131	...	...	70	3,062

[1] The table is not found in any printed document or book. It has been compiled and arranged from the separate colonial budgets. Certain minor details including the subventions (some of which will be found in Table A) have been omitted, so that the figures in the last column will not always tally with the addition of those in the preceding columns.

[2] Native taxes.

AUTHORITIES

Deschamps, L.—Les colonies pendant la Révolution, 1898.
Dislère—Traité de législation coloniale, 2 vols., 2 ed., 1897.
Duval, J.—Les colonies et la politique coloniale de la France, n.d.
Garnier—Législation domaniale des colonies Françaises, 1897.
Girault, A.—Principes de colonisation et de législation coloniale, 1895.
de Lanessan, J. L.—L'expansion générale de la France, 1886.
de Lanessan, J. L.—La colonisation Française en Indo-Chine, 1895.
de Lanessan, J. L.—Principes de colonisation, 1897.
Le Bourdais des Touches, J.—Etude critique sur le régime financier des colonies Françaises, 1898.
Leroy-Beaulieu, P.—La colonisation chez les peuples modernes, 4 ed., 1891.
Petit, Edouard.—Organisation des colonies Françaises, 2 vols., 1894.
Rougier, J. C. Paul.—Précis de législation et d'économie coloniale, 1895.
[NOTE: Since this essay originally appeared, two works of merit on the colonial tariff policy have been published:
Ermels, R.—Frankreichs Koloniale Handelspolitik, 1910.
Girault, A.—The Colonial Tariff Policy of France, 1916 (in the Series published by the Carnegie Endowment for International Peace).]

INDEX